THE ROWING MARINE

THE ROWING MARINE

Crossing the Atlantic: The World's Only Physically Disabled Person to Hold the World Record in an Endurance Event

LEE SPENCER

THE ROWING MARINE
Crossing the Atlantic: The World's Only Physically Disabled Person to Hold the World Record in an Endurance Event

First published in Great Britain in 2025
by Frontline Books
An imprint of
Pen & Sword Books Ltd
Yorkshire - Philadelphia

ISBN 9781036132767

A CIP catalogue record for this book is available from the British Library

Typeset by Lapiz Digital
Printed and bound in the UK by CPI Group (UK) Ltd,
Croydon, CR0 4YY.

Printed on paper from a sustainable source by
CPI Group (UK) Ltd, Croydon, CR0 4YY

The Publisher's authorised representative in the EU for product safety is Authorised Rep Compliance Ltd., Ground Floor, 71 Lower Baggot Street, Dublin D02 P593, Ireland.
www.arccompliance.com

For a complete list of Pen & Sword titles please contact
PEN & SWORD BOOKS LTD
47 Church Street, Barnsley, South Yorkshire, S70 2AS, England
E-mail: enquiries@pen-and-sword.co.uk
Website: www.pen-and-sword.co.uk
or
PEN & SWORD BOOKS
1950 Lawrence Rd, Havertown, PA 19083, USA
E-mail: uspen-and-sword@casematepublishers.com

CONTENTS

LIST OF PLATES

ACKNOWLEDGEMENTS

I would like to sincerely thank everyone without whom this book wouldn't exist:

- Liz Williams, for turning up at my hospital bed straight after I lost my leg with notebooks and encouraging me to start writing about my life and experiences.
- Liz McConaghy, for urging me to contact the publisher with my manuscript and then making the introduction.
- Megan Meyrick, for continuously reviewing my writing and assisting with the final edit.

I am also grateful to a few former colleagues who helped me organize timelines, recall personalities, fact-check, and ensure I did not unintentionally disclose HUMINT modus operandi. Protecting HUMINT sources and current operations was my primary focus during the editing process. You know who you are, and I can't thank you enough.

A special thank you to Mark Time for his unwavering support throughout the entire process, organising the manuscript and helping edit it down to something manageable.

And finally, to my brother Frank and his daughter Zanele, without you I wouldn't be here, let alone this book.

AUTHOR'S NOTE

In a post-truth world where 'My Truth' is often given the credence it doesn't deserve, I want to say a few words on perspective. We all have consensual realities that are not open to debate, they are truths. But we can all have opinions on how those truths affect us. A table is a table, but we can have opinions on whether it's a good table or maybe even what type of table it is. In early 2024, after most of what is in this book had been written down and I was well into the editing phase, a memory that I had subconsciously subdued, popped back into my conscious mind. It completely changed my perspective of my Mum, my Dad and my whole childhood. Perspectives and opinions change.

This book is not an accurate historical account of the world I encountered. It is instead an honest description of my life as seen through my eyes. It is at times the perspective of a child, a very unhappy teenager, a soldier and a disabled veteran. I have tried to write it without the benefit of hindsight because it was those eyes that not only shaped how I saw the world and how I saw myself, but more importantly it gave me my place in that world. This book is about my interactions with the truths I encountered. It is written through my perspective as it was, to the best of my memory.

Where I have deviated from fact, or truths, it is only to protect Human Intelligence (HUMINT) Sources, Operational Procedures and current HUMINT Operations. I have tried to be as accurate as possible whilst maintaining the central core of the story, but I have intentionally changed names and personalities as well as geographical locations and dates. Where I haven't changed facts, I have been intentionally vague and it should be obvious to all who read this book, where these changes and vagaries occur.

This book is presented as a story and with all stories it has heroes and villains. The stories we were told as children were full of both and through a child's eyes, I often saw people as heroes and villains. With hindsight and dare I say a bit of maturity, I know there are no heroes or villains as we understand them. Most of us are just bungling our way through life trying to do our best. We can never truly know what is going on in other people's lives and the reasons behind the choices they make. I hold onto my belief in the fundamental goodness of the vast majority of people, as a choice.

If there are any heroes in this book, it's the ones who saw something in me that others, including myself, didn't and gave me a chance. It is to those optimistic fools that I dedicate this book. I do it in genuine and heartfelt gratitude. I shudder to think where and how I would be now without the little piece of belief they had in me. I also write in hope that this book inspires others to believe in someone and give them a chance. None of us truly understand our own potential, let alone the potential of others. Of all those that saw some potential in me and gave me a chance, Claire my wife stands out in the colossal optimism vested in a 16-year-old, born-again Christian wally, on a youth training scheme and perhaps the worst breakdancer in Dagenham (she claims she just lacks ambition). Without her love, support and friendship I would have nothing. I owe her everything.

Devon 2025

GLOSSARY OF TERMS

2 i/c – Second in Command: The subordinate officer or NCO who acts as a deputy to the commander of a section, troop, or other unit.

Autohelm – A mechanical piston that drives a boat's rudder as part of the autopilot system.

Automatic Identification System (AIS) – A short-range, automatic system used on ships and boats to automatically broadcast and receive vital navigation data, including identity, position, speed and course, via VHF radio waves.

Beasting – Royal Marine slang for correctional physical training exercises used as a punishment. Also called a 'thrashing'.

BFT – Within Royal Marines training. An acronym for Bottom Field Test. A mandatory pass or fail test specific to Royal Marines basic training that consists of rope climbs, fireman's carry, a regain and a timed run around the assault course on the bottom field at CTCRM.

BFT – In the wider military. An acronym for Basic Fitness Test. A mandatory military fitness test, consisting of exercises like press-ups, sit-ups and a timed run.

Binner – DHU-specific slang for office where the Operators worked in a DHU Detachment. Can also refer collectively to all the Operators within a DET.

Bootneck – A slang term for a Royal Marine taken from the historical practice of taking some leather from a boot to protect the throat from a cutlass slash. Incidentally, American Marines call themselves 'Leathernecks'.

Bow – The front of a boat.

CO – Short for Commanding Officer. Normally a Lieutenant Colonel and in command of a whole unite or Commando Group. Example CO 40 Commando.

Course Over Ground (COG) – The actual direction of travel regardless of the heading and variations in tides, currents, wind and wave direction.

CSM – Acronym for Company Sergeant Major. A Warrant Officer Second Class (WO2) appointed as the Sergeant Major of a Company-sized group responsible for all administration and logistics at the company level. It is an appointment not a rank.

CTC – Shortened version of CTCRM. Acronym for The Commando Training Centre Royal Marines. Also known as just Lympstone. Where all Royal Marines undergo basic and command course training.

Daggerboard – A flat fin underneath a boat that provides lateral resistance and stability in side winds and swell preventing sideways drift.

Day Sack – A military term for a small rucksack used to carry essential equipment for a day's patrol, separate from a larger Bergen (main rucksack).

Defence HUMINT Unit (DHU) – A tri-service military unit within the British Armed Forces whose role is the recruitment and running of Covert Human Intelligence Sources (CHIS) in support of British Military Operations.

DET – short for Detachment. A subunit within the DHU deployed on Operations.

Dhobi – Slang for cleaning; both for laundry or showering.

DL – Acronym for Drill Leader. A specialisation within the Royal Marines from Corporal onwards whose role is ceremonial duties and parades as well as recruit training in dress standards and drill.

Drogue – A conical or funnel-shaped device with open ends, towed behind a boat, aircraft, or other moving object to reduce speed or improve stability.

EFOY – A mini generator that converts chemical energy into electrical energy based on DMFC (Direct Methanol Fuel Cell) technology.

FDO – Forward Deployed Operator: A DHU operator positioned close to the fighting units to provide real-time human intelligence.

FOB – Acronym for Forward Operating Base. A small base, sometimes just a fortified compound, used as a base for a subunit to patrol from. FOBs varied in size form a company location commanded by a Major to a smaller outpost housing a less than fifteen soldiers and occasionally commanded by a corporal.

Galley – Term used for all kitchens, whether shore-based or on ships within the wider Naval Service

GPMG – The General-Purpose Machine Gun is an air-cooled 7.62mm belt-fed machine gun usually carried in at the troop level.

HESCO – A brand name for collapsible wire mesh containers lined with heavy-duty fabric and filled with sand or rubble, used to build protective barriers in military zones.

HUMINT – Intelligence gained from a Covert Human Intelligence Source (CHIS).

IED – Acronym for Improvised Explosive Device. A homemade bomb, the leading cause of casualties during the Afghanistan conflict.

Irons, 'Going into irons' – When a boat drifts without direction and is forced sideways to the wind and waves.

KFS – Acronym for Knife, Fork, Spoon. The standard-issue metal cutlery set.

LZ – Acronym for Landing Zone. An area specifically designated for helicopter landing.

Minimi – The FN Minimi is a Belgian 5.56mm light machine gun usually carried at the section level.

Minuna – An Afghan term for any buried explosive device, either IEDs or legacy land mines from the Soviet-Afghan war.

NAAFI – Acronym for Navy, Army and Air Force Institutes. A British military organization that runs canteens and stores for servicemen and women but generally used as a term the NAAFI shop. A shop on military camp.

OC – Short for Officer Commanding. Normally a Major in rank and often a Company Commander. Example – OC Charlie Company

O Group – Orders Group: A command briefing where a leader issues detailed orders to subordinate leaders for an upcoming operation.

OP – Observation Post: A military position from which soldiers can observe enemy activity or maintain surveillance.

OP MINIMISE – The procedure of closing all communication back home whilst on deployment to allow the family of a seriously injured or deceased soldier to be informed.

OPSWO – Acronym for Operations Warrant Officer. The detachment Sergeant Major within the DHU. Similar to a CSM.

Port – The left side of a boat from the perspective of looking forward.

Provy – Short for Provost and refers to the Provost section or Provost Sergeant that commands it. The Provost section is responsible for discipline within a unit. Each unit within the Royal Marines has a Provy Sergeant and Provy Section.

PTI – Physical Training Instructor.

PW – Acronym for Platoon Weapons. A specialisation within the Royal Marines from corporal onwards. PWs are concerned with all weapons training and live firing as well as recruit training.

Regain – Part of the Bottom Field Tests within Royal Marines recruit training where a recruit must hang horizontally from a rope and pull themselves back up onto it.

RIPA – Acronym for Regulation of Investigatory Powers Act 2000. A UK law that established a legal framework for public authorities to conduct covert surveillance and Human Intelligence operations.

RSM – Acronym for Regimental Sergeant Major. A Warrant Officer First Class (WO1) appointed RSM of a unit and is responsible for overall discipline, standards and administration within the unit. It is an appointment and not a rank.

Safety Stays – Two safety straps that extend along the length of the boat on both sides approximately 20cm and 40cm above the deck. They offer some protection from falling overboard.

Sangar – A fortified position or tower with a sentry post inside.

Scran – Royal Marines slang for food and / or a meal.

Section – The basic unit within Royal Marines unit structure. It consists of eight men broken down into two fire teams of four men, Delta and Charlie. It is commanded by a Corporal with a Lance Corporal as 2 i / c who commands the Delta fire team.

SF – Acronym for Sustained Fire. Supporting fire from heavy machine guns at the troop, company and unit level. Often GPMG's in the SF role mounted on tripods and 50-calibre machine guns.

Snatch Vehicle – An armoured Land Rover used during the Afghanistan conflict, often criticized for being vulnerable to IEDs.

Starboard – The right side of a boat from the perspective of looking forward.

Strop – A safety lanyard or strap used to secure a person to a boat or structure to prevent falling overboard.

UKSF (often abbreviated to just SF) – Acronym for United Kingdom Special Forces, comprising of the Special Air Service (SAS), the Special Boat Service (SBS) and the Special Reconnaissance Regiment (SRR).

UTC - Acronym for Universal Time Coordinated and also known as Greenwich Mean Time (GMT). As apposed to Local Time which is the time adjusted for location around the Earth in time zones.

Vallon – A brand name for a type of highly sensitive metal detector issued to the British Military and carried by patrol members to find IEDs.

Wadi – An Arabic term for a dry riverbed or ravine, which typically contains water only during the rainy season.

Waypoint – A point or location on a route and often used as a point at which direction is changed or in maritime navigation a point or location that is navigated towards to give a heading, but never reached.

Wrapp – Royal Marine slang for giving up, verb 'to wrapp'.

Yomp – A long-distance march carrying heavy gear over rough terrain, a staple of Royal Marines training and operations.

BEGINNING

At midday on 9 January 2019, the bow of my little rowing boat *Hope* slowly drifted away from a pontoon in Portimao a small town on the southern coast of Portugal. As she drifted around to point at the far shore of the Arada river, I looked up over her stern at Gaz, holding her.

'Ready?' he said.

I nodded and he pushed her out towards the middle of the water, the ripples gurgling under her small hull as she drifted away. I dropped both oars into the still water. Pulling on the starboard oar and pushing on the port, *Hope* swung round to point at the harbour wall a kilometre to the south, and the Atlantic Ocean beyond.

I turned to look at the pontoon. My friends Jonathon, Gaz and Mike, and my wife Claire with one arm across her body nervously holding her other arm that hung by her side. They stared back in silence. Izzy, who was in charge of the media campaign, looked busy with the camera crew and I could faintly hear the buzz of their drone above. I hooked both oars under the crook of my knees, their blades dripped as they hovered over the still water. I waved back with both hands in the air. Everyone on the pontoon most likely waved but my eyes were fixed on Claire. I grabbed the wooden handles of both oars, slid as far forward on the rowing seat as I could, pushed my arms out in front and took a deep breath. I then plunged the oars into the water and pulled. *Hope* surged forward on the start of our 3,639-mile journey across the Atlantic, from Portugal to South America. If I was successful, I'd be the first physically disabled person to row solo and unsupported across the Atlantic Ocean from mainland Europe to mainland South America and only the fourth person in history.

I should mention I only have one leg.

But I wanted to be the fastest. I wanted to beat the 2002 able-bodied record of Norwegian Stein Hoff who completed the row in 96 days, 12 hours and 45 minutes. I wanted to prove that no one should be defined by disability. I wanted to prove that I wasn't defined by my disability. Most of all, I wanted to prove to myself I still had some worth.

The journey across the Atlantic would prove to be the defining journey of my life so far, but as with all journeys of significance, they rarely start with the first step or in this case the first pull on the oars. This seed was planted with a chance encounter with a tiny, dehydrated puppy caught between two fences in the oppressive heat of an Afghan summer in what seemed a lifetime ago. This is not just the story of my journey across the vast expanse of empty ocean, it is the story of how I got to the start line.

Eleven years before, I'd been a Sergeant in the Royal Marines and volunteer for Special Duties. I was serving in a detachment of the Defence HUMINT Unit (DHU) in Lashkar Gah, the provincial capital of Helmand in Afghanistan. It was 6 May 2008 and my friend Ed, a ridiculously intelligent Gurkha officer, called me on the radio. He was acting as an overwatch from the nearby sangar – a fortified tower with a sentry position inside.

'Frank, there's a puppy stuck in the fence just outside the gate.'

'What shall I do?'

'Go and get it. I'll give you a shout when it's clear.' The radio fell silent then crackled back into life. 'Clear.'

The huge green metal double gate had a small door to the right. I unlocked the overly large padlock, drew my pistol, slid open the rusting bolt and stepped through the doorway. Down to my right about five metres from the gate was a tiny, tan-coloured puppy caught in a small gap between the two large metal link fences surrounding the camp. I knelt and the puppy stared up at me with the saddest hazel eyes I'd ever seen. I pulled on the bottom of the fence as hard as I could, producing a small gap and pushed my arm in. 'There, there,' I said, soothingly. I was worried that I'd scare the poor thing and it would jump out of range of my outreached arm. I gently grabbed it by its scruff as firmly as I could and pulled it back through the gap in the fence. I scooped it up in my arms and ran back into camp. I turned and locked the gate and radioed Ed that I was in, and the door was locked.

'Wait there,' said Ed as one of the detachment vehicles pulled up.

Back in the Operations room, the rest of the DET had heard Ed and I talking over the radio and had come down to see the puppy.

I called the puppy Hannah and gave her some food and water as soon as we got back to the DET. She was famished and very dehydrated. I tried to slow her eating and drinking as I was worried wolfing everything down could cause problems.

After emailing friends and family a picture of Hannah, I was inundated with parcels containing puppy food, treats, flea and worming tablets and toys. She received more parcels than anyone else in the DET. Soon after, I received an email from my cousin telling me about a charity he had seen on Crufts called Nowzad Dogs founded by a Royal Marine called Pen Farthing. They rescued dogs and cats that service personnel had adopted from Afghanistan and Iraq, then transported them back home.

I emailed Pen the story of Hannah and he arranged to fly her back to the UK. Hannah started her three-month journey to England in what we called a jingly taxi, a peculiar Afghan form of transport consisting of a Chinese Honda motorcycle pulling an ornately decorated covered cart, with bells and tassels and a seat inside for the passenger. We tried to make it as comfortable as possible for the journey to Kandahar. From Kandahar she then spent some time in Kabul before moving to Islamabad where she received the required inoculations before the final leg of her journey to quarantine in a kennels near Ilchester in Somerset.

Hannah beat me back to the UK by a few weeks. As soon as I got home, I, Claire and the kids visited her in kennels to introduce her to her new family. I visited her every Friday, stopping off on my weekly commute down the A303. After six months in quarantine, I was finally able bring her to her new home. Hannah became a part of our family, and we all loved her, especially my boy Billy who formed a deep bond with her.

Day 1

Hope slid through the calm waters of the Arada river estuary towards the sea wall and the Atlantic Ocean beyond. As the pontoon drifted away, I had an overwhelming sense of relief. In the past few years, I had doubted that this day would come and I would let down the people who backed me and prove the doubters right. I'd already postponed the row twice, once the previous year when my Mum died and once before Christmas when I couldn't get a clear weather window. I needed three days of favourable weather to get clear from land and I'd spent December fruitlessly waiting in Gibraltar for the weather to change. I'd planned to row out through the Straits of Gibraltar and into the Atlantic – a journey made more difficult by the fact that the Mediterranean Sea is slightly lower than the Atlantic Ocean. Rowing slightly uphill against the incoming current meant that a favourable weather window was even more critical. I'd spent the whole of December poised in Gibraltar ready to row before postponing.

I returned to Gibraltar straight after the new year, ready to start for the third time. A weather router checks the weather forecasts and ocean currents and sets an optimum course for an ocean rower to follow. My weather router was the most experienced ocean rower on the planet,

Leven Brown. I'd been speaking daily to Leven since the turn of the year, getting updates on the weather and my chances of leaving.

Leven called me on the 7th from his home in the Borders, 'Hi Captain,' he said in his calming soft Scottish brogue. 'I can't see anything showing on any models that looks favourable for a departure any time soon.'

'How far are you looking out?' I asked.

'It's hard to be precise on anything over a week, but all the models are quite consistent which usually means a fairly settled pattern, I'd hedge my bets on nothing for a couple of weeks. But,' he continued, 'if you can get yourself to Portugal tomorrow for a Wednesday start, then there's a perfect weather window for the get going.'

It was an opportunity I couldn't miss.

The following morning, I said a goodbye to everyone in Gibraltar. I'd been based on the Rock for nearly two years and raised a lot of money and received lots of support. I was disappointed that I couldn't start my row from there.

The RIB from the Royal Naval Squadron based in Gibraltar escorted me out past the runway to the start of Spanish waters. I shouted my thanks to them, they had looked after *Hope* whenever I was away from the Rock. I then changed the small Gibraltar courtesy flag to a Spanish one as I entered Spanish waters. I rowed around the tip of the runway and into the harbour in La Linea, Spain. Waiting for me there was Claire, Gaz, a wiry former Royal Marine Physical Training Instructor, and Mike, a very Northern ex-rugby pro. We raised *Hope* from the water with the harbour boat crane and set her down on her trailer before driving to Portimao, pulling *Hope* behind us.

Saying goodbye to Claire on the pontoon had been horrific. The thought of what was coming, the isolation, the fear, the utter exhaustion and doubts that I wouldn't be up to it, had gnawed away at me since the moment Leven had given me the green light to go. It had built through the road journey from La Linea, through a busy morning of last-minute preparations and exploded as I sat down on the pontoon with Claire. We've had many hard goodbyes through 24 years as a Royal Marine, but as I held Claire I was filled with utter dread. I felt sick to the pit of my stomach and tried to hide the terror that filled every inch of my being. I reluctantly dragged myself away from her as the noon departure time approached, and was filled with nerves as I clambered onto the boat. As I pulled on the oars for the first time, I pulled my focus away from the pontoon, away from Claire and the life that she was a part of. With mental dexterity practiced through many similar goodbyes, I thought only of the journey ahead.

The terror I felt moments before drained away. I was here. I had only one direction – out into the ocean. I had to get on with it. I rowed out through the gap of the sea wall past the red-striped Lighthouse of Praia da Rocha on my left and the green striped harbour light on my right and into the Atlantic.

The sea was flat calm and the sun beat down from a cloudless sky. My instructions from Leven were to row directly south for the first few miles to clear land before turning south-west. I hadn't decided on a routine for rowing, I had a vague idea that I'd try two hours rowing to one hour rest and would need to test how this affected my body and adjust it accordingly. I wanted to row as much as possible, but I knew that whatever routine I decided on, it needed to be sustainable for what was most likely to be three months at sea. Getting into a rowing and resting routine would be critical in getting across.

Routine is everything. It breaks the day rowing up into physically manageable periods, it helps to ensure that you eat and hydrate regularly, it gives you time to do the small but vital daily jobs that keep both your body and the boat going. But ultimately a routine keeps you sane. Getting into a routine was high on my priority list, but for now I needed to get as far out to sea as possible. I rowed for the rest of the day constantly, only stopping to drink and as the sun sank low on my left out to the west, I was still heading south. As daylight faded, along the southern coast of Portugal I could see the small, flickering lights of normal peoples' homes leading their normal lives inside. After six hours of constant rowing, I decided to take my first rest. I climbed into the small cabin and wiped the salt off my body and tried to get some sleep.

An ocean rowing boat is seldom still. The currents, the motion of the waves and the wind all keep it moving. As the boat moves through the water, even at a very slow speed, the motion of the water over the rudder keeps the boat on course. Further out at sea this motion is critical in keeping the boat safe. If the boat was to drift about aimlessly it'd be prone to going sideways to the waves and wind. This is called 'going into irons', it's where the wind presses the boat sideways against the water. Because *Hope* was so small and low in the water, even the slightest breaking wave from the side would almost certainly capsize her. *Hope* was designed to capsize and right herself but capsizing at sea in a small rowing boat is often catastrophic. Many ocean rows have failed in the past with a crashing wave sweeping vital equipment away. With the sea flat calm there was no danger from a breaking wave but as I tried to get an hour's sleep, a light breeze came from the south and pushed *Hope* back about half a mile. I woke to find myself closer to land than before I'd slept and realised that I was in for a long sleepless night of near-constant rowing to get away from land.

During the night a pod of dolphins came to see *Hope,* no doubt curious about this strange craft. The moonlight shimmered off their wet skin as they broke the surface of the water next to me. The lights of Portugal slowly became fainter and just before dawn I had the first of many close encounters with large container ships. *Hope*'s Automatic Identification System (AIS) alarm rang out warning me that another vessel was going to come close. I raised them on the radio and explained that I had limited manoeuvrability and asked if they would box around me, which they then did.

The sky to the east began to lighten and the pod of dolphins disappeared, as if their duty as guardians through my first night at sea was done. As the final stars disappeared the sun rose out of the sea, its yellowy orange light glinting off the small waves. I could just make out the slight brown smudge of the Portuguese coast through the morning mist. I decided that as part of my routine, I'd start each morning at 8am local time, recording everything of significance that'd happened the previous 24 hours along with my position and how far I'd rowed. It'd also mark the new day and draw an end to the last.

Day 1 Logbook Entry

Position at 0800hrs on 10th Jan 2019 UTC	*Distance travelled 21nm at 213°*
36°48'.087N 008°41'.958W	*Total distance*

Headwinds and side winds light. Most of the night a pod of dolphins followed from about 0400hrs until sunrise at 0755 hrs. At 0530 close call with passing cargo ship on head on collision course.

In September 2008 I finished my six-month tour in Lashkar Gah and I asked Pen Farthing if there was anything I could do to repay the charity for bringing Hannah home. Pen suggested I could do a charity event to raise some money. Doing an event for charity was something I had never previously considered. I'd never have thought of myself as someone able to do something impressive enough to deserve asking people to give me money for charity. Despite being a Royal Marine and physical fitness being part of my daily life, I still thought myself as the antithesis of an athlete. In early 2009 for the first time in my life, I applied for an endurance cycling event. I completed a 100km cycling sportif called The Exmoor Beast, raised over £600 for Nowzad Dogs and I firmly got the bug. I absolutely loved every part of it.

The next couple of years were taken up with the Advanced phase of my Special Duties course and another six-month tour of Afghanistan, this time in Kandahar and Sangin. I came home from Sangin in the late summer of 2010, the bloodiest year in Afghanistan. Whilst I had been away in Afghan, whenever a British Service person had been killed or badly injured, the welfare phones and the internet were switched off in something called OP Minimise. Its purpose was to allow the families to be informed first and in a dignified way. OP Minimise was often inforce a couple of times a day and each time I was overwhelmed with the knowledge that somewhere, a husband, a wife, mother, father, son or daughter was about to have their whole lives shattered. I wanted to do something for a charity that helped these families. When I returned home, I decided to run a cross-country marathon over Dartmoor on Christmas Eve in aid of the Royal British Legion. My plan was to run from Okehampton Battle Camp on the northern edge of the moor to my local pub in the village that I live, a total of 26 miles. Christmas Eve in 2010 happened to have one of the biggest dumps of snow on Dartmoor in recent years.

In training for the marathon, I was regularly running the first 12 miles to Postbridge in the middle of Dartmoor in about two and a half hours. On the day of the marathon, in places the snow was knee high and I stumbled into the car park at Postbridge nearly seven hours after I set off. Finally, in just over nine hours after I started, I staggered into the pub exhausted.

After another tour of Afghanistan in 2012, I started a secondment away from the military which meant I was able to spend a lot more time at home in Devon. I live in a village on Dartmoor, that was once the home to the married quarters, military housing for the men of 42 Commando just a few miles away in Bickleigh Barracks. Because of the historic association with the Royal Marines through the married quarters, many old Marines made the village their home.

In the village lived a young Royal Marine called Dom who had become paralysed from the neck down after an accident in Norway. He had recently moved into a specially adapted house and needed 24-hour care. Dom had some very basic movement in his arms, but those movements weren't anywhere near dextrous enough to allow Dom independence in his daily life. A Devon-based technology company called Advanced Control Research needed £70,000 to develop what it called a 'handroid' system – a kind of robotic exoskeleton. Dutchy, a serving Royal Marine who lived in the village, suggested that we could do something as a village to help raise money towards the £70,000. I couldn't run a marathon because I'd already done that,

I also couldn't do two marathons on consecutive days. Eddie Izzard, the comic, had just recently completed 27 marathons in 27 days. We needed something impressive enough to get people to donate. There was nothing for it, I would have to run two marathons back-to-back, a total of 52 miles across Dartmoor. The whole village got behind the idea and we all worked hard at raising as much money as possible. I set off from the village pub at midnight on 22 June 2013, with former servicemen spread across Dartmoor manning checkpoints along my route. I eventually ran back into the village later that morning to what seemed like the whole village cheering me in, an amazing moment for me personally. But what was even more incredible, as a group we raised nearly £20,000 towards the robotic exoskeleton. The Royal Marines Charity paid for the rest and Dom got his 'handroid'. It gave him enough independence to enrol in a university course and train as a counsellor, helping others in difficulty. Within six months of running the Dartmoor Double Marathon, my life would be turned upside down and I'd be in hospital having lost a leg.

Day 2

I wrote my first of many entries into the logbook and ate my first breakfast at sea, a rehydrated freeze-dried high-energy porridge. I decided to rest and start rowing again at 10am, then row two hours on and one hour off until 6pm where I'd have another two-hour rest around the evening meal. As I slowly crept further from land, its influence over the sea and wind conditions waned and the Canary Current began to push me south. The Canary Current originates far out in the Atlantic, travels south, off the coast of southern Portugal, past the Canary Islands that give it its name and down towards the Cape Verdes. From there the trade winds would hopefully push me across the Atlantic.

The wind started to pick up from the east and drove small choppy waves from the side, tossing *Hope*'s small hull about. The exaggerated movement of the small boat made sitting in the cabin unpleasant. The sun turned the cabin into a sweatbox during the day and sitting inside was like sitting in a hot sweaty tumble-dryer. Laying down was OK, but sitting made me nauseous, something I was expecting and knew would pass in a couple of days. At around 2pm, I started to cross a busy shipping lane, essentially a dual carriageway for shipping with a lane going in one direction and a lane going in the other. Just like crossing a normal busy road, I had to cross this one by the shortest route. I changed direction to south-south-west so I could cross it at a right angle and started rowing hard. My plans for rowing two hours on and one off and a two-hour dinner break went out of the window. I cleared the first lane at about 8pm and turned south again to get as much time between the two lanes. I managed to get 45 minutes rest before turning south-south-west again and started to cross the second lane. I finally cleared the shipping lane at 4am and utterly exhausted after a near-constant 14 hours backbreaking rowing, I crawled into the cabin and fell asleep.

Day 2 Logbook Entry

Position at 0800hrs on 11th Jan 2019 UTC	*Distance travelled 47nm at 240°*
36°48'.087N 008°41'.958W	*Total distance 68nm*

Strong sidewinds all morning then when they change to easterlies I had to change course to SSW to transit shipping lane SSW of Portugal. Hard Rowing from 1400hrs until 0400hrs when finally crossed shipping lane. Loads of ships v busy. Several AIS alerts. Good speed through the night.

On the night of 6 January 2014, I woke up in an intensive care hospital bed without my right leg. I was groggy and a bit sore, but absolutely elated to be alive. The first couple of days after losing my leg are hazy and I'm not sure when or in what order things happened. There was a conversation with the doctor who explained that there was a lot of debris in the wound and she would most likely have to operate and I'd need two of three more trips to the operating theatre.

Although elated at being alive, I felt the person I was, the person who defined himself by what he could do physically, had gone forever. I was no longer that person. I was now disabled. But if I was going to have to redefine who I was as a disabled person, then I was determined to be the best disabled person I could possibly be. I'd already completed a few challenges for charity, the Dartmoor marathons and cycling sportif, so it was a natural next step to set myself new challenges. The first was to raise £10,000 for the Royal Marines Charity in my first year as an amputee. I now had a new mission in life and a renewed focus. But first I needed to learn to walk again. I was determined to throw myself wholesale into rehabilitation and I set myself the first of many personal goals. It was obvious that my career as a soldier was over. I'd worked hard for nearly 22 years in one direction, now my life had turned in another. The well-trod path of completing challenges for charity before losing my leg gave the new direction in my life clarity. It really felt like my life had just changed direction instead of being completely turned upside down. Rescuing Hannah the puppy in

Afghanistan inadvertently but directly enabled me to make some sort of sense out of the calamity of losing a leg. The simple, human instinct to rescue a helpless puppy had a very positive effect on me in my hour of darkness.

My left leg had been completely dislocated at the knee, all the ligaments had been shattered and I needed a major operation to rebuild and reattach them. The operation took several hours and opened my entire knee up like a butchered piece of pork. When I woke after the operation, the pain was unbearable. It felt like it was invading every part of my being. It was so bad that I cried. Pain, like all negative emotions, is transient and it soon passed. Once my knee had been operated on, I felt that I could now get on with getting better and focus on walking again. I finally left St George's Hospital five weeks after losing my leg, but because our house wasn't suitable, I was released into the care of the Royal Marines. Through Afghanistan and Iraq, the Royal Marines had suffered a disproportionately high number of seriously injured soldiers. Responding to that need, they had formed Hasler Company, a unit dedicated to rehabilitation and recovery. The Royal Marines Charity and Help for Heroes had built purpose made accommodation that included family rooms, one of which Claire and I moved into.

Hasler Company was commanded by Major Scotty Mills, a black lad from Peckham in south London who'd gone through the ranks and was one of my oldest friends in the Corps. Scotty was a PTI and this was the first time I had met him since he commissioned as an officer. I'd followed Scotty around the Royal Marines, him always a rank above me. We'd served together in a variety of different roles within the Corps, from invading Iraq with 40 Commando to spending three months solid partying on the Commando Display Team. But I don't think either of us foresaw our paths crossing again in these circumstances. We met in one of the corridors next to the company offices and I looked up at him from my wheelchair.

'Hello mate,' I said.

Scotty looked sternly at me. 'Shouldn't you salute an officer?'

Royal Marines have an uncomfortable relationship with saluting. It's not something we like doing if it's avoidable. I once spent seven weeks at the Royal School of Artillery, the epitome of pointless military regimentation. I was on a course with eleven other Bootnecks. Someone had put in a complaint that we weren't saluting officers. The next morning while sauntering from our accommodation to the classroom, we spied a young Second Lieutenant, walking towards us. We quickly and very obviously rearranged ourselves into single file with about twelve paces between us then for the first time whilst at the Royal School of Artillery, marched smartly. As we passed him, we each shouted in turn 'MORNING SIR', 'MORNING SIR', 'MORNING SIR', chucking up a salute. We were told off again, this time presumably for saluting too much.

I looked up at Scotty confused and without thinking tried to salute him from my wheelchair. Scotty's face cracked into a massive smile, 'I've been dying to do that,' he laughed. 'Ha, I can't believe you fell for it.'

Day 3

The brisk, easterly wind continued all day and night (by convention, wind is always described in terms of where it's coming from), and I finally got into a rowing routine of two hours on and one hour off during the day, then switch to two on and two off through the night. Down each side of the boat were two hand lines attached to the rudder, pull on the left one and *Hope* turned to port and the right turned her to starboard. I could lock the hand lines off and therefore keep the rudder in place. When hand steering like this it's very difficult to keep a constant course over a long distance. The tiniest movement in the hand lines translate to a larger movement in the rudder. You must find a happy medium between constantly correcting your course, putting down the oars each time, or to zigzag across the ocean. Also, the speed the boat moves through the water changes the boat's course. The faster the boat moves, the more water moves over the rudder and the more effect the rudder has over the boat, increasing the turn.

At the end of each two-hour rowing shift, I'd spend five or ten minutes of my precious hour off setting the rudder to keep the same course at the much slower speed. I had several autohelms with me, a long black piston that attached to the rudder and connected to the navigation system in the cabin, auto steering the boat. I had several due to the fact they were designed for a much larger vessel like a yacht. The continued movement of *Hope* being pummelled from side-to-side, even from the smallest of waves, overworked the autohelm as it continually corrected the movement to stay on course. Because of this, they were prone to burning out. A good working autohelm makes life in an ocean rowing boat a lot easier as it keeps you on course so you can concentrate on just rowing, but they are difficult to configure in a small rowing boat. Before I left Gibraltar, I'd gone through the system and set it up ready to go. But now I just couldn't get it to work. It kept turning *Hope* from side to side, slewing violently and making rowing nigh on impossible. On my first row across the Atlantic in a crew of

4 other amputees, we had had a similar problem. Cayle, a double above-knee amputee from South Africa, had skippered us across and I knew he'd have the answer. I detached the autohelm for the moment and hand steered through the day. I rowed in shifts of two-hours on and one off until 6pm when I stopped for two hours to eat my evening meal and then called Cayle on the satphone. Together we went through the various settings, menus and sub-menus on the touchscreen control panel in the cabin. It all seemed to be in order. I put on my life jacket, opened the hatch door and as quickly as I could, attached myself to the safety strop on the deck with a carabiner. Once on deck I closed the hatch door before a wave could crash over, drenching the cabin. At the rear of the boat the rudder was housed in a small cabin. It was too small to keep anything in, as the rudder arm needed to be free to swing unhindered. I unhooked the steering lines, then as quickly as I could keeping the time *Hope* was not being steered to an absolute minimum, reattached the autohelm then switched it on. I heard the familiar grinding sound kick in as its internal motor and gears whirred into action, turning *Hope* back onto course. I waited for a couple of minutes, but everything seemed to be OK, the waves and wind gently nudged *Hope* forward and the autohelm kept her on course. Back in the cabin I called Cayle to tell him everything seemed OK.

Day 3 Logbook Entry

Position at 0800hrs on 12th Jan 2019 UTC *Distance travelled 52.1nm at 240°*
35°58′.221N 010°29′.097W *Total distance 120nm*

Kept a good course on a 240° bearing.

Brisk easterly all day and night. Problem with the bilge pump, it won't auto switch off and autohelm just moves the back of the boat all over the place. It's been hand steering all day.

I first met Cayle in March 2014, on my very first admission to Headley Court, the military's rehabilitation centre built around an imposing red brick eighteenth-century manor in Surrey. Dutchy, the Royal Marine from my village, was now working at Hasler Company and he drove me down to Headley Court.

'C'mon then, Royal,' he said as he went to get my wheelchair from the boot of the car. He unfolded it and put the wheels on and held it steady as I awkwardly tried to ease my way backwards out of the back seat onto the wheelchair. Dutchy loaded one of my bags onto my lap and allowed me to wheel myself away. I'd already developed an aversion to being pushed. I hated the helplessness of someone else being in control. Just by the entrance was a small reception desk where the duty nurse showed me to my room. The building looked and smelt brand new and the room was laid out exactly like a hospital ward with six hospital beds in two rows. Dutchy had carried my other heavier bag and guitar and dropped them by my bed, 'Right I'll see you Friday, Royal,' He said as he left.

Sat on the bed opposite mine with his curtains open was a double amputee, his two prosthetic pins leaning against his bed. 'Hi,' he said. 'I'm Cayle.'

'Kyle?' I asked.

'No Cayle, like the crap vegetable.' He laughed. He had a slight accent I couldn't place. Cayle had an air of assumed authority and I mistakenly thought he was an officer. He had an impressively huge black beard almost touching his chest. Beards in the military are an oddity and tend to stand out.

'What's with the beard?'

'I've just got back from rowing the Atlantic.'

I looked at the two stumps where his legs should've been in disbelief. 'You just rowed across the Atlantic?'

I put 100 per cent effort into everything I was doing, driven by a hatred of my wheelchair. My physio Joy was an older lady with a slight frame and a stern look. If I ever felt sorry for myself and put less than 100 per cent in, Joy would have none of it. She pushed me when I needed it and she held me back when I was overreaching. I was very lucky to have the best physiotherapist at Headley Court. Joy was away the day I walked for the first time and I wish she could've seen my first steps. I wheeled myself into the physio room with a pair of crutches attached to my wheelchair and the first of many prosthetic legs on my lap, itching to get up and walk. The stand-in physiotherapist asked if I was ready.

'Yep, I think so.'

I leaned forward, and with the help of the crutches, pushed myself out of the wheelchair into a standing position for the first time in three and a half months. Then at about 2pm on 15 April 2014, I took my first steps. I was concentrating on every single movement, expecting it to be alien. But it felt natural, my balance was still there and as I took a few more steps towards the physio who was recording the moment on my phone, the emotion hit me. It was like a basketball-sized lump of pure happiness in the pit of my stomach that slowly climbed up into my throat. I was aware of the silence that had suddenly descended on the usually bustling physio room as the other physiotherapist watched.

I turned to the right following my physio with the camera, fighting to keep hold of my emotions and looked up. Sat on a bench a few metres to my front was another physiotherapist, she was beaming at me, her face lit up with pure joy. I supposed it was moments like this that drove the obvious passion they had for their job. I started crying with pure happiness.

That first year without a leg was spent between Headley Court and Hasler Company, each day a positive, achieving something I couldn't do the day before. Small victories took on a whole new meaning, like walking to the pub for the first time and standing at a urinal, a genuine milestone on my recovery. My goal of raising £10,000 for the Royal Marines Charity gave my rehab a focus. I walked my first mile as a sponsored walk and was invited to Gibraltar to do the Rock Run. Whilst in Gibraltar I had a chance meeting with an old friend from the Marines who I hadn't seen for years and who would go on to have a pivotal role in the planning of the row. Ivor is a Welsh Del Boy Trotter. He is a huge strapping former Welsh national swimmer and he was stood in front of me in the Lord Nelson pub in Casemates square, an old fortified bastion at the end of the main street in Gibraltar.

'Frank.' he boomed, standing with his arms outstretched. 'Now then, someone told me that something bad happened to you,' his face creased in drunken concentration. 'Now what was it?' He then looked down at my prosthetic leg and smiled. Even over the din of a packed bar full of drunken Marines, I heard the penny drop. He pointed down and said, 'That was it.'

'Ivor, I thought you were dead. Where have you been?'

'Now don't be taking any pictures for Facebook, I've been yeare for five years now. I think they've forgotten I'm yeare.'

Ivor was the storeman in Gibraltar. He was effectively his own boss and in one of the most lucrative jobs in the Corps. Royal Marines change jobs, called going on draft, every two years, and year extensions in good jobs are rare. The drafting system in the Marines can often be brutal, but Ivor had managed to stay in Gibraltar for five years, a testament to his ability to wheel, deal, duck and dive and get things done.

Including the sponsored walk up the Rock, charity gigs and events, I eventually raised over £12,000 for the Royal Marines Charity. But whilst I achieved what I had set out to do in my first year missing a leg, I had no idea what I was going to do in my second. I needed a focus. I also had no idea what I was going to do for a job. I was a soldier and every professional competency I had, relied on a physically fit and strong body. With no idea how I was going to provide for my family,

I started an Open University course, with the vague plan of maybe becoming a teacher.

As I came to the end of my first year as an amputee, I was deeply worried about how I was going to provide for my family into the future and had no focus. Then I received an email forwarded by BLESMA, the limbless veterans charity. The email was from an organisation called Row2Recovery who were looking for amputee volunteers to row across the Atlantic Ocean. I immediately applied.

Many of my admissions to Headley Court overlapped with Cayle's and we talked a lot about his row across the Atlantic. I met him again at the first selection gathering for Row2Recovery at the river rowing museum in Henley-upon-Thames. Ten other amputees turned up and I eyed my competition which became fiercer when told that there were only three places on the boat up for grabs as Cayle would be the skipper. As well as prospective rowers, several of the past Row2Recovery crews turned up to cast their eyes over us potential new recruits. I mingled with the other amputees in the conference room at the back of the museum waiting for the selection process to start. The day was organised and run by Paddy, the chairman of Row2Recovery. The day consisted of interviews, testing rowing mechanics with the various disabilities and finished with rowing an old ocean rowing boat up and down the Thames. As I returned to Devon, I vowed that I would do everything I could to get a place on the boat.

Making the first Row2Revovery all-amputee team was now my priority for the coming year, even if it was as a reserve. What I didn't know as I drove home, was that I was already on the boat. Cayle had said that he wanted me, and the others agreed with him, although it would take another four months before I would find out. The Royal Marines lent me a rowing machine that I installed in my garage and would sit rowing for hours watching programmes on an iPad to combat boredom. Paddy finally called in August to let me know I had made the crew and then followed a frantic few months of packing, media interviews and training courses where I met the rest of the crew. Patrick, an Irish Guardsman who'd lost his leg in Afghanistan in an IED blast, and Nije, a former RAF physical training instructor who'd lost his leg above the knee in a parachuting display accident.

After all the preparations and training, we finally set off for La Gomera for the start of the Talisker Whiskey Atlantic Challenge. La Gomera is one of the smaller Canary Islands. It's where Christopher Columbus set off and its dramatic and harsh volcanic coastline testament to its relative geological youth. We finally set eyes on our boat for the first time on the quayside of San Sebastian harbour and the full enormity of the task of getting her ocean ready before the start of the race hit us.

We only had three weeks to turn a fiberglass shell into an ocean rowing boat and also meet all of the stringent safety criteria of the race rules. Not only did we need to prove the boat's seaworthiness, but we had to prove ours as well. We needed to complete a set amount of hours' sea training in the boat. Most of the other crews had already achieved this before arriving in La Gomera so we were playing catch up from the very start. Only having three legs between the four of us, didn't help. We were in a race against time to pass all the inspections before we could launch her so we could complete our statutory minimum hours training at sea. Our days started early and we'd graft all day before going to the local bar called the Blue Marlin. All the crews would congregate in a strange atmosphere of looming dread and serious drinking.

As we worked on the boat, in a strange way she became part of the team, it felt that she shared our adversity. We nicknamed her 'HMS *Legless*' and slowly but surely, we started to get her ready. But there was a problem that we couldn't fix, one of the rowing positions needed to change from a fixed rowing seat for Cayle, with no legs, rowing with upper body only, to a moving seat for when he handed over to Patrick, with one. The date for the start of the race was 15 December 2015. As it approached, we still didn't have a workable solution to Cayle's rowing seat. We were facing the awful choice of not being ready for the start of the race or going to sea with an unworkable system for one of the two rowing positions. Fortunately, just days before the intended race start, an Atlantic storm blew in and the start was postponed. The new race start date was set for 20 December and the five-day reprieve saved us. With the help of a German engineer who worked in the marina, we finally fashioned a workable solution to the seating problem.

I was a Royal Marines Commando. It defined me and I was extremely reluctant to let that person go. I knew deep down that I wasn't physically able to be that person again and that I had lost the person I had struggled all my life to become. Someone I was happy to see staring back in the mirror. The slow realisation that I had lost that part of my life gave my drive to be a member of the Row2Recovery all-amputee crew an added impetus. As I slowly let go of a life that defined who I was, rowing the Atlantic Ocean became a crucial cog in the wheel of redefining myself as the best disabled person I could be. I was not only setting off to row across the Atlantic, I was setting off to look in a mirror on the other side of an ocean in hope that I liked who I saw staring back.

Day 4

On my first row across the Atlantic with Row2Recovery's all-amputee crew, I had really struggled at the very start and was expecting the first week of this row to be just as horrific. The first three days I was waiting for a sudden realisation of exactly what I was doing to hit me. I'd worried about how I'd cope with complete isolation and assumed that this would be a massive problem that I'd have to overcome. But it never came. I woke for my last nighttime rowing shift at six in the morning and watched the new day arrive as the sun rose from the sea into a stunning sunrise. I felt privileged to be here. After two hours rowing, I filled out the logbook and ate breakfast, then started the first of my daytime rowing shifts at 10am.

I was now firmly in the Canary Current with the wind and waves behind me. It was perfect rowing conditions and every now and then, at the crest of a wave, I'd flick the oars with practiced timing and *Hope* would surf down the front. The wave would break, foaming around me as I quickly pushed down on the oar handles raising the blades up and out of the water. At midday, when the sun was at its hottest, I switched the water maker on and made fresh water. The water maker draws seawater from under the boat, up into its desalination plant, where it's forced through filters under huge pressure to remove the salt. It requires a lot of power to run, hence why I only ran it when the sun was at its strongest. The solar panels were trickle-charging two car batteries inside the boat that drove all the nav systems, radios and the autohelm. In the afternoon the sky clouded over and I was worried about the amount of power left in the batteries after using the water maker. I had invested in an EFOY, a mini marine generator that burned methanol to generate electricity. It wouldn't generate enough power to run anything directly, but it would continue to trickle-charge the batteries in the same way that the solar panels did. I'd considered it a necessity starting the row this far north. Most Atlantic rows start further south from the Canary Islands where the sun is a lot more reliable. I switched it on for a couple of hours to get the batteries up to full strength. I ate my evening meal as the sun set behind grey wispy clouds then settled into the night routine.

Day 4 Logbook Entry

Position at 0800hrs on 13th Jan 2019 UTC	*Distance travelled 63.9nm at 133°*
35°20′.252N 011°32′.259W	*Total distance 184nm*

Good rowing with up to 1.5 – 3 metre swells, good surfing down waves.
Top speed 4.8knots
Cloudy in the afternoon using the EFOY to top up the batteries. Continuing to bend round to the south.

On the morning of 20 December 2015, we pulled out of San Sebastian harbour to the blast of an air horn. Patrick and Nije were rowing while Cayle steered and I stood waving at the crowds who'd come to see the start of the race. Once we were clear of the harbour, we settled into our rowing routine of two hours on and two hours off. We would do one three-hour rowing shift at night from midnight to three or from three to six in the morning to allow for a three-hour block rest. The three-hour rowing shift also changed the order of rowing each day, so that one morning we'd see the sun rise and the next day the other pair would. I'd come to dread the three hours rowing at night. I was sharing the front cabin with Nije, but we'd become ships in the night, passing each other every couple of hours to row, me rowing with Cayle and Nije with Patrick.

As we rowed south away from La Gomera and the shelter it offered from the northerly wind, the waves began to pick up. Later that morning another pair from the race, Shane and Theo, rowed past us. We'd struck up a great friendship with them in the Blue Marlin bar and they'd be the last humans we'd see for over 40 days.

During the first day's rowing, a side swell developed, and my lack of experience rowing began to show. The boat kept tipping from side to side and gaining any purchase with the oars became a real problem. I just couldn't create any rhythm, which was crucial in trying to stay in time with Cayle who set the cadence. Patrick had grown up on a small island on the west coast of Ireland and the sea was very much in his blood. As La Gomera disappeared behind us, the swell grew and so too the sense of being completely out of my depth. I'd been to sea before, but only on large troop transportation ships from the Royal Fleet Auxiliary or the Royal Navy. Nothing I'd ever done before had come close to this. The further we rowed from land and into this totally alien environment, the worse I felt. Ten minutes before the end of each rowing shift, whoever was rowing would wake the next rowers so that they could get ready to change exactly on the hour. Just before dawn on the second morning, Nije banged on the cabin door shouting, 'Ten minutes.'

Rowing the Atlantic had been my focus for nearly a whole year, but stupidly I'd never stopped to think exactly what it involved. Now I was in a tiny rowing boat, surrounded by the vastness of the ocean in all its visceral power, I felt so insignificant with the whole of the Atlantic Ocean stretching out before me. I felt utterly helpless. I had made a massive mistake. The stupidity and arrogance of thinking I was able to do this consumed me. The seconds ticked away to when I was supposed to get out of the cabin and I forced myself to get ready. As I did, a panic set in.

'I'm going to be the weak link'. I thought. *'I can't do this'*. Terror ran through me. *'I'm the one who's going to let everyone down.'*

I sat up and glared at the hatch, unable to move. I couldn't get out of the cabin. I was breathing like I'd just run 10,000 metres, and I could feel my pulse racing. The awful realisation emerged that I was having some sort of panic attack. I delved deep into myself looking for any scrap of courage I had left and forced myself to shout 'Ready.'

Getting in and out of the cabin smoothly was critical. With the hatch open the boat was vulnerable to a cabin-drenching wave at best and a catastrophic capsize at worst. Nije and I had a routine and as he shouted, 'Go,' I went into autopilot. Seconds later I was sat with Cayle on deck. I picked up the oars and pulled and as I did, I felt the tension, panic and total inadequacy wash out of me. *'I can do this.'*

In fact it would be easy. All I had to do was get out of the cabin every four hours and pull on the oars for a couple of hours. It was that simple. Breaking challenges or problems up into smaller, more manageable pieces is a massive cliché, but as with all clichés, there's an element of truth. I'd looked at the entirety of the ocean stretching out before me and rightly felt totally inadequate before it. Now I'd only focus on each rowing session. The ocean row completely changed for me in that moment.

Gradually I got to grips with rowing in time with Cayle and my confidence grew. Moving around the extremely unstable small rowing boat on one leg was often precarious and it wasn't long into the journey when I took a tumble. I moved to the rear of the boat to help Cayle prepare meals when a small wave hit the boat and I fell overboard. My leg got caught between the hull and the safety stays and as I tumbled over there was a sickening crack. Patrick let go of his oars and grabbed my upper arm with lightning speed and held me in a vice-like grip. He held me there for a couple of moments, our hearts thumping, before pulling me back into the boat. Luckily my prosthetic was the cause of the sickening crack, breaking as I fell overboard and therefore repairable, unlike a real leg. But it shook me. Even though I was tied to the boat, it brought home the precariousness of our existence out in the ocean. Falling overboard without being tied on is almost certainly a death sentence and it was a few days before I ventured down the other side of the boat and only then shuffling on my bum.

As the days went by, I grew into the row and even started to enjoy it. *Legless* was a newly built and designed ocean rowing boat with the front cabin the largest of the two. It was an extremely fast boat to row down wind, but any side wind would push the larger front cabin round to face down wind. To counter this, underneath the front cabin was a retractable daggerboard, a two-foot-long plank that acted like a keel. We soon found out that ours didn't work and was stuck in the 'up' position. The side wind for the first couple of days was constantly trying to push the front of the boat off course and the stern rudder was constantly trying to turn her back on course. We burnt through the first of our three autohelms in a couple of days.

The wind changed to a preferable north north-easterly and we soon made great progress pushing south from the Canaries towards the trade winds to take us across the Atlantic. I quickly got into a routine and my body adapted to the enormous strain I was putting on it. The average person burns between 2,000 and 2,300 calories a day. Rowing an ocean burns between 8,000 to 10,000 calories a day. We'd rationed 6,000 calories per person per day yet I'd lose almost three stone in eight weeks. The only comparable challenge in terms of physiological demands placed on your body by rowing an ocean is walking solo to the South Pole. After a couple of weeks came the day when we turned *Legless* from a south-westerly direction to a westerly direction, pointing her towards the finish line in Antigua. It felt like we were really making progress.

We were then hit by a few days of really quite strong side winds that produced some nasty waves. Cayle decided to go to hand steering to save our remaining autohelms. Because the dagger board was stuck in the 'up' position, we couldn't lock the rudder in place. In our pairs, one would row and the other would steer using the handlines whilst staring at the compass trying to maintain a constant course. The margin for error in steering was tiny. The wind and waves kept turning the boat downwind or if you steered a tiny bit too far the other way, she would go into irons. The waves would press *Legless* on her side and it was almost impossible to turn her. The waves were big, angry breaking beasts and being side on to them was a very dangerous position. Whoever was on deck would shout and we'd try and get three on deck, two on the oars and one person steering and it would often take forty minutes to dig the boat out of irons. There was also a long lag between pulling on a steering line and that action transferring to the boat changing direction. Steering took absolute concentration and any lapse would immediately put *Legless* back into irons. We all deteriorated quickly as mental and physical exhaustion set in. At its worst, changing steering position became impossible without going straight into irons again. Cayle sat steering for close to 18 hours without any rest. It is the most astonishing example of mental endurance I have ever witnessed.

Everything is transient. The wind dropped and changed direction, enabling us to continue back into our rowing routine. Those few days took a huge amount out of all of us, none more than Cayle. We were all desperately exhausted but slowly recovering when Cayle called us together. We had just swapped rowing with Patrick and Nije and I was settling in for two hours rest. I opened the hatch to hear what he wanted. Cayle was sat up in the rear cabin with the hatch open. 'We've just received a text on the sat phone, I'll just read it out. It says "Hurricane coming. Row south".'

Nije and Patrick stopped rowing. 'What?' Patrick asked.

'Yep, that's all it says. "Hurricane coming. Row south". I guess we better start rowing south.'

Three days later, Hurricane Alex hit us. It was the earliest hurricane for 78 years and the strongest January Atlantic hurricane for 61 years.

We put out the para-anchor, a large parachute that sits just under the water attached to the strong point on the front of the boat. It keeps the boat at its most stable facing into the waves and wind, with the added benefit of reducing how far we'd be blown back. Cayle and I tied ourselves to the deck and fashioned some flat surfaces as best we could to ride out the storm.

I slept for hours, I must have occasionally been woken by huge waves crashing over me, but I can't remember them. The worst of the storm lasted 24 hours, but we had to wait another two days before we could pull in the para-anchor and continue the row.

Hurricane Alex enforced us into a three-day rest. Shortly after it had passed, I was out on deck rowing with Cayle. The sun shone down from a deep blue sky with only a few wispy clouds streaked across it. We were making good progress in near perfect rowing conditions and I felt strong, confident in what I was doing and happy knowing that I was experiencing something that very few people get to do. It suddenly dawned on me that I was the same person I was, before I lost my leg. That person was somebody I had strived all my life to be, someone I could finally be happy with staring back at me from the mirror. I thought that person had gone forever when I lost my leg. I had set off to redefine who I was from my hospital bed believing that what defined me now was disability. I set off hoping to be proud of the person I saw staring back in a mirror on the other side of the ocean. When I lost my leg, I lost who I was, I lost that sense of self that the vast majority of us take for granted and regaining it was the most significant thing to happen to me since losing my leg. It was more important to me than walking for the first time. In the shock of that realisation, I stopped rowing. Cayle noticed and turned round, 'Everything OK mate?'

'Yeh sorry.' I said, slightly dazed. I thought about how to explain the emotions I was feeling, decided I'd tell him later, then carried on rowing with a big smile on my face.

I'd rowed every session with Cayle and we had talked and laughed the whole way across the ocean and never once had a cross word. Twelve hours a day, seven days a week we laughed, joked and told each other pretty much all there is to tell. Three days out from Antigua, I finished regaling him with another story from my life, stopped rowing and then went quiet. Cayle sensed something was wrong, stopped rowing himself and turned around.

'I've got nothing else to tell you,' I said.

'What?'

'That's it. I've told you everything.'

'Well make something up,' he laughed.

'I have. I've been lying for two weeks now.'

We laughed together for about ten minutes.

Before we set off for the Canaries, we'd been interviewed by a film maker called Gavin. He'd followed us out to La Gomera and documented every part of the preparations and the launch of the row. He was making a film about us and became very much part of the crew. He'd chartered a yacht to take some footage of us at sea and had brought my son Billy with him. It was amazing seeing Billy even if he did look a little green.

'Hi mate,' I called over to him. 'How's it going?'

'Shit,' he called back. 'I hate boats.' Gavin, Billy and the yacht turned and left us after Gav' got his footage. They were the first people we'd seen since Theo and Shane had rowed past us on the first day. They were only a few miles behind us.

The following day we planned our arrival into Antigua. At our current speed we were looking likely to finish at around 2am. We'd dreamt of the reception that awaited us all the way across the ocean and a middle of the night finish seemed like it would be a disappointing washout. We were currently 8th out of 26 boats, not too bad for four disabled soldiers and it was a position we wanted to keep. We decided to rest for two hours and aim to finish at first light. It would be close but reckoned we'd keep our slender lead over Shane and Theo.

It was a beautiful sunny day and fairly calm so we all dived overboard for a swim. We made some extra fresh water and washed for the first time in eight weeks. It felt amazing and the excitement of finishing began to build in all of us. After two hours we set off towards Antigua and the finish line. As the afternoon drifted into what we hoped would be our last evening at sea, a headwind began to develop.

'Where the fuck is that coming from?' Cayle frowned. 'That shouldn't be happening.'

He looked worried, but it was only a slight breeze and we could still row into it.

The sun set behind a huge cumulonimbus cloud that seemed to fill the whole sky in front of us. It loomed menacingly like a sentinel guarding the finish.

Later that night we saw the lights of Guadalupe shimmering in the distance off to the south-west. At first, we thought it was the lights of a large container ship, but we soon realised that it was our first sight of land. Any euphoria we had quickly disappeared as the huge cumulonimbus cloud we'd seen earlier in the evening slowly drifted towards us. The headwind dropped and we felt the ocean pause as if taking in a breath. From the flat calm, a ferocious wind thrashed the sea into angry crashing waves that smashed over our tiny boat. Cayle and I were on the oars and pulled with all our might as the deafening rain whipped our faces. I could barely see Cayle only metres away.

The storm battered us for about an hour then as quickly as it arrived, it disappeared. We could see it drift away behind us, set against the dark sky, highlighted by the moon. Another huge cloud with its squall underneath rolled towards us. Cayle opened up the rear hatch and looked at the navigation system chart plotter.

'Shit,' he said. 'That's pushed us too far south.'

He quickly adjusted the heading as the next mini storm hit us as ferociously as the first. We pulled as hard as we could, but the winds were pushing us south of where we needed to be.

Above the din of the crashing sea and wind he screamed, 'It's pushing us past Antigua.'

Throughout the whole row I'd never seen Cayle look as worried and it made me realise that this was serious. 'Fucking hell, we're going four knots sideways.' he swore in astonishment.

The wind and vicious crashing waves were pushing us sideways as fast we could row forwards. The huge clouds with their ferocious squalls crashed over us throughout the night with brief interludes where we tried to recover lost distance from being blown south. If we continued to be pushed south and west past Antigua it would make it near impossible to row back east to the island. We'd have to be rescued and the result would be failure.

The whole row hung by a thread. We desperately fought the squalls and storms through the night, rowing our hearts out as we edged slowly towards Antigua, its lights now tantalisingly close.

The coming dawn was completely blocked out by the monstrous black clouds retreating to our east, but we started to make out the dark shape of Antigua looming out of the sea. As we slowly approached the lee of the island, the last of the squalls drifted away, off to bother someone else.

'Frank, get some rest.' Cayle called over to me. I'd been rowing continuously for 8 hours 40 minutes.

We rowed into English Harbour, Antigua 46 days, 6 hours and 49 minutes after we'd left La Gomera and into the record books. We had done it. Around 70 per cent of rowing power is drawn from the legs and we only had three between us yet had beaten the majority of the fleet that rowed out of La Gomera.

After 46 days at sea with only the sky and the sea as a backdrop; the colours, noise and people waiting to see us finish was overwhelming. It was a sensory overload and utterly amazing. My Mum and sister were there with Claire and my kids. Billy still looked a little green from his excursion on the yacht. Paddy from Row2Recovery was there and we drank champagne together out of my prosthetic leg before being whisked away for a video call with Prince Harry who congratulated us.

Lots of media interviews followed as I got slowly inebriated. The interviews were eventually called to a halt as I started talking about Cayle's arse live on TV. I was half asleep, very drunk and had no idea what I was saying.

Before the media circus, Claire had taken me to the toilet, something she would need to do for a few days. We were all swaying about and needed help standing. Rowing across the Atlantic to look in a mirror wasn't just a cliché. For me it was a very real thing. I had lost who I was and that moment of realisation that I was still the same person I was the night before I lost my leg, was the single most important thing to happen to me since. My life changed the moment I lost my leg. Rowing the Atlantic changed it back just as dramatically. As I stared into the mirror, I looked into my eyes and I knew I had rowed across the Atlantic and I'd been OK. I got into a proper bed for the first time in nearly seven weeks. The cool, clean sheets felt like undeserved opulence and I savoured the simple luxury of the hotel bed. It felt utterly amazing. Before falling to sleep, I turned to Claire and said, 'You know I'm thinking about doing it solo'. And I was.

Day 5

Near-perfect rowing conditions continued throughout the day and I was now firmly in my routine. I finished my last two-hour day shift rowing at 6pm and started to prepare my evening meal. The freeze-dried high-energy rations were the same as we'd used on my first row and for this one I'd allocated myself 6,000 calories per day for 90 days. If I didn't beat Stein Hoff's record of 96 days, then the end of the row would be a hungry one and that was a good incentive to row faster.

The freeze-dried meals were excellent, packing as much energy as possible into each meal, but that made them quite sickly – like eating a cross between the richest, most indulgent chocolate fudge cake and a pot noodle. The meals were as flavoursome as they could be, but most meals, in my opinion, benefit from a large dash of chilli sauce and I'd packed bottles of the stuff. Even through the lashings of chilli sauce, I could tell that tonight's meal didn't taste right. It was one that I hadn't tried before and hoped that the odd taste was just down to that.

I tried to get some sleep before night rowing so set my alarm for 8pm. I woke up feeling slightly nauseous and put it down to lingering seasickness. The light from the waxing half-moon shimmered on the small waves around me. It would be a very welcome companion illuminating my way. When it wasn't there, I dreaded the pitch-black emptiness.

My stomach started to rumble and the nausea I felt earlier worsened. I thought that the meal I'd eaten earlier had probably had its packaging damaged and had gone off. I'd packed the rations for this row a year before and left them sitting inside the holds and I was now beginning to regret that decision. I continued to row, then three things happened at once. One of the two mini navigation screens at the rear of the boat went blank. *Hope* suddenly slewed off course and, from the cabin, the navigation system started beeping in alarm. I quickly grabbed the steering handlines and yanked, forcing the autohelm off the rudder via a system of clever pulleys and steered *Hope* back onto course using the compass screen that was still working. I locked off the handlines fixing the rudder and *Hope*'s course through the black sea settled. I then dived into the cabin. The navigation screen was blank flashing the message 'Loss of GPS Signal'. I tried switching the system off then on again and still nothing was working. The alarm continued to beep as I frantically tried to find what had gone wrong. On the opposite wall from the navigation system was a removable panel and inside was the GPS that ran the Automatic Identification System (AIS). I unscrewed the panel and looked inside. I'd used the space to store my spare fleeces and foam mats to cushion the rowing seat. I removed them and unplugged the GPS. I checked the lead looking for an obvious fault. While investigating, my stomach started to rumble badly then had the awful realisation that I had seconds before whatever was in there, was going to come out. I opened the hatch in a panic and awkwardly clambered out. Getting in and out of the hatch with only one leg isn't easy, especially whilst clamping my arse cheeks together. I barely made it to the side before exploding overboard. This was going to be a very bad night.

Day 5 Logbook Entry

Position at 0800hrs on 14th Jan 2019 UTC	*Distance travelled 43nm at 222°*
34°48'.180N 012°07'.418W	*Total distance 227nm*

AIS dropped out at 2100h then GPS fix also dropped out, at the same time started with v bad sickness and diarrhoea, no vomiting but nausea and v bad diarrhoea.

A v bad night.

In the summer of 2016, I made the decision that I would row the Atlantic again, but this time solo. I wanted to continue what Row2Recovery had set out to do, raise money for military charities and keep wounded and injured servicemen and women in the nations' conscience. The Endeavour Fund, the precursor to the INVICTUS Games Foundation, helped wounded and injured servicemen and women rediscover their adventurous spirit through physical challenges, had financially underwritten much of Row2Recovery. Rowing across the Atlantic had such a positive effect on me, I wanted to raise money so that others in a similar situation as me, could have the same opportunity.

Rowing again would be a massive undertaking, especially as I would be ending one career and starting a new one and I still didn't have a clue what I was going to do for a job. In March the decision was made that I would be Medically Discharged from the Royal Marines in the coming September. It suddenly seemed that I had an opportunity and if I didn't do it now, I might never get the chance again.

I would be raising money for both the Royal Marines Charity and the Endeavour Fund. I was also acutely aware of the enormity of the task I had set myself. There is a saying in ocean rowing that 'it's much harder get a boat to the start line than it is to row it to the finish line' and I gave myself until the following summer to raise the enormous amount of sponsorship required to put an ocean rowing boat in the water.

I announced on a couple of ocean rowing social media pages that I was thinking about going solo. Almost straight away I received a message from Phil, who'd rowed as one of a pair of Americans who'd beaten us by a day on the Talisker Whiskey Atlantic Challenge. Phil is like the all-American dream, tall, athletic and looking like he'd just walked off a Tommy Hilfiger fashion shoot. He offered me the use of his two-man boat *Hope,* an unbelievably generous offer that would save me tens of thousands of pounds. In the hospital bed next to me when I first lost my leg was a south London businessman called Tim. We'd become close friends since and after I told him I was going to row the Atlantic again he took me round to meet many of his business associates. At the end of the day, I not only had a boat, I also had my first sponsors. The row was firmly underway.

On Monday, 26 September 2016, my time as a serving Royal Marine finally came to an end. It was over 24 years after I first got off the train at Lympstone Commando, nervously clutching my suitcase and wondering if I really had what it takes to get through training.

On 28 October 2016, the Corps birthday when Royal Marines everywhere celebrate the formation of the Corps, I happened to be in the Senior Non-Commissioned Officers' Mess on board HMS *Victory* having a drunken conversation with General Ed Davies, the Governor of Gibraltar. He suggested starting the row from the Rock. Initially the thought of rowing through the Straits of Gibraltar and out into the Atlantic seemed ridiculous, but after a bit of research, I realised that there was potential to beat a record. If I rowed from mainland Europe to mainland South America solo, I'd be only the fourth person in history to do so, but I could also have a go at beating Stein Hoff's able-bodied record of 96 days. If I, as a disabled person, could beat an able-bodied record in something as physically demanding as rowing solo across an entire ocean solo, it would send a positive message that no one should be defined by disability.

I believed I'd have to redefine myself as a disabled person when I lost my leg and only through rowing the Atlantic did I realise that I was wrong. I now saw an opportunity to change how society viewed disabled people and maybe how disabled people view themselves.

As soon as I made the decision to row from Gibraltar, I contacted General Ed and flew over to meet him. Even though the Royal Marines rank structure is more egalitarian than the rest of the armed forces, meetings with Generals, especially those appointed as Governor, are rare. I was aware of how fortunate I was to be meeting with him and how generous General Ed was being with his precious time. I also rang my old mate Ivor, the storeman in Gibraltar who I'd last seen doing the Rock run. Between Ivor and General Ed, I soon had a firm plan for rowing from Gibraltar and set 18 January 2018 as the departure date. Throughout 2017 I threw myself into putting the row together, logistically and financially.

My Mum had been diagnosed with pulmonary fibrosis soon after getting back from Antigua and she deteriorated quickly. Because of living in Devon and being consumed with preparation for the solo row, I didn't really comprehend exactly how ill she was. My sister on the other hand dealt with it on a daily basis as she lived around the corner from her.

It finally hit home when I went to see my sister Julie finish the London Marathon in 2017. My Mum couldn't walk without oxygen. I accompanied her to an appointment to see a lung specialist. In my ignorance I couldn't understand why I was being asked to come all the way from Devon to drive her around the corner to what I thought was another routine appointment in Essex.

Throughout my life I've had a very difficult relationship with my Mum and couldn't express any form of loving emotion to her. For years I would involuntarily flinch whenever she tried to touch me. I saw how much this hurt her, so I worked hard to control it, but still it remained, just beneath the surface. The appointment was to give my Mum her biopsy results to identify how aggressive the fibrosis was, and she asked me to accompany her to see the consultant. It was bad news. My Mum started to cry and sounded like a frightened child as she tried to ask questions. I felt helpless sat next to her. I knew I should hug her, but I couldn't. I could sense the consultant urging me to comfort her and felt embarrassed at appearing heartless or emotionally retarded, then felt heartless at thinking only about how I appeared to the consultant. It was such a simple thing to do, and I knew how much it would mean to her, to just put my arm around her and say 'Come on, Mum'. I just couldn't do it. I've forced myself to confront death, I've forced myself to overcome utter exhaustion and carry on, but I just couldn't do this one simple thing. I felt utterly hopeless.

In January 2018 I flew out to Gibraltar with Cayle, his brother Seth and my mate Bondy, and along with Ivor we started to pack *Hope*. We were working long hours getting everything ready and Cayle's experience was invaluable, but the previous year was beginning to catch up on me. I was exhausted, but everything was starting to come together.

With two weeks to go and the weather looking promising, we were joined by Lucy who was running the media. As well as packing and preparing *Hope*, I was pulled sideways to do interviews, photo shoots and filming as Lucy ramped up the media campaign. Since starting to plan the row, it had always been a concept in my head, but as it became real, the full enormity of what was about to happen started to become clear. As departure day creeped closer, I became more run down. With a week to go, the previous year finally caught up with me. We'd all taken a break from prepping *Hope* to grab some lunch with Lucy and I wasn't feeling good. I felt slightly nauseous but put it down to the previous nights' beers. I excused myself to go to the toilet but didn't make it clear of the table.

'Shit.' I said. 'Sorry guys I've literally just shat myself. I'm going to go back to change.'

With that knowledge, I left them to their lunch. By the time I reached the accommodation, I had full-blown gastric flu, or H3N2 Aussie flu to be precise. I was sweating, shivering, felt sick and had horrendous diarrhoea.

I called Cayle. 'I only ever get the flu for 24 hours, I should be OK tomorrow.' And went to bed.

The next morning I felt worse. My sister Julie called to tell me that Mum had been taken into hospital with a chest infection in the early hours of the morning. She'd been struggling to breath and Julie had called an ambulance. I went down to the boat with Seth, Cayle and Bondy but just couldn't function so returned to my bed.

I spent the next couple of days trying to get as much done on the boat, in between regular updates on my Mum from Julie and retreating to bed with the flu when I couldn't carry on. I was ill for 72 hours and as I started to feel better, so did my Mum. On 14 January, four days from setting off, I spoke to her. She sounded a lot better. Julie said that she was passed the worst and should be out of hospital the next day. I felt that everything had turned a corner and we'd all gone through the worst. I was still exhausted and the flu had really knocked me for six, but I could at least see the light at the end of the tunnel. I could now focus solely on the 18th and the start of the row. Claire joined me and my weather router was flying in the next day. Everything was finally coming together.

Claire and I woke with a growing sense of both excitement and foreboding. The row became very real and with three days to go it felt that I had started the final countdown. As we were walking to meet everyone for breakfast, my phone rang. It was my sister.

'Mum's had a really bad night,' she said.

'What shall I do? Do I need to come back?'

'Wait for the consultant to come round. Don't do anything yet.'

Claire saw the sudden change in my demeanour. 'What's happened?'

As Claire and I walked over to the boat to meet everyone we discussed whether to start the row or not. The team from Ocean Village, where I planned to depart from were waiting for details about the start. There was a real excitement and energy surrounding everyone, but I was on a different planet. I told Cayle of my conversation with my sister and that I was waiting for another call.

Julie called again. I could hear slight sobs in her voice as she said, 'The Doctor came round and said that there wasn't anything more they could do for Mum except make her as comfortable as they can until the end.'

Ivor drove Claire and me to Malaga to get the only flight to Stanstead in Essex, close to Basildon Hospital where Mum was. During the flight I looked out of the window at the wispy clouds below and knew. I don't know how, but I just did. When we landed Claire switched on her phone and it immediately beeped with an incoming text. It was from a second cousin, sending us her condolences. Billy met us at the gate.

'It's alright mate,' I said, saving him the task. 'I already know.'

My mum died of pneumonia while we were in the air. The row was over before it began.

Day 6

With frequent bouts of diarrhoea and constant nausea, rowing through the night was impossible. I concentrated on remaining hydrated and waited for the morning to call Tim, a boat engineer in Gibraltar who'd helped me set up the navigation system before I left. I spent the next six hours disassembling, reassembling and changing components over with the spares held, with sporadic episodes of jettisoning myself out of the cabin to squirt overboard, often at the most awkward point. It was incredibly hard work, but by 2pm, with Tim's help, we'd exhausted every option for a fix at sea. The navigation system was gone.

I rang Leven to ask his advice. Although the electronic navigation system was broken, I still had a back-up hand-held GPS and charts. The electronic compass at the end of the boat was also working. So, with the handheld GPS and charts, I could tell where I was, where I needed to go and with the compass, I knew which way.

'You know, Lee, it's a back-up system for a reason. It would be remiss of you to venture out to sea only with your back-up system for navigating. My advice, Captain, is to call in to the Canaries and get the necessary repairs there,'

His soft Scottish voice always reassured me as he recalled something similar happening to him from one of his many ocean rowing sorties, yet it didn't register. My mind told me the row was over. My aim was to beat the able-bodied record for rowing across the entire Atlantic

Ocean solo and I'd got as far as the Canaries, the start-point of my first row across the Atlantic.

I rang Claire and Izzy, who was running the media campaign for this row, to tell them the news. I was utterly devastated, but not surprised. My entire life I'd failed at everything I had ever set out to achieve. I started to think how ridiculous I was to allow myself to start to believe this time would somehow be any different.

I repeated the call to Cayle. 'Mate, it's like the last three and a half years has just gone up in smoke in front of my eyes.'

I was overtaken with a sense of utter unfairness. I'd genuinely set out to do something worthwhile, how I had worked myself into the ground putting the whole thing together, my Mum dying just before the first start date, and now just five days in, it was over.

As I talked the situation through with Cayle, I knew I'd have to carry on to South America. Too many people had backed me with their time and money to just give up. The prospect of failing even before getting to the Canaries loomed in front of me. There was nothing I could do about it other than play yet another shitty hand life had dealt me. The rest of this row would now be not just physically demanding, it would also be both mentally and emotionally draining as well.

I rang Claire to tell her I'd continue the row regardless.

'The record is still on,' she said.

Her words confused me.

'Tatiana from the Ocean Rowing Society has literally just emailed me back. No ocean rowing record is worded "non-stop," so you can stop for essential repairs. She said the clock will still be ticking though. But the world record will still stand.'

The Ocean Rowing Society are the custodians of all ocean rowing records and Guinness World Records look to them to ratify ocean rowing records. After hours of exhaustion trying to fix the navigation system through a bout of chronic diarrhoea, the roller coaster of emotions of failing and finally getting myself ready to carry on regardless, the row was back on.

The last few hours had reminded me of how closely failure stalks me. Throughout my life failure has been my constant companion. When I thought the row was over, those thoughts hidden deep came to the forefront of my mind. It was the same when I lost my leg that same feeling was there. That this was *'just bloody typical, everything I do goes wrong.'* Failure and self-loathing are the monsters that have lurked in the shadows of my mind through my entire life. As much as I convinced myself of my altruistic motivations for rowing, running from those two monsters had driven me, from Dagenham to the

Marines, from the Marines to Special Duties and was now driving me across an entire ocean. To fully understand the row, you have to know where those two monsters came into my life.

Day 6 Logbook Entry

Position at 0800hrs on 15th Jan 2019 UTC	*Distance travelled 35.9nm at 176°*
34°12'.009N 012°03'.611W	*Total distance 263nm*

Spent all morning with v bad diarrhoea and feeling nauseous whist on the phone to Raymarine engineer.

By 1400hrs had exhausted all possible options of a fix at sea left with no AIS (transmit only) and limited internal GPS that kept dropping. After speaking to Leven the only option is to head to Gran Canaria Las Palmas to try and get it fixed. No rowing all day due to sickness.

DAGENHAM

My Dad was a violent alcoholic. He beat my Mum before I was born, through her pregnancies and right up until she left him when I was seven. He'd grab my Mum around the neck, throw her around and punch her in the face and her body and kick her when she was on the floor. After a particularly vicious beating where one of her eyes had completely closed over, our family doctor told her that she should leave my Dad before he killed her. My Mum often had black eyes when she dropped me and my sister off at school and even at that early age, I felt somehow different to all the other kids. We were the problem children from the problem family. Whenever my Dad beat her, my Mum would scream for me to come and help her. I'd run to where in the house he was hitting her and freeze in the doorway, petrified with fear.

He also beat me. I remember being at the family doctors with bruises across my forehead and being off school for two weeks with concussion.

Any recollection of him hitting her or me had been locked up in a box, deep in my subconscious. I had vivid memories of the immediate before and aftermath, but a complete blank of the violence in between. I only knew that my Mum called me to help her and me freezing with fear, because she talked about it in later life with a lot of regret. She felt guilty for the pressure she put on me at such a young age.

Then, many years later whilst driving, a memory appeared as if from nowhere, like it just popped into existence. Except it had the familiarity of a memory I've always had with a rawness that belied the 50 years that separated then from now, like it had been stored, pristine in a jar, in a dark corner of my mind.

I was five or six years old, downstairs in our front room looking at the orange, brown and black circular patterns of the carpet. I was trying to make sense of the swirls, trying to find a pattern in the seemingly random. I knew my Dad was drunk and I could hear shouting and bangs and thuds.

I heard my Mum cry out, 'No John. No,' a desperate pleading in her voice.

I anxiously tried to tear my mind away from what was happening upstairs by concentrating on the carpet. My sister Julie was in the room with me, sat on the sofa.

'Lee. Lee.' I heard her cry.

I ran upstairs. My Mum was on the bed propping herself up with her arms, her cheeks wet with her tears. My Dad was stood on the other side of the bed from me, silhouetted by the window with its half-drawn curtains. He had a handful of her long, dark hair in his right fist, his face screwed into a snarl. He was biting his tongue, something he did when angry and it protruded from the side of his mouth. My Mum was looking at me and sobbed, her eyes begging me to help her.

'Stop hitting her!' I shouted from the doorway. I was too scared to set foot in the bedroom.

'I'm not hitting her,' he snarled. 'If I wanted to hit her, I'd knock her fucking head right off.'

He then yanked her head back and raised his left arm to punch her again. She closed her eyes and covered her face in desperation. He held her there, my Mum flinching and him mocking me. I was terrified and felt utterly useless. I hated that I wasn't brave enough to help her and hated myself for being a coward. He let go of my Mum's hair then grabbed her by the throat and pulled her face inches from his and spat something incoherent.

A few days later, I had to retell what had happened to my maternal nan, her mother my great nan Woods and great aunt Em. I was stood in the middle of the room with my great nan Woods sat in front of me. I felt I was on trial and I was guilty of not doing anything to help my Mum.

'My John would sort him out,' said great aunt Em

My great aunt Em had married and divorced 'a' John before I was born. I had no idea who John was but felt the implied accusation that someone should have sorted my Dad out because I hadn't. It carved a canyon-sized rift through my very being, where to the very core of my soul, I believed I was a coward and hated myself for it. But the memory of the raw fear in her face as my Dad gripped her throat gave me an empathy and understanding of what she went through that I wished I had before she died. I knew my Dad was a 'wife beater' and what my Mum went through, but it was as if I read about it once, long ago. It had no emotional resonance or meaning with me.

There is a definite before and after in how I viewed my Dad. Before my Mum left, I hated him. I was petrified of him and repeatedly asked her to leave. After she left him, I yearned for his approval. Although I knew that he'd beat both my Mum and me on a conscious level, it was never spoken of between us and the actual memories of him doing it were locked away deep in my subconscious. Conversely, when my Mum left my Dad, my relationship with her rapidly deteriorated. I felt that she was constantly angry with me. Practically my Mum was meticulously fair. Chores and Christmas and birthday presents shared equally between my sister and me. But emotionally I felt that she had a near constant underlying rage directed solely at me and we would argue constantly.

My Mum's sister would often say to me, 'You know your Mum loves you really.'

The word 'really' hung in the air conspicuously trying to convince me against my lived experience. Unsurprisingly I wasn't the easiest child to bring up, but my behaviour wasn't especially delinquent, not to Dagenham standards anyway. Perhaps I was angry at her for leaving my Dad, even though I begged her to when they were together. That alone cannot account for how she changed towards me. Once my Dad left and he stopped beating us, I undoubtedly craved my Dad's approval and that must have upset her, but again that alone cannot explain how deeply our relationship changed. Later as an adult, my Mum said she was frightened of me and was scared that I would hit her.

She said that, 'A line would've been crossed,' with a forceful conviction, so that fear was real to her. She clearly saw a lot of my Dad in me, but didn't see the deep revulsion I had of being violent towards a woman like him. I wasn't my Dad. It is maybe a large part of why our relationship changed. Whatever changed, it clearly sat deep within her and was conspicuous in the chasm of difference between how she was emotionally towards me and my sister.

My Mum's life with my Dad was unimaginably difficult and then bringing me and my sister up on her own was incredibly hard. I have no doubt that she tried her hardest with the cards life had dealt her. The memories of my Dad beating my Mum and me were purged when he left, but the memories of the near constant arguing with my Mum were my constant lived experience.

Football was a big part of my early life. My maternal grandad Horder was an avid Arsenal fan, so were all my Dad's brothers and the majority of the kids in Ingleby Road. Two doors down lived the Roses, their Dad, George took me to all the Arsenal home games. Not that I ever saw any football. The North Bank at Highbury was a typical football terrace with sloping steps and barriers to stop the crowd surging forward. We would sit on the barriers to see a little of the game and when the Arsenal scored, we were thrown off in the mayhem of the crowd jumping up and down celebrating.

My paternal nan and grandad Spencer and my Dad's youngest brother, Kevin all live around the corner in the banjo, which is Dagenham for cul-de-sac. At the other end of Ingleby road was Tony Watson. Although he was seven years older than me, he took me under his wing. He knew that my Dad regularly beat my Mum, as did the whole street and treated me like the little brother he never had. I looked up to Tony who had a crossbow, air guns and used to catch lizards and snakes over the local waste ground behind Western Avenue. Catching newts, lizards and snakes with Tony Watson is where my love of nature and the outdoors was born.

In the Dagenham that I grew up in there was a hard man culture. My Dad was respected and carried a hard man reputation. I would often find myself saying 'I'm Johnny Spencer's son', with a sense of pride. However, I was never a fighter. I hate confrontations and always felt that he was disappointed in me for being a coward.

My Dad would also nick anything that wasn't nailed down but that came from a background of stealing often being a necessity for survival. My paternal grandad Spencer, talked about the hardship of growing up in Poplar in the Eastend of London after the Great War. He had to steal as a young boy to put food on the family table. His Dad, my great-grandad John Joseph Spencer, was blinded by gas and honourably discharged from the Great War on 24 March 1918. My great nan Lilley was then forced to work as a bookies' runner, an illegal occupation that brought in a few crucial pennies. A big step down for a Royal Naval officer's daughter who once won a scholarship for playing the piano.

The local corner shop was owned by one of our friends called Spud. His uncle often helped out in the shop and when he did, the news would rapidly spread that he was there. Spud's uncle was deaf and all the kids would take it in turns to go in and ask for something in the rear of the shop and when he turned around, they would fill their pockets full of whatever they could grab. Except me. Not through moral objection, but because I was a coward. This bothered me as I wanted to be like my Dad who was described as, 'a brilliant thief.'

I only once tried to nick something from the local off licence. After loitering in the tiny shop looking guilty, I eventually grabbed a bag of crisps, the loudest thing in the shop. The manager, a youngish burley man, heard the almost deafening rustle and looked directly at me, from whatever he was doing.

'Put them back,' he said.

I panicked and ran out of the shop and straight home. The manager just followed me. My Dad was an alcoholic, he managed the local Off Licence, he knew both me, my Dad and where I lived and knocked at the door. That was the end of my criminal career. As well as believing that I was a coward, I was also a terrible thief.

Day 7

Feeling better, I was rowing again, but without the navigation system driving the autohelm. I was hand steering, and with it came the inevitable zigzagging across the ocean. The tiniest adjustment to the steering lines transferred to large changes in direction. I had no way of knowing what direction *Hope* was travelling or Course Over Ground (COG). The COG screen at the rear of the boat was blank. Only the compass screen was working to show the way she was pointing.

The direction a boat is pointing and its COG are seldom, if ever the same. Wind, currents and waves all influence the direction of travel and meant I had no immediate way of knowing my COG. To get this I'd have to determine position on my back-up handheld GPS and then plot it on the chart. By comparing current and previous positions, I was able to get a recent COG. The more frequently I did this, the more accurate the COG would be, but the more frequently I did this the less I was rowing. I was now aiming for a 200m gap in a sea wall in Las Palmas from nearly 400 miles away. Accuracy was now critical.

I was struggling to hold my course. A westerly wind was pushing me too far east towards the African coast. Early in the afternoon a small orange turtle, about the size of a dinner plate, swept past the port side of *Hope*. I was about to plunge my oar in the water at the start of a stroke but just managed to stop myself from hitting the turtle. Its startled head popped up and looked back at me as I rowed away. It was a small highlight in an otherwise frustrating day.

Day 7 Logbook Entry

Position at 0800hrs on 16th Jan 2019 UTC	*Distance travelled 45.7nm at 175°*
33° 26′.516N 011°59′.186W	*Total distance 308nm*

Cloudy, frustrating day and night. No cog and only compass to nav, felt that I've spent the last 24hrs zigzagging about. Pushing due south and trying not to get pushed too far east.

Saw an orange turtle right next to the boat in the afternoon, stuck its head out to look at what was happening, nearly hit it with the oar.

1976 was a long hot summer and one sunny afternoon at the start of the six weeks' school holiday, I walked straight into my Mum being beaten by my Dad. Hearing I was home she called for me to get help. I ran upstairs where my Dad had her pinned to the bed. My Dad said something that I couldn't hear as I turned and ran down the stairs and out of the front door. I ran straight to our neighbour George.

'My Dad's hitting my Mum and she needs help.'

'I'm not getting involved in that,' he laughed nervously. 'Go and get your nan.'

I ran into the banjo and straight into Nan Spencer's. I told them that my Mum needed help. They weren't interested. My nan and grandad were in complete denial about my Dad's alcoholism and that he regularly beat my Mum.

Yet nan kept me there, away from the 'nothing' happening back home. After what seemed like an age, I walked home and as I turned the corner of the banjo, my Mum was walking out of the door with her granny shopping trolley full of washing to take to her Mum's. It was my nan's washing that she did for her for a few extra quid a week in an old twin-tub washing machine. Because of my Dad's drinking there were extended periods where he didn't work and spent what little we had down the local British Legion club. Money was very short throughout my childhood so those few extra pounds were extremely handy.

My grandad Spencer walked around the corner just in time to see my Mum with her washing, clutching my sister by the hand and mistook the situation as my Mum finally leaving my Dad.

'I'll make sure you never get housed. You'll be homeless if you leave him,' he yelled.

My Mum grabbed my hand and carried on walking out of Ingleby road to my nan and grandad Horder's half a mile away. And that was that, the final nail in the coffin that was my Mum and Dad's marriage.

We spent the school holidays at my nan and grandad Horder's in the same clothes that we'd left with.

Just after the end of the summer holidays, my Dad moved out of our home and into my nan and grandad Spencer's so we moved back into our home. There then began a protracted cycle of court cases, reconciliations with him staying over with the inevitable arguments that led to a beating for my Mum, then another break up.

Massive clumps of hair started to fall out when I was bathing and bald patches appeared on my head. I was diagnosed with nervous alopecia. I also began to have recurring nightmares about rats in my bed and I'd wake screaming and run into my Mum's bed too scared to be in my own.

My Dad moved into a high-rise just around the corner from Ingleby road and as my relationship with my Mum deteriorated, my nan and grandad Spencer's became my second home. I was the eldest grandchild and was undoubtedly their favourite, much to the detriment of my sister, who may as well have not existed. My grandad Spencer ran the local British Legion and it was the hub of our family. If my nan and grandad Spencer's was my second home, then the Legion was a definite third. I'd walk past my Dad's flat and straight to the Legion if I wanted to see him. In the British Legion, my Dad sat on a table full of old Royal Marines. They called their table 'The Royal Marines Mess Deck' and it's where I first encountered Bootnecks. Almost everyone in the Legion had served in the Second World War, but the Royal Marines were different. They socialised together and were noticeably prouder of their Corps and their green Commando berets. They had a definite identity. I'd sit listening to their war stories, very few about fighting the Japanese or Germans: most were of fights in bars or getting drunk and being driven back by the POWs they'd meant to be guarding. I had a deep respect for the Second World War veterans instilled in me by both sides of my family, but I looked up to the old Marines most of all.

I'm dyslexic and found school difficult. I was always told that I was clever but lazy and this was reflected in every single school report. In my first year at Junior school, the whole school auditioned for the choir for the upcoming Christmas carol concert. We all lined up in the hall, singing our little hearts out. The teachers walked in between rows of singing children, stopping at each in turn to listen. Those they tapped on the shoulder were told to go onto the stage.

Mrs Fox was a fill in teacher who didn't have a class of her own but took random lessons. She was a severe, religious woman and I thought she always disapproved of me. She walked behind me, and I could sense her head dip down to my right side. I sang for all I was worth. She paused a second, straightened and just before walking on to the next child, tapped me on the shoulder. I thought my chest would explode with pride. I strutted confidently onto the stage and joined a few children who'd also been tapped on the shoulder. I sat on one of the seats and continued to sing with the broadest smile across my face.

The teachers continued walking up and down until they had listened to the whole school, by which time there were perhaps a dozen of us on stage, with 90 other kids standing in rows down on the hall floor. I couldn't wait to get home and tell my Mum I was in the choir and already imagining her at the concert beaming with pride.

One of the teachers then said if anyone who was in the choir really didn't want to be, they should go up onto the stage. I couldn't imagine why anyone wouldn't want to be in the choir, why wouldn't you want to sing in front of your parents at a Christmas concert? Even more confusing, one of the kids on the hall floor put his hand up.

'You sure?' said the teacher to a quick nod. 'Go on then up on the stage.'

The penny slowly dropped as he walked along his row to the edge of the hall then towards the stage where he climbed up the few steps and sat on the only free chair on the stage. I was absolutely devastated. The school choir was virtually the whole school except for us – twelve tone-deaf children. Even at that young age I thought, *'Are we really going to make that much of a difference?'*

They could've told us to sing quietly. It was then I realised that life at school wasn't going to be easy.

As I progressed through early school, I became less and less engaged. The teachers had marked me down as the problem child from the problem family and gave up on me. Being placed daily in an environment where the only test of your worth is the ability to regurgitate what you've learned onto a page only added to my already overburdened sense of uselessness. School rapidly became something else I was rubbish at and added to my sense of self-loathing. I hated school. Not surprisingly I got into a lot of trouble in junior school. There was a group of six of us who were separated between different classes. It wouldn't be unusual for any of us to have physical fights with teachers and throw chairs around the classroom.

My last teacher in junior school, Mr Venables, was a Spitfire pilot in the Battle of Britain and I treated him awfully. I also bullied an Asian girl in my class. I'm still very ashamed of this and the memory smarts of how I behaved to them both.

My Mum met Charlie around the middle of junior school at Gingerbread, a club for single parents and he soon moved in with us. From the very start our relationship was fraught. I thought that by being nice to him was somehow disloyal to my Dad. My Mum slowly pushed me away emotionally. My nervous alopecia and nightmares worsened, and I'd often run screaming into Mum's bedroom. Charlie told my Mum to be harder with me.

I was referred to a child psychiatrist who told her, 'Charlie would never be any good for your son. What are you going to do?'

For a child psychologist to be that frank seems almost incredulous. In hindsight, the bluntness of that statement holds more truth about our relationship than my memory can account for. Charlie was never stepdad of the year but in comparison to my Dad, he wasn't bad. Ultimately my Mum chose Charlie over me and that decision haunted her. It was a very difficult family set up for him to walk into to start with, but our household became even more unstable with constant arguments between Charlie and my Mum.

It was with this as a backdrop that my relationship with my Mum deteriorated dramatically. We'd argue constantly, I felt that I could do no right and the only 'logical' explanation I had for my Mum's anger towards me, was that she hated me. Maybe she resented the fact that she'd been told to leave Charlie and because she didn't, she blamed me for the guilt she felt.

Despite her new relationship she still loved my Dad and talked about him positively. Incredibly, to the point of her saying he made her feel safe. Whenever my Mum talked about him positively, I heard 'Unlike you' in everything she said.

Charlie and my Mum seemed an all too familiar cycle of arguing, splitting up, reconciling, marry, divorce, reconcile while mine and my Mum's relationship continued on a downward spiral until we couldn't be in the same room together. I hated my home, I hated Charlie and I hated my Mum. But mostly, I hated being me.

Early in my Mum's relationship with Charlie, we took a camping holiday to Cornwall. Charlie, wanting to go fishing, had rushed us to the cliffs overlooking the sea shouting in frustration that 'tide and time wait for no man'. I don't know why, but that simple sentence resonated. At first, I didn't understand his anger and his sense of urgency. To my mind the sea wasn't going anywhere. But as we finally sat on the cold granite rocks of the Cornish coast, looking out over the vast Atlantic Ocean with its huge swell driving ferocious waves, I was filled with a sense of smallness. How utterly insignificant I was compared to the ocean, and I suddenly understood Charlie's frustration. I knew that time and tide do indeed wait for no man and my utter insignificance up against both. I had a clear understanding that time is inexorable, that even if I wanted the bad times to continue, they wouldn't.

Whenever life was almost unbearable from that point on, I had the feeling that I was in a tunnel that had an end. All I had to do was close my eyes and keep pushing through to the other side. Everything is transient.

Day 8

The handlines for the hand steering rig could be locked in place either side of my legs. If I needed to make a tiny adjustment to, say, the port side, I could release the starboard and pull the port line in a millimetre and then lock off the port side again. With these miniscule adjustments to the rudder, I could set a more accurate COG and zigzag less. But I was still struggling to claw back the west I lost the day before. The best I could manage was almost due south. A few squalls came past during the day, instantly whipping the sea into a frenzy of white topped waves. One minute there'd be hardly any wind, the next a 20-knot gust pushing me east. The squalls left behind a choppy, dirty sea and the irregular waves made it difficult to row with any rhythm. The squalls also brought a smattering of rain and the cold fresh water was blessed relief in washing the salt from my face and body.

Another small orange turtle swam past late in the afternoon before the sun set behind grey clouds, tinged with yellow edges. I called Ivor in Gibraltar. I needed someone to coordinate getting me into Las Palmas port, and looking at the chart I could see that the marina was on the northern side of the port. It appeared that I'd have to round the southern point of the sea wall of the port and row back north to enter the marina. This would most likely be into wind and therefore I needed a boat to shadow me in. Ivor had helped me every step of the way getting *Hope* into the water and he readily agreed when I asked him if he could fly to the Canary Islands in the next couple of days.

The squalls continued through the night. Thankfully the strongest winds were from the east so each time a squall passed through, I tried to claw back as much west as possible.

Day 8 Logbook Entry

Position at 0800hrs on 17th Jan 2019 UTC	*Distance travelled 54.6nmnm at 188°*
32°32′.632N 012°08′.600W	*Total distance 362nm*

315 miles to Las Palmas.

Have been struggling to get west. Been heading almost due south but need 210°-220°.

Weather has been v changeable with lots of squalls passing through all night. Wind is one minute 0.5knots then gusting 10-20knots with a lot of easterly.

Saw another small orange turtle.

Today has started wet, grey and choppy.

In 1981 I finished junior school and, unlike all my friends at William Ford Juniors who went to Dagenham Priory comprehensive, I went up to Bishop Ward Catholic Comprehensive. All the male members of my Dad's side of the family had gone there including my Dad who was expelled for hosing down nuns during a choral concert, something my nan Spencer was inexplicably proud of. My nan only converted to

Catholicism when she married my grandad and was the most Catholic person I knew. Before being accepted into the school as a non-Catholic, I had to be interviewed by the headmaster, a fat old Irishman called Mr McDermott.

He asked my Mum a few half-hearted questions about my schooling and did his best to sound interested in the answers, then asked what team I supported.

'Arsenal,' I replied.

He perked right up and said, 'Oh that's OK then, you're in.'

My Mum laughed nervously and waited for the next question, but that was genuinely the end of the interview.

The main difference between Bishop Ward and Dagenham Priory was that Bishop Ward had a school uniform. Because we were on benefits, we had to go to one of only a few shops that stocked the uniform for Bishop Ward. I was given two government-issue shirts and trousers and government issue jumper, shoes, blazer and tie. I cried my eyes out and was dreading starting a new school dressed like a pauper having to queue up for free school meal tickets. I knew I'd be a beacon for bullying.

The top streams in secondary school studied for O Levels and the bottom streams studied for CSEs. School was little more than a sifting exercise for those who'd go on to work in an office and those destined for the factory floor and this was done by a set of tests to filter the O Levels kids from the CSE kids. Unsurprisingly I was firmly a CSE kid.

The majority of my teachers at Bishop Ward were terrible. Teaching was replaced with copying from books. At one open evening a top stream 'O' Level class put on a comedy sketch show purely for their parents. I peeped through the window in curiosity and saw their teacher beaming with pride at his students. I was genuinely shocked. I'd never seen a teacher the slightest bit interested in anything his students were doing. My maths teacher, Mr Buhaja, never once showed anyone in my class how to do anything. Computers were just becoming popular and he sat in class reading books on programming. At the end of my schooling he refused to enter me for the exam, saying to my Mum that it wasn't worth it. I assumed that he must know what he was talking about and that I was stupid. I played schoolyard football every lunchtime, but never made the school team and despite trying as hard as I could in the cross-country team trials, I came a miserable 53rd in my year.

I was rubbish at all sports, I wasn't academic, and I was a benefits kid.

I hated the stigma of being on benefits and got a paper round from the local newsagents. I spent all my money on clothes. In the early 1980s large, branded fashion names were made popular by football hooligans and casuals and if you didn't wear a certain fashion name, you were a nobody. I saved up my £3.50 a week money from a paper round and bought a bright blue Sergio Tacchini tracksuit top that was about £60. I wore it continuously for a year.

Through secondary school, my home life was difficult with constant arguments with my Mum and school wasn't an escape. I was extremely unhappy and often thought of suicide as a relief from the constant feeling of worthlessness. There was an incessant monologue, like another person in my head, constantly accusing me of being rubbish at everything, for being a coward, for being thick. Fear of hurting myself stopped me seriously attempting to kill myself, reinforcing my perception as a coward.

I idolised my Dad and craved his approval. I thought he felt I was a bit of a wally. Some of my decisions were incomprehensible, as if I was purposely giving ammunition to my inner monologue.

The breakdancing craze spread from America and I enthusiastically took up spinning on my head, becoming a member of Dagenham's premier breakdancing crew, 'The Popping Wizards'.

Every Saturday, my friend Darren and I would get on the Tube to hang out with all the cool breakdancers at Covent Garden. If that wasn't uncool enough, I got a perm and called myself Jiwi Rock. Every other Wednesday a local pub called the Robin Hood held a disco for body poppers and breakdancers. Every week there was a 'burn off' – a dance competition between two people where the level of crowd cheers would determine the winner. The DJ would walk through the crowd and approach talented dancers for the burn off. Anyone decent would attract a circle of on-lookers who'd gather to admire their moves. The DJ spotted a young lad ardently throwing himself about the dance floor and asked if he would like to participate in that week's burn off. He declined, but I incomprehensively volunteered.

I followed the DJ to his decks where the other dancer waited. Announcing the burn off the DJ asked the other dancer his name and where he was from before starting the music. The dancer started rhythmically stepping faultlessly from side to side in time with the tune, before flipping onto his back to start a windmill. 'Oh bugger' I thought. Windmilling was the holy grail in breakdancing. It's hard to describe, let alone actually perform. I waited with a foreboding feeling building in my stomach as I knew exactly what was about to happen. He finished with a flurry of head spins before flipping from his back onto his feet like a kung fu master to rapturous applause.

I stepped forward. The DJ asked my name and I mumbled 'Jiwi Rock,' down the microphone. The music started and anything that I thought I was mildly good at, completely vanished from my mind. It's hard to describe what I did, I started moving instead of doing nothing and this slowly turned into a rather bad robot dance. It was the single most uncool thing I could ever do. Inside I was screaming at myself to stop but I couldn't. It was the longest song of my life and had to carry on until the music stopped. The crowd stood silent.

'Let's hear it for Jiwi Rock' cheered the DJ to a muted giggle.

From the crowd someone shouted, 'Wanker!!'

I walked embarrassed through the crowd to find my mates who seemed reluctant to be near me. I left the breakdancers' disco utterly dejected, got two buses home and added breakdancer to the ever-growing list of failures.

In 1982 Argentina invaded the Falkland Islands, a relatively unknown place to most I knew. During the subsequent war, the Royal Marines were all over the news. After the conflict, there was a lot of interest in the Marines who were portrayed as super humans and there followed a documentary called 'Behind the Lines' that documented the Royal Marines Mountain Leaders course.

Before the Falklands War, I dreamed of being a soldier, someone brave and strong who would look after their Mum. I was 11 years old when the Falklands War happened and afterwards there was only one thing that I wanted to be – a Bootneck.

A Royal Marines Commando was everything that I wasn't. They were fit, strong and physically robust. But most importantly, they were brave. Since watching, paralysed with fear unable to help my Mum as she was being beaten by my Dad, I'd dreamed of being brave enough to help her. I didn't really want to do a Marine's job. I wasn't interested in the Marines as a career, I just wanted to be one of them.

At 13 my school held a careers fair before we chose our options. I headed straight to the Royal Marines recruiting Sergeant and said that I wanted to join the Marines when I left school.

'Are you a captain of the school football or rugby team?' he asked.

I shook my head.

'Do you play for any of the first teams?'

Another shake of my head,

'Second teams?'

Another shake.

'Sorry, we're only looking for the captains of the sports teams. You're not what we're looking for.'

Deflated, I asked, 'Can I have a booklet?' pointing to the huge pile behind him.

'Sorry. I've only got a few left.'

I was devastated. I wasn't even worth a booklet. I'd only ever wanted to be a Royal Marine and if the recruiting sergeant was the expert on the right attributes to be one, then my career aspirations were over before they started. I had no idea what else I wanted to do.

The dream of being someone brave and tough stayed with me. Dreaming had become a refuge from a real world so callous and unforgiving. Dreaming became my coping mechanism and drifting away into my own little world was something I'd done since before I could remember. Often my daydreams would be startlingly vivid and I'd find myself silently mouthing imagined conversations. I'd return to the real world with a jolt and quickly look to see if anyone noticed. Being a Royal Marine as a serious career choice may have been over, but crucially, I never lost the dream.

Day 9

The squalls of the previous day drifted away on the back of a northerly wind that drove a clean, new swell. The waves built to between 10–15 feet and coming directly from the north. At first light I started to push south-south-west. The waves, although big, didn't break and I was able to surf down them at an oblique angle maintaining a near perfect course. I dropped the daggerboard a third down. It steadied *Hope* perfectly in the oblique wind and reminded me of the hard time we had in the side wind on my first row with Row2Recovery when the daggerboard was stuck in the up position.

These were perfect rowing conditions. I called Leven who told me the weather looked consistent all the way to Las Palmas. I checked my COG after each rowing session. I was holding a decent course. A near full moon kept me company through most of the night and in the morning, I logged the previous day's stats. I'd rowed nearly 70 nautical miles in 24 hours.

Day 9 Logbook Entry

Position at 0800hrs on 18th Jan 2019 UTC	*Distance travelled 68.9nm at 210°*
31° 32.9'.50N 012°50'.211W	*Total distance 377nm*

245nm to Las Palmas, good rowing all day. Big wind and swell through the night. Expected rowing conditions continue all day today.

My Mum grafted every hour she could and often went without a proper meal so me and my sister could eat. Amongst the many jobs she had was a Provident Lady and would cycle alone, carrying lots of cash around Dagenham's dark streets, collecting money from people who'd taken out a loan. She also studied to get a qualification as a company secretary and, shortly after, started work in the City. My Mum had one goal in life – to buy her own house to pass on to me and my sister to give us the financial boost that she never had, and she selflessly worked towards it with a will of iron. As soon as she could, she bought the new council house in Victoria Road we had recently moved to.

My friends and I started to attend a youth club run by a born-again Christian church, part of an evangelical outreach programme. We'd go along to take the micky out of the happy-clappy Christians who played the guitar, clapped along to the church songs and even danced when they got carried away. The youth club was fronted by two older Christians called JP and Tim. Both were in their mid-twenties, professionals, graduates and part of what people would now call the educated middle-class elite. They were very un-Dagenham.

The possibility there might not be a God was something that hadn't crossed my mind. I was baptised a protestant, but my Dad's side of the family were Catholic. I went to a Catholic school where each day started with prayers often doled out by the deputy head Mr Brown, with all the enthusiasm of a manic depressive counting out the most boring moments of his life in alphabetical order. My uncle Kevin was an altar boy and would make me go to church with him because my nan would give me money for the collection. He'd take the money for himself as soon as we were out of the door. My experience of God and church had not been positive and seeing people who were happy about God was strange yet, in a way, refreshing.

As I sat through the religious bits of the youth club I started to feel uncomfortably like a hypocrite. I believed what they believed, and I started feeling very uneasy about continuing to make fun of them. The Christians all knew that we were all taking the piss but were just nice in return. We all knew that they were too decent to react to the micky taking and to continue knowing that was cowardice. It felt like bullying. They were all thoroughly decent people. This unease built up until I decided to take the most unpopular step of my life.

At one of the meetings, the lead person asked if anyone wanted to become a Christian. After a long hesitation, I raised my hand and instantly lost nearly all my friends. My two best friends, Steven and Darren, did the same as me. We all became Christians at the same time. Although having Darren and Steven join the church the same time softened the blow of losing all my other friends, becoming a Christian was social suicide that brought a totality. There was going to be no half measures and I threw myself into my new life. The church was like a new family and gave me a sense of belonging.

Being a Christian was immensely uncool and a sense of shame to my Dad. Being a born-again Christian in the very macho-led culture of Dagenham's working men's clubs stood out. I once visited my Dad over the club and sat talking to him and his friends. I was drinking Coke as a good Christian, and when my Dad asked me to get a round of drinks in I refused, as to do so would be illegal as I wasn't yet 18. He became angry and started being abusive, but I stood my ground. I could see I'd let him down again. Even though I was now a born-again Christian, the desire to be a strong and hard man, like I believed my Dad was, still burned deep. My Dad's shame in me reaffirmed to myself that I was weakling and a bit of a wally. I felt that I was about as for from the person who would be able to protect his Mum as it was possible to be. I cried when I left the club to walk home.

I was a Christian when I left school at 16 with my one qualification – O Level grade 'B' in art. I started work at a local Chemical plant on a Youth Training Scheme. I worked in the laboratories, a job I hated from the moment I started. Part of the YTS was a day release to a college to get a B-Tech qualification that ran alongside vocational training. One of the first exams was a basic maths test. I came top of my class with 86 per cent. Being on a YTS, I was in the minority in my class as most had proper jobs and most had O Level maths as well. It was the first inkling that I wasn't necessarily thick.

The youth club outreach programme had been quite successful for the church in not only attracting us, but keeping many teenagers from leaving. Many were only involved because their parents were Christians. Steven, Darren and I joining kept them a lot more involved than they otherwise would. Amongst the other teenagers in the church was Claire who had been a Christian since the age of 14. Her mother, Olive, was also a Christian but her Dad George had died shortly before I joined the church. George was quite old when Claire was born, he was a 6'6", stone-deaf docker who'd fought in North Africa during WW2 where he lost his hearing in an explosion. Because Claire was a bit older, she was given a kind of responsibility as a mentor to those who had just joined the church. Claire was two years older than me, a big deal when you're 16, had a proper job and was buying her own house. She was also very pretty. Most of the young men in the Church had a thing for Claire. Her Mum was of Jewish descent and loved to feed everybody. You couldn't leave Olive's without eating your body weight in cakes, sandwiches and sausage rolls. Although Claire was two years older, I could always make her laugh. Then I'd tease her until she was fit to burst with anger, then make her burst out laughing again. I was there as much for Olive's cooking as I was for Claire.

The Church organised holidays and it was on one of these holidays on the Isle of Wight that I decided that I'd ask Claire out, not out on a date, just out. That's how pre-Tinder teenagers started dating. You'd ask a girl, 'Do you want to go out with me?' And if she said yes, you were then girlfriend and boyfriend. I spoke to my friend JP about asking Claire out.

'That's probably not a great idea, 'he replied. 'She's quite a bit older than you.'

'I know. But I think I'll ask her anyway.'

What I didn't know is that JP had just that day, asked Claire out on a date. He was the most eligible bloke in the church, he wasn't bad looking, had a car, a flat with a PhD in biochemistry. He was everything I wasn't. When Claire told her Mum that JP had asked her out, she was so excited she bought a hat for the wedding.

The next day I asked Claire out.

'No,' she replied.

'I know you like me so I'm going to ask you again in a month.'

I've no idea where the confidence came from. My relationship with my Mum hadn't got any better and I still had suicidal thoughts but was managing my feelings better. I had two coping strategies that I used and were both very effective in bringing me out of my dark thoughts. One was physical exercise. Whenever I felt down, I'd wrench myself out for a run. The other was playing the guitar. Playing became a meditation, I'd completely focus and afterwards feel a relief and calmness.

A month to the day after I first asked out Claire, I was at her house with a Christian friend Keith. Claire's dates with JP had fizzled out and Keith was obviously interested in Claire and I was waiting for him to leave so I could ask Claire out again. It became a Mexican standoff; we both knew that the other was only there for Claire and neither of us wanted to leave first. Finally, he broke and I took my chance to ask her out again.

'No,' she replied again.

'I know you still like me, so I'm going to ask you one more time in a month. After that, I'll never ask you again.'

A month later and good to my word I asked Claire again. We'd been to a birthday party. Keith and I jostled to walk Claire home afterwards. I eventually won and whilst walking her home, I asked.

'It's been a month and I said I'd ask you again, do you want to go out with me?'

Claire hesitated. As she was about to answer, I said, 'I promise you I'll never ask you again. This is it, so think carefully. I know you like me.'

'OK, yes.' she said.

We were now boyfriend and girlfriend. As we reached her front door I thought *'Do I kiss her.'* Before any chance to find out, she'd closed the door with a quick 'Goodnight.'

The next day Claire telephoned me before I went to work. 'Can we meet later to talk?'

I knew she'd had second thoughts and I thought I knew why. I met Claire over Old Dagenham park. There was a slight drizzle in the air and we sat under an old slide that had a shelter with seats built into it. Claire started to prepare me for the bad news that she had changed her mind by telling me how great I was and that she does like me but not necessarily in that way.

'Listen Claire.' I broke in. 'I know you like me and I know I haven't got a proper job and I'm a bit younger than you, but that doesn't matter. I know you fancy me. And I will never ask you out again, ever. Don't let what other people think change your mind.'

'Yeh, OK.' She said and if we didn't kiss for the first time then, we did later that day.

Not long after I started dating Claire, I applied for a job in a laboratory in London. The pay was incredible for someone with my experience and qualifications. I was interviewed and, after what felt like a lifetime, I received a phone call offering me the position.

I found out that I was third choice out of three candidates interviewed. The first choice received a better offer elsewhere. The next person on the list declined the job for personal reasons and then, in desperation, they called me. I also heard that I'd been so bad in interview they'd considered readvertising the position. So began my stint as the worst ever employee of Sandoz, the Swiss pharmaceutical giant.

I continued to throw myself into being the best Christian possible and a big part of that understanding the bible. A cornerstone of the church's belief system was that the bible was 100 per cent the word of God. The problem was the more I read the more inconsistencies I found.

The Church was Pentecostal, meaning they believed in speaking in tongues. This has its origin in the New Testament when the Holy Spirit descended on the disciples, and they started speaking the language of angels. Speaking in tongues, can be controversial with video clips of evangelical American preachers comically spouting nonsense on the internet. But in 1984 I'd never come across it before. When I first heard people singing together in tongues in harmony, it had an ethereal beauty that sent a shiver down my spine.

Speaking in tongues was a rite of passage into the church and another cornerstone of their belief system. I started to notice a difference in the way people from different areas of the church spoke in tongues. The church was part of a much larger organisation of about seven churches. The people who attended Ilford like JP and Tim, spoke in tongues with very soft sounding words, almost French sounding. When the people of Dagenham church spoke in tongues it sounded harsh and guttural, almost Russian or German.

It began to occur to me that if this really was the language of angels then it should all be the same. The only logical explanation for the different sounds, was that people were subconsciously picking up and regurgitating nonsense words. I realised that if the Bible isn't 100 per cent the word of God and if speaking in tongues is just well-intentioned people regurgitating nonsense, then what was real about being a Christian? Claire and my relationship also became physical which is inconsistent with the church who believed in strictly no sex out of marriage. Leaving the church eventually came down to a choice between boobs or Jesus. In the end boobs won.

Day 10

The excellent rowing conditions continued. I headed into an imaginary funnel where the closer I got to Las Palmas the more accurate I had to be. Further away, any deviation from a direct line to the port was easily corrected without having to make any dramatic turns or row in a side wind. Now as I closed in on Las Palmas, the less I could deviate from a line drawn directly to the port.

My COG became critical. At the beginning and after each rowing session I'd plot my position, compare it to the previous and gain my COG for the last two hours. Constantly plotting my position was taking precious time away from rest and I knew the closer I got, the more I'd have to check my COG.

During the night, the wind dropped slightly but the sea became choppier. Waves were sizeable, were more irregularly and started to break, often side on, drenching me each time. My last rowing session of the night from 6–8pm was under a dull grey sky filled with drizzle. I was glad to finish and shelter in the cabin, cold, wet and miserable. When I worked out my stats for the previous 24 hours, I was astonished to find out I'd rowed nearly 71 nautical miles.

Day 10 Logbook Entry

Position at 0800hrs on 19th Jan 2019 UTC *Distance travelled 70.8nm at 216°*
30° 35′ 333N 013°38′.762W *Total distance 448nm*

174nm to Las Palmas.

Good rowing conditions continued all day and night. Very choppy sea.

19th Jan started grey, drizzly with light NNW wind. Anticipate hard days rowing today.

I hated my job in the lab and hated myself for doing it. In Dagenham, it was hard, physical labour or a well-paid office job that were respected and defined who you were. My Dad still called himself a steel erector. In between long bouts of unemployment I'd known him as a coalman, crane driver and builder, never a steel erector. I'd no idea what defined me or who I was. My job was neither physical labour or well-paid and I couldn't look myself in the mirror and be proud of the person who I saw staring back. I yearned to be someone who was strong, brave and hard, everything that I thought I wasn't. I didn't want to just join the Army and be a soldier, I'd dreamed of being a Royal Marine.

I not only hated my job but was also terrible at it. Often, I'd wait on the platform at Dagenham East Underground station looking down the tracks for the next London-bound train and think, *'Nah, not today'*, then walk home and call in sick.

I also stopped going to college on day release and when work was given a breakdown of my college attendance, I was called in to explain. Somehow, I wasn't sacked but given a final warning. Working in a lab with no academic qualifications also put me at the very bottom of the social pile. I had absolutely nothing in common with the other people who worked there, I imagined them all as audience members on Radio 4 comedy shows intellectually laughing at jokes that weren't meant for me. I was utterly lost.

Although I was born in Barking and brought up in Dagenham, I always yearned to be in the wild. The nearest rural area growing up was the waste ground behind Western Avenue where I caught, snakes, lizards and newts. I often loaned 1:50,000 Ordnance Survey maps from the local library and dreamed of camping trips to all the distant and exotic places like Devon and Wales.

My friends, Steven, and Darren had drifted away from the church about the same time as me along with John Brown, who was a member of the church before we joined. In spring 1988 John and I went wild camping in Mid-Wales inspired by an OS map. We caught the train to a town called Machynlleth and walked south on a road for a couple of miles before jumping over a fence into a farmers' field to set up camp in a small copse.

Machynlleth sits in the Dyfi valley with the hills slowly rising north into Snowdonia National Park. We sat on a hill looking at majestic mountains and promised ourselves the next trip would be to explore Snowdonia. After a few days camping, we returned home.

A couple of months later, John Brown came round to see me. He had very recently qualified as an electrician. After years of being skint as an apprenticed he'd bought himself a motorbike. We went up to my room and he asked to put Pink Floyd's *Comfortably Numb* on my stereo. We listened to the track and then just after it finished, John announced that he was leaving.

'OK, see you mate,' I said slightly baffled by his fleeting visit.

They were the last words I said to John. He died on his motorbike two days later.

It was as if he was saying goodbye and we never got the chance to return to Snowdonia.

When John died, I went to see him lying in the funeral home. I couldn't believe he looked anything other than asleep. It was very surreal and had a profound effect on me.

John's brother had died years earlier when John was just a toddler but remembered his brother dying in his mums' arms outside their house after being run over by a car. John's Dad, unable to cope, left her to bring up John on her own. How could any God allow this to happen? It belied all logic and reason and no amount of 'God works in mysterious ways' could account for the devastation inflicted on her. That was the final nail in the coffin of any faith I had left.

I started playing football with my uncles Michael and Kevin. They were short of players and in desperation Kevin rang me and told me I was playing. The team was in the interdepartmental league of the massive Ford plant in Dagenham and was called Becket House Finance. Because they were sponsored by one of the players who had his own fish stool business, the team badge was a couple of prawns.

I ran enthusiastically for 90 minutes without touching the ball. They were short again the following week and was told that I was playing again. Despite my abject performances they had no other option, so I soon became a permanent fixture in the team. We ended up at the bottom of the second division. I was forced to play as a centre forward, the logic being that I could do less damage to my team up front as far away from our goal as possible.

As it was Ford's interdepartmental league, rules stated that many of the team had to work for Ford. Most of our team played under assumed names of actual Ford's employees. My uncle Kevin had played under five different names as he kept getting banned.

Sunday league football was mainly played by fat, hungover, old men and I spent every Sunday morning getting kicked up in the air trying to run past them. One game, a particularly nasty defender who'd taken a dislike to me, took the opportunity to have a go. I squared up to him then almost immediately found myself on the ground curled up into a ball being enthusiastically booted about by several other defenders. This turned into a mass brawl. My uncle Kevin grabbed a metal spike used to portion off the cricket green and chased the whole opposition team off the pitch. As this was fairly normal for Sunday morning football, the game carried on. Kevin only got a yellow card and probably banned again for accumulated yellow cards. It's only memorable as it's one of only two games in four years where I scored a goal. As a centre forward. That's half a goal a season.

Although having been told at school that I wasn't what the Royal Marines were looking for, I'd never lost the dream. I started running as a coping mechanism to deal with the self-hatred. As I became fitter, I started to dream more about joining the Marines. In early 1988, I took the plunge and in my lunch break entered the Armed Forces career's office near Holborn Tube station in London. After an initial talk with the careers officer there, I formally applied to join the Royal Marines.

Over the next few weeks I sat a psychometric test, had medical examinations and studied Royal Marines history ready for interview, hope slowly growing. I confessed to my Dad and all his Bootneck friends in the British Legion that I'd applied to be a Royal Marine. I asked for the time off from work to attend interview, something my boss was overly eager to do.

On the day of the interview, I put on my suit and excitedly travelled to the careers office. I was interviewed by a Chief Petty Officer from the Royal Navy. After the interview he left the room saying that he was going to check the availability of a Potential Recruits Course, a four-day course at the Commando Training Centre Royal Marines in Lympstone and the next step in the selection process. After a couple of minutes, he came back into the room.

'I'm sorry, but I don't think that you're good enough to warrant a place on a Potential Recruits Course. They're quite full up at the moment.'

Devastated, I got the Tube back to work. I'd told everyone that I was applying for the Marines and was embarrassed when I told them

I hadn't got beyond the interview, although I think my boss was more devastated at not getting rid of me.

Day 11

The drizzle and light northerly wind continued through the day and moved west into the night. The swell decreased and I was pulling hard on the oars with little forward momentum. After each rowing session I'd return to the cabin exhausted, but still had to accurately plot my position and COG. The north north-westerly wind, though light, was still pushing me east and I was rowing as obliquely as I could without going into irons. I experimented with dropping the daggerboard both full and half down but found it most stable in the quarter down position. In the morning, I was gutted that, despite my efforts, I'd narrowly missed out on rowing 50 nautical miles in 24 hours.

Day 11 Logbook Entry

Position at 0800hrs on 20th Jan 2019 UTC	*Distance travelled 49.5nm at 206°*
29° 50′ 957N 014°03′.845W	*Total distance 498nm*

Hard day and night rowing. At 0100hr wind moved round to NNW. Trying to keep heading at 180°- 200°. 125nm to Las Palmas

In the autumn of 1988, I met a friend from school called Nick at the Jean-Michel Jarre concert in the derelict London docklands. I hadn't seen him since leaving school and we arranged to meet for a drink.

I told Nick about how I'd gone camping in Mid-Wales with John Brown and looked across the Dyfi valley to the higher hills and mountains of Snowdonia. Camping in Snowdonia felt like unfinished business and Nick seemed keen to go. We arranged a long weekend over Halloween. We caught the train to Machynlleth and then hitched a lift north into the lower hills of Snowdonia. By the time we unpacked at the bottom of a mountain called Cadair Idris it was dark and we pitched our tent under a cloudless, star filled sky.

The late autumn weather was unbelievably good, and we didn't see a cloud in the sky throughout the whole weekend. The days were unseasonably hot and the nights freezing in my useless sleeping bag I'd owned since scouts. The first morning after shivering my way through the night, we got up and saw for the first time the surrounding landscape. We were in a deep valley with the impressive cliffs of Craig y Llam in shadow to our south and the rising sun just hitting the eastern peak of Cadair Idris, Mynyth Moel. The craggy outcrops and cliffs glowed orange in the autumnal morning sun. It was stunningly beautiful.

We hiked up the Minffordd Path that climbs through a steep-sided oak wood and then opens out onto an impressive bowl shaped vista with a lake of the deepest ultramarine called Llyn Cau surrounded on three sides by majestic, rugged cliffs. The Minffordd Path slowly climbs up to the south of Llyn Cau above the cliffs that then follows around the lake in a series of three peaks, the last of which is the summit, Cadair Idris. We climbed slowly, weighed down by our camping equipment and were passed by many day hikers.

We stopped between the first and second peaks to take photos at a viewpoint where the cliffs dropped almost vertically down to the lake below.

Llyn Cau shimmered the deepest blue as the early afternoon sun caught the grey cliffs, casting deep shadows amongst the crags. Before we set off again, two guys stopped to chat. They were destined for the summit where they intended to sleep in a mountain refuge shelter. They set off and we followed on slowly behind. We finally reached the second summit and looking over the eastern stretches of Cadair Idris, the cloudless blue sky was tinged almost violet at the horizon, a sure sign that the afternoon was wearing on. We decided to take a few more photos.

'I can't find my camera.' said Nick. He frantically searched his rucksack, pulling everything out, but it soon became apparent it wasn't there.

Realising he must have left it on the path, we left our rucksacks and climbed back down to the point we'd previously stopped. By the time we found Nick's camera and climbed back up to our rucksacks, the sun had disappeared and the sky was darkening as evening approached. We were alone and the mountain deserted. After a brief discussion, we realised that if we turned around and climbed back now, we'd be walking for the majority of the time in darkness. The only option left was to carry on up to the refuge shelter. We set off quickly, but by the time we got to the start of the final climb dusk had settled on the mountain with the first stars appearing above our heads. It was going to be a moonless night and we had no torches. We continued up the path as best we could. I offered to go ahead to see the two lads who'd passed us earlier and ask to borrow a torch. I left my rucksack with Nick and climbed up alone into the almost pitch black. I carefully felt my way up the mountain, in places hunched over on all fours.

The refuge shelter was a basic stone building with a corrugated tin roof set just off to the side of the triangulation stone on the summit and

I found it by soft glow of light escaping the open door. The two guys were cooking their evening meal and chatting to an older bloke who'd ascended on his own. They all laughed when I explained that we'd gone camping without a torch between us and readily offered one of theirs. I scrambled down to Nick who had begun to get seriously worried as I'd taken a lot longer than he thought necessary. We slowly slogged up the final slope to the summit and our home for the night.

We ducked into the shelter, saying hello to everyone tucked up in their sleeping bags. The two lads sniggered at our totally inadequate camping equipment. Sniggering turned to laughter when I retrieved my old scout sleeping bag from my rucksack. I slept little and spent the whole night shivering. At around six in the morning an alarm went off and the other three guys started to get out of their sleeping bags and put their clothes on.

'Are you off back down already?' I asked.

'I've only come up to watch the sunrise,' said the guy who was on his own.

Nick and I slowly got out of our sleeping bags, grabbed our cameras and followed on out of the shelter. I didn't need to get dressed as I'd worn every piece of clothing I'd brought in a failed attempt to keep warm. As soon as I cleared the shelter's entrance, I was blasted by biting wind that gained in strength the closer we got to the summit.

To the west looking out towards the Irish Sea the sky was still black and the stars glimmered, but facing east into the bitter cold wind, along the horizon the sky was pale blue with the coming dawn. Gradually the sky lightened. Pale blue turned to the faintest hint of orange. The landscape stretching out to the east began to take form. Barely visible at first, the lower slopes of Cadair Idris fell away into a void with the next hill rising up beyond. As the sky lightened and turned increasingly salmon pink, the lower hills of the Cambrian Mountains became clearer, rolling on towards the horizon, their tops tinged pink by the dawn, each one fading into mist filled valleys. I was stunned by the sheer beauty of it all.

Light now engulfed us with only the brightest stars visible to the west. As I stared out towards the increasingly brighter eastern horizon, I was filled with anticipation, then scarcely contained excitement. The air around me felt electrically charged and crackling. Then, higher above the horizon than I was expecting, a thin bright orange strip appeared. It quickly grew in length and then magically became a fiercely bright orange ball. In that instant I felt the whole universe change and night became day. As the sun climbed slowly up from the east, the rolling hills and valleys in between changed colours as their shadows cast towards us. It was the most moving and spectacularly beautiful thing I'd ever seen.

A couple of days later, I was walking the grey streets of home to Dagenham East station. I passed a man I'd seen nearly every working day for about three years. We passed each other at the same spot nearly every morning. I was suddenly struck by the absurdity of the situation.

'Morning,' I said as we passed.

He stopped in shock, then smiled. 'Good morning,' he said.

I carried on and as I reached the entrance to the station I looked over to my left. The sun peeked over the train tracks and waste ground where I'd spent many years catching newts and lizards as a kid. It looked beautiful and I wondered how many similarly beautiful sunrises I'd passed without taking any notice.

On my journey to work, I sat in my usual seat on my usual train where I'd seen the same people for many years. I'd seen more of some of them over the last few years than many of my relatives.

I repeated my 'Good morning.'

It was like a set of dominoes falling. Everyone said, 'Good morning,' and started talking to each other.

I finished my journey at Euston Square Underground and whilst rushing through the station as I'd done for many years, I suddenly stopped. *'Why am I rushing?'* I thought.

I wasn't going to be late. I looked around at everyone rushing. I thought *'I bet none of them are going to be late either'*. Something in me had fundamentally changed.

I continued in my job and used every bit of annual leave on long weekends away. I discovered youth hostels and Claire often came with me to either Mid-Wales, Dartmoor or Exmoor. I still had no idea what I wanted to be, but realised if I waited for a better career, I'd blink and ten years would have gone by. I'd still be in the same job I hated and more importantly, hated myself for doing.

I handed in my months' notice, probably just before I would've been sacked. Months later, on a youth hostelling trip to Wales with Claire, I was in conversation with another guest and mentioned that I'd watched the sun rise from the summit of Cadair Idris.

'Oh, you've heard of the legend of spending the night on Cadair Idris?' he asked.

'No.' I replied.

'Apparently,' he said with a smile, 'If you spend the night on top of Cadair Idris, you either become a poet, die, or go mad.'

Whenever I look back I doubt I'd have left my job if I hadn't spent the night on Cadair Idris. I may not have become a poet or died and my sanity may be questionable, but spending the night on Cadair Idris did have a profound and lasting effect on my life.

Day 12

I was now closing in on Las Palmas and navigation was absolutely critical. Claire and Ivor had arrived in Gran Canaria to meet me. I spoke to Ivor over the satphone and explained how important it would be for a safety boat to shadow me in. The wind forecast from Leven was showing strong northerly winds all the way in and it would make turning back into wind to get to the marina near impossible.

The wind was blowing from the east all morning and I was rowing at almost a right angle to it. The swell was mainly coming from the north-north-west, but the steep waves were 15–20 feet.

In the afternoon as the sun dipped into the west, I could just make out land to my right. I was surprised to see it as I didn't realise how close I was to Lanzarote and Fuerteventura. As the sun began to set in the west the wind swung round from almost due east to north-north-west, and I was now rowing at almost right angles to the wind and swell. I was heading in a south-westerly direction towards Gran Canaria with little or no room for manoeuvre. I was following a busy shipping lane between the Islands of Fuerteventura and Gran Canaria. All day large container ships came and went, two miles to my west. The wind and waves were doing their best in pushing me towards it and several times *Hope* would turn too far east and go into irons. The wind and waves pushed her sideways, holding her against the choppy sea. The swell and breaking waves were steep enough to make capsizing a real danger. Each time she went into irons, I'd quickly turn her due south and row my heart out to get out of irons. I was steering on a knife edge of maintain the COG I needed to get to Las Palmas, staying away from the shipping lane and not going into irons. The lights of Fuerteventura kept me company through most of the night as I constantly checked my position and COG.

Day 12 Logbook Entry

Position at 0800hrs on 21st Jan 2019 UTC	*Distance travelled 55.6nm at 204°*
29° 00′ 363N 014°30.023W	*Total distance 543.5nm*

Distance to Las Palmas 71nm @ 222°

A hard day of 2 halves. From 0800 wind came from almost due east. First 22nm were due south. At approximately 1730 the wind turned suddenly to

NNE managed 36.2nm @ 220° first half hard rowing at almost right angles to the wind. Luckily the largest swell was still NNE turning NNW for the majority of the day. After wind turned found it was hard to maintain enough west and went into irons a couple of times. Spent off watch monitoring directions and COG which was hard without the Nav systems working. Had to keep dropping way points and measuring back from current location to get a COG

In September 1991, I found myself unemployed and without a plan. I started filling in on bar shifts in the local clubs plus the odd bit of labouring. I knew that I needed a proper career and the direction in life that it would give me. I started to think about the Royal Marines again and I really couldn't see anything else that I wanted to do. I decided that I would give myself three months to get as physically fit as possible and then apply again.

Far from being a career choice it was still a dream. I was also aware that this would most probably be my last chance. I started training hard. I had continued to run almost daily so had a decent base to start from. To running I added pull-ups as I knew from my previously unsuccessful attempt at joining they'd be the first thing I'd be asked to do in the careers office. I installed a pull-up bar in my bedroom and wherever I was working, I found something I could do pull-ups from. Pull ups became a habit.

In the late summer of 1991, I nervously went back to the Careers office and full of trepidation, applied to join the Royal Marines. As expected, the first request was to do pull-ups. This time I managed fifteen. Not a massive amount but a definite improvement on the seven I manged before.

The interview was conducted by a large Colour Sergeant from the Royal Marines called Curley. At the end of the interview, Curley said I'd passed and would be loaded onto the next available Potential Recruits Course (PRC). He led me into another room to watch a video on the PRC after which he handed me a load of paperwork, including a physical training manual, to prepare myself for the PRC. He told me to expect the formal letter inviting me to the Commando Training Centre Royal Marines and a rail warrant to come in the post.

I was one step closer to my dream of joining the Marines. The physical training manual contained a circuit that I completed daily. It contained exercises using only body weight, like press-ups, burpees, pull-ups and sit-ups.

The letter came within a few weeks and the rail warrant to 'Lympstone Commando' made it all feel suddenly very real. The night before I was due to leave for the PRC my uncle and aunt came round to visit Mum. I told my uncle that I was going to join the Marines and that in the morning I'd be getting the train to Devon to attend the PRC.

'You'll never pass,' he said. 'They're not interested in you, you'll never be able to hack it, or the discipline and you'll give up.'

I arrived at the small railway stop called 'Lympstone Commando' on the edge of the River Exe estuary. I looked up nervously at the camp. The assault course with its ropes and various obstacles ran ominously next to the train line. There were a few other nervous looking young men who alighted the train and we were met by a Royal Marine with his distinctive green beret and led up through the camp to what would be our temporary home for the next few nights. We were taken into a large room full of bunks and left to make up our beds. I grabbed a top bunk and introduced myself the very athletic looking lad below. I noticed with envy how much bigger his biceps were compared to mine. We had a few lectures on what to expect over the next couple of days and were then issued our kit, including some very ill-fitting combat trousers and jacket. The hardest part of the day was trying to sleep.

After an early breakfast, our first detail was in the gym for the United States Marine Corps (USMC) tests, a series of timed exercises. But first came the warm-up. We were all sent sprinting from one side of the gym to the other, stood up, sat down, rolled over. Press ups, sit-ups, more sprints, running on the spot, it seemed to go on for ever. The PTI's with their pristine white vests and shorts were quick to identify anyone they deemed to be 'loafing', not giving 100 per cent, so I tried to be the first on every sprint and the first to finish every exercise. By the time we lined up in pairs ready for the press-ups, the start of the USMC test, I was exhausted. The warm-up felt like an arduous gym session. The person opposite me would be counting my press-ups and laid down on his belly and placed a clenched fist out in-front. I would be doing press-ups with my hands either side of his clenched fist and he would only count every time my chest touched his fist. I knew I had two minutes to do 60 press-ups to get maximum points.

The PTI in-charge shouted, 'Standby, Knees away.'

I braced myself in the press-up position

'Go!'

I bent my arms until my chest hit the fist in front of me. The other PTI's stalked up and down the line checking on every press-up and occasionally I heard them shout, 'Don't count that one, all the way down.'

After the first few press-ups, I realised that the exercise that I thought was a press-up, wasn't quite a Royal Marines press-up. I clearly hadn't been going all the way down in my training. My arms were also tired from the warm-up and as my number of press-ups slowly crept into the teens, I began to panic. This was already a lot harder than I'd imagined. I only managed a pitiful twenty-nine press-ups and the rest of the exercises followed a similar theme. Next came sit-ups, then burpees after which I ran outside to vomit. Finally the pull-ups, something I'd trained hard on, but still only managed twelve. With my uncle's words of 'You'll never pass', ringing in my ear, we went outside of the gym for the final part of the USMC Test, the sprints. I ran my heart out and vomited again.

Next came the swimming test. As I waited by the pool I was sick again.

'Staff!' I shouted with my hands cupped full of vomit.

'Out there, you gopping creature,' he shouted as he pointed to the exit.

I struggled through the morning and through the afternoon on the endurance course. The endurance course is a set of tunnels, hills and pools on Woodbury Common. On exiting the tunnels, I had to shout my name and realised they were checking to see who was slowing down and resting out of sight in the tunnels.

I was determined to exit on the heels of the person in front. 'Spencer, Staff!' I shouted.

'Spencer? I thought you would've wrapped by now,' said the corporal.

For a second I was shocked and thought *'how dare you'* and looked back at the corporal who'd just said it, with anger written all over my face. The group of corporals with him all burst out laughing. At the end of the day after showering, the lad who I was on the bunk below me, started packing his kit.

'What's happening?' I asked.

'I'm off,' he replied. 'I don't want to do this.'

I was shocked. He looked a lot fitter and had done way better than me on the USMC test. I'd assumed he'd be a definite pass.

The second day was the bottom field assault course that ended with an extremely long thrashing. If the first day was about physical fitness, the second was about determination. The PRC Sergeant Major followed me around and even offered a little encouragement on some of the obstacles. I didn't know it at the time, but my scores for the gym tests were so poor that I was close to failing the PRC and the Sergeant Major had come to look at someone who was a borderline fail. The thrashing seemed to go on for ever, but the little bits of encouragement and being under his beady eye kept me going.

Then a curious thing started to happen. I started to catch some of the people up and overtake them. Up until that point, I felt totally out of my depth. Now I was starting to pass other people and I started hunting them down, one after the other. I'd finally found something I was good at, not giving up. I started to revel in catching and overtaking all those that I'd thought better than me. All my life I'd been rubbish at everything, but now I really felt for the first time that I wasn't a complete failure. As hard as it was physically, mentally I began to relish the hardship. The harder it got, in comparison to everyone else, the better I performed.

On the last morning the whole course lined up in the corridor. They called out the names of all those that had failed, about two-thirds of the course and they walked back to pack their kit. My name hadn't been called out and I stood with the remaining third. We were taken through into a classroom where we sat down.

'Congratulations, you've passed the Potential Recruits Course,' said the corporal.

I had finally succeeded at something. It was that 'not giving in' that got me through the PRC. We sat through a lecture on the next steps before joining, physical training we should be concentrating on and given paperwork to take back to the careers office. A few names were called out, mine amongst them, and we were told to wait outside the Sergeant Major's office. When my turn came, I knocked at the door and walked in. I recognised him from the previous morning when he'd followed me around the assault course. He explained that I'd scraped a pass by the smallest of margins on all the gym tests and that I would need to work 'really hard' before I came back and joined a troop to start training proper.

As I walked out from his office he called out, 'Spencer.'

I turned round to look at him and replied, 'Sir?'

'You'll be a fucking good Marine.'

Slightly shocked, I walked out of his office, all the way down the corridor to the accommodation and packed ready for the journey home to Dagenham.

Walking back down to the train station and the Exe estuary beyond, I felt that my life had suddenly changed from one of little direction to one of purpose. I stared training in earnest and eagerly waited for the postman to deliver a letter offering me a place in training. I felt an enormous sense of pride when telling anybody that would listen that I was joining the Royal Marines. I soon realised that no one had believed that I would pass the PRC from the universal look of shock when I told them. My uncle had only articulated what everyone thought. Of course, I knew that the hard work was yet to come with actual Royal Marines training, but just getting over the first big hurdle of the Potential Recruits Course was a massive personal achievement. My grandad Spencer beamed with pride when I told him that I had passed the selection and soon I would be off to start training as a Royal Marine.

Day 13

My run into Las Palmas was well and truly underway. The wind and swell, still predominantly from the north-north-west, steadily increased through the day. *Hope* held her course perfectly, surfing easily down the steep 20-foot waves.

By now I was well practiced at setting the rudder and fine tuning the difference between rowing and rest periods. I considered the option of continuing across the Atlantic without repairing the navigation and IAS systems. I felt capable in navigating across the vastness of the ocean with my handheld GPS, compass and charts. But Leven's wise words of not venturing out across the ocean on only my backup system rang in my ears, and I knew he was right. If my handheld GPS broke, or was washed overboard, I'd be resigned to rowing west and hoping.

Plotting my position and COG was now an hourly chore and took priority over rowing, eating, drinking and resting. At midday, I spoke to Claire and Ivor on the satphone and Ivor explained that he'd managed to get a boat to shadow me in, but could only meet it at 0930 the following day.

'I tried everywhere, bud. The marina, I've asked in the chandlery, everywhere and we were beginning to get worried bud. And then, today we were having breakfast in this restaurant by the marina and the bloke who owns it, cracking guy he is, and knows everyone. He's sorted one for you. But it can't get there before 0930, bud.'

'Hoofin, cheers, Ivor.' I replied.

'It's called *Obelix*,' he said, before passing Claire the phone.

'Ralph left this morning,' she said.

Ralph Tuijn is an incredibly experienced ocean rower and had been planning on rowing the same route hoping to beat the same record. Originally, we were due to leave on consecutive years, but when my Mum died and I postponed the row by a year, we were now rowing against each other. We'd spoken fairly frequently throughout the previous December, both waiting in vain for a decent weather window. Ralph was also planning on a six-person crossing from Africa to South America later in the spring and I'd assumed that he'd given up rowing solo this year after not getting away in December. Not only was I up against it, trying to beat an able-bodied record with one leg and having to stop for repairs, I was now in a race with one of the most experienced ocean rowers on the planet.

As the day progressed and I closed in on Las Palmas, it began to look increasingly likely that I'd have to slow down. Even without rowing I was steaming along at nearly three knots. I considered rowing in as close as I could and deploying one of the two anchors I was carrying for just this sort of situation. But the chart showed nowhere suitable. My route into Las Palmas port would take me just to the east of the prominent rocky peninsular of La Isleta in the north-east corner of Gran Canaria. I'd then have to row south alongside the three-mile-long sea wall that protects the port in Las Palmas before turning into the harbour itself and the marina. Anchoring anywhere on my route would put me too close to the rocky coastline or sea wall and big breaking waves could smash *Hope* against them. If I arrived at the end of the sea wall before the safety boat, rowing back north-north-west directly into the now strong wind to the marina through a busy port harbour would be extremely difficult and potentially dangerous. My course in was at an oblique angle to the wind and waves, if I deployed the para' anchor I'd drift south south-east into the busy shipping lane I was skirting. My only option was to continue my current course, or as near as possible, but slow *Hope*'s progress. I was carrying three different-sized drogues. A drogue is a tapered, funnel-shaped tube designed to be dragged behind a boat to slow it down. Where a para' anchor is always attached to the front of a boat, facing it into the wind and swell, it stops a boat in its tracks and lets it drift with the weather and current. A drogue is dragged behind the boat and because its smaller and has an open end, it will allow a boat to stay more on course.

At 7pm I attached the middle-size drogue to the rear of *Hope* and it immediately slowed my progress to one knot. But it changed my course towards the shipping lane. I constantly monitored my position through the night with the lighthouse on La Isleta and the lights of Las Palmas giving me a good visual reference point. By one in the morning, I was right on the edge of the shipping lane and had to bring the drogue in, also if I went any more east and I would be rowing at a right angle to the wind and breaking waves to get into Las Palmas. There was nothing else I could conceivably do but start my run in to Las Palmas and hope I'd slowed down enough. The bright flashing light of the La Isleta Lighthouse was joined by the more distant Punta Sardina Lighthouse in the far north-west of Gran Canaria and the twinkling lights along the coastline in-between. They all looked deceptively close, but as the dark night turned pale grey with the coming morning, I began to relax and by 8am, I still had twelve nautical miles to go.

Day 13 Logbook Entry

Position at 0800hrs on 22nd Jan 2019 UTC *Distance travelled 59.5nm at 220°*

28° 14′ 359n 015°12.870w *Total distance 603nm*

Distance to Las Palmas 12nm @ 233°

Strong NNE winds all day and night would have meant getting to Las Palmas before the recovery boat at 0930hrs. Deployed drogue at 1900hrs until 0100hrs. Kept slow track in waiting to hear from the boat. Dolphins around the boat at around 0400hrs. Drogue slowed progress to 1knt. Boat was running at 3knts-3.5knts without any assistance.

Passing the PRC gave me new-found confidence so decided to try rugby. We'd never played it in school but after watching matches on the television from the Rugby World Cup, it looked like something I could do. '*All you have to do is run forwards and throw the ball backwards,*' I thought.

I took myself off to the nearest rugby team, Romford and Gidea Park, for a training session. They put me in the fifth team and stuck me on the wing for the following Saturday's home game. After scoring a try and drinking a specimen bottle of various spirits in a mix-up with the worst player from the returning first team, I ended up outside Claire's front door. She answered the door and asked me what I was doing,

'Can I come in?' I asked and stumbled into her hallway. I attempted to get down on one knee but due to the fact I was so drunk I fell over.

'What are you doing?' she asked.

I tried again struggling to one knee. I unsteadily looked up to Claire and grabbed her hand and asked, 'Claire, will you marry me?'

'Get up, you silly arse.'

'No, I mean it.'

'You better not be joking,' she said. Then paused. 'OK'.

And that was it, we were engaged.

I've never played rugby since. I tell people that rugby ruined my life much to Claire's annoyance.

A few weeks before I was due to leave Dagenham to join the Marines, I was walking past the British Legion when I saw my Dad walking towards me.

'Alright Dad?'

He looked far from alright, he looked confused and obviously drunk. 'They won't let me in my flat.'

I assumed that he was too drunk to get his key in the door. Not an unusual occurrence, so I offered to help him. I'd been walking from the direction of my Dad's high-rise and I turned to walk back with him to his flat.

'No not that one,' he said, flicking his arm to indicate the high-rise where his flat was, 'That one in there,' he continued pointing at the back of the British Legion. 'I've got a flat up there and they won't let me in it.'

I'd never seen him like this before. I'd seen him paralytic drunk on many occasions but never confused about where he lived. 'Come on, let's go up to your flat there,' I said pointing at his actual block of flats. 'And I'll go and sort it out for you.'

I walked him to his block of flats and left him at the outside door fumbling with the key fob. I ran as fast as I could around the corner into Ingleby road to my nan Spencer's house to get help. I explained what had just happened and my nan dispatched my uncle Keven to see what was going on. Kevin quickly realised that my Dad wasn't right and brought him back to my nan's. My Dad was having an episode of alcohol-induced psychosis. He moved into my nan's house for a couple of weeks where he slowly returned to his version of normal.

In the aftermath I had a conversation with two of my cousins, David and Mathew, about who was the maddest in the family. To give this some perspective, when they finally came and locked my uncle Keven up for nearly two years in a mental health hospital: he was running down the road naked with a knife. He didn't even make the shortlist. David was arguing in favour of his mother Maria being the family loony, but Mathew and I were arguing in favour of another cousin, who admittedly wasn't as mad as Maria, but having achieved plenty of lunacy at such a young age, had a lot of potential.

'It makes you think about their upbringing, doesn't it? They've all got hang ups,' I said.

'They're not all mad,' said David, 'Your Dad's not mad.' He said before looking in the air. 'Oh, there was that time he thought Harry Secombe was living in Nan's bread bin.'

My Dad's mental collapse made me realise that I was finished with Dagenham. I couldn't end up like my Dad. I'd dreamed of being a Royal Marine for as long as I could remember, but I also wanted out of Dagenham and the life that it inevitably offered.

Day 14 Las Palmas

The wind and waves stayed consistently big all the way into Las Palmas, but as the morning wore on, the waves became noticeably steeper.

On my first row for a couple of days we had huge 20-foot waves, but almost 200 metres apart. To me they resembled hills gentle rolling away to the horizon. Occasionally there'd be a random wave doing its own thing, going in a completely different direction. When it converged with another wave under our boat, it would lift us up and it felt we could see for miles. Cayle and I would stop rowing and stare in awe. It was like being on top of a huge mountain with the horizon below us in every direction. It's rare when the sky makes up most of your world.

These current waves were in stark contrast. One second, I was at the bottom of a huge steep valley with only a tiny bit of sky above me and the next I was riding the top of the wave and craning my neck round to catch sight of land. The La Isleta peninsula was clearly visible with the white buildings of the lighthouse perched prominently on brown and dark grey cliffs. I started to hear the radio traffic from the port in Las Palmas and, waiting for a break in the radio traffic, informed them of my approach. I was still rowing at a tight oblique angle to the waves. As I came level with the lighthouse, I could see the sea wall stretching south and now had something definite to aim for.

My main VHF radio was inside the cabin and it'd be difficult to row and, concurrently, jump in and out to talk to both the port and the escort boat *Obelix*. I had a handheld VHF radio as a back-up, just for this situation. It was attached by a lanyard next to me and crackled into life.

'*Hope, Hope, Hope* this is *Obelix*. Over.'

I grabbed the radio and called back, 'Hello *Obelix*, this is *Hope*. Go to channel seven two. Over.' Channel 72 is one of the channels set aside for general chat.

I quickly grabbed my GPS anticipating that *Obelix* would ask for my position and then switched the channel on my VHF radio to 72.

'Hello *Hope*, what is your position?'

I then read out my position in latitude and longitude. A couple of minutes later, *Obelix* powered up next to me. She was a huge dark blue and black sided tugboat with a white cabin perched high at the front. Standing on her deck was Ivor and next to him, perched on his two long pins for legs and with his distinctive black beard was Cayle. We tried shouting to each other but the waves were too big for the large tugboat to get close enough for a conversation.

I was astonished that Cayle had come out to surprise me. I sat back down and carried on rowing as *Obelix* shadowed me. The sea wall seemed to go on for ever, as I slowly rowed along its length. I had to row about 50 metres from the wall. Big waves rebounded from it and crashing into waves going the opposite way made rowing particularly difficult.

Finally I rounded the southern tip into the sheltered water of the port of Las Palmas. Once in the marina, I pulled *Hope* up to a pontoon next to the Port Authority. Waiting for me on the pontoon was Claire and Ivor's partner Sharron.

Obelix also came alongside and I shouted my thanks to her crew as Ivor and Cayle came ashore. Cayle tied *Hope* to the pontoon and with the help of Ivor, I stood on dry land again. Claire held me. It was a bittersweet moment. I was obviously very glad to see her, but I wished it was at the end of the row, not at a forced stop. I'd been at sea for two weeks and was unsteady on my foot. The constant movement of *Hope* in the open ocean had become normal and now the sudden change to motionless dry land threw my senses and standing became a challenge.

'You've gotta do your passport.' Claire said as she helped me up the ramp from the pontoon to the Port Authority building.

Before I went to the desk to check in, I staggered with Claire's help to the one thing I was really looking forward to – a porcelain toilet.

Ivor and Cayle took charge of *Hope* while Claire and I took a taxi to a hotel in Las Palmas. Once showered I laid on the bed. It's impossible to describe how good, clean, dry, cotton sheets feel after two weeks at sea laying on a thin plastic mat. I laid there in bliss, savouring the luxury of a bed that didn't rock from side to side, before falling into a deep sleep.

The next morning I rowed *Hope* from the Port Authority office temporary mooring to the other side of the marina. Cayle and Ivor had already sorted me a berth next to the Restaurante Embarcadero owned by John who'd arranged for *Obelix* to follow me in.

After tying *Hope* up, I followed Ivor into the restaurant to meet John.

'John, this is the idiot who's rowing across the whole ocean,' said Ivor as John held out a hand.

'I can't thank you enough,' I said.

John asked about the row so far and offered up his restaurant as a temporary base whilst we worked on *Hope*. Cayle and Ivor stayed with the boat waiting for the engineer and I went back to the hotel.

Cayle called me later that afternoon, 'Dude, the problem's sorted. The engineer thinks it was water or moisture getting into the connectors in the rear cabin.'

When I arrived at the boat, Cayle showed me the problem. In the rear cabin with the autohelm and EFOY power supply was a small plastic strip connector with wires that connect the screens at the rear of the boat to the main navigation system in the front cabin. Cayle explained that water had got into the connector and had stopped the rear navigation screens from talking to the main navigation system in the front. The navigation system relied on all the parts talking to each other and if there was a break in that chain, as had happened, the whole system would fail. I'd been carrying a few spare strip connectors with me the whole time but wasn't to know that had been the problem.

'Let's take her for a spin and test it out,' Cayle suggested.

I could tell that he was eager to get back out on the water in an ocean rowing boat.

We rowed out of the marina into the port. We set waypoints into the navigation system, (imaginary points for the navigation system to navigate to) and I rowed back and forth, testing the system. It all seemed to be working perfectly. After taking *Hope* back into the marina I rang Leven Brown to see how soon I'd be able to get away.

'Hello, Captain,' he said in his soft Scottish border's brogue. 'It's all looking a little tricky at the moment with a lot of uncertainty. There may not be an opportunity to get away for a week.'

'You know Ralph has set off?' I asked in reference to Ralph Tuijn.

'Yes I saw.'

'I just keep thinking that the best I can hope for is to beat him in, so I at least break the able-bodied record and then Ralph'll just come in and then take the record off me.'

'There's a lot of ocean between then and now,' Leven said. 'And the only thing we can control, is the start.' He continued with his mantra on being cautious about getting safely away from land. 'We'll talk again the morrow captain.'

I acknowledged his better judgement. There was nothing I could do about Ralph slowly catching me and with at least a week before I'd be able to get away, I decided I may as well let my hair down and went out for a few beers.

The next day, despite hangovers, we needed to be as productive as possible and stripped the boat out as much as we could. We laid the lines I'd used for the drogue to dry in the hot sun. Whilst the ropes dried, we cleaned out all the holds and checked through all the rations. The ration pack I ate that most likely gave me diarrhoea was the only one that was damaged. After packing the rations and ropes away, *Hope* was now ship shape and ready to go. I just had to wait for the weather. Leven messaged saying that there was no change and it could still be at least a week before the weather settled. As frustrating as waiting for a change in the weather was, if I was honest with myself, I wasn't looking forward to getting back in the boat and all the time I was waiting, Ralph was chasing me down.

That evening John took us to his favourite restaurant and I relaxed. I felt conflicted between not wanting to get back in the boat and the need to get away before Ralph caught up, but accepted that I couldn't change the weather so enjoyed the meal.

Leven rang the following afternoon. 'Hello Captain. A few of the models I'm looking at are settling down and it's looking likely that there's an opportunity to be on your way tomorrow.'

I'd resigned myself for a prolonged stay in the Canaries and was now thoroughly enjoying being on dry land – not rowing through the day and night with the constant movement of the boat, not rehydrating every meal, sleeping in a bed with soft, clean cotton sheets. And the isolation, I had just got used to being around people. I hadn't realised how much I'd allowed myself to forget why I was in Las Palmas in the first place and now the row came crashing back into my life.

'I'll call in the morning to confirm, but it's looking good. I'd plan for a midday departure.'

I looked over to Claire. 'I'm going tomorrow.'

That night we went into Las Palmas for some food and beers, but it felt very much like a condemned man's last meal.

The next morning Leven called, 'Hello Captain. It's a go.'

Day 18

I rowed over to the Port Authority to complete the paperwork needed to exit the Canaries and, for the second time, said goodbye to Claire.

Ivor pushed *Hope* away from the pontoon and I rowed out of the marina and through the port. Claire stood on the wall overlooking the port occasionally waving and as I rowed away, she slowly disappeared from view.

My instructions from Leven were to row south-east away from Gran Canaria and then as I cleared the southern tip of the Island, head almost due south. Late in the afternoon, a huge dolphin and calf came and swam around *Hope*, checking her out before swimming away.

Late afternoon turned to dusk and then the lights of Gran Canaria kept me company through my nighttime rowing shifts. I finished my first night at sea for five days happy to be finally on my way. I'd adjusted straight back to my routine on *Hope* as if I hadn't stopped. Far off, beyond the hazy blue grey hills of Gran Canaria, the snowy top of Mount Teide, the volcano on Tenerife poked out of the mist.

Day 18 Logbook Entry

Position at 0800hrs on 27th Jan 2019 UTC	*Distance travelled 34.6nm at 182°*
27° 33′ 227n 015°23.971w	*Total distance 650nm*

A steady slog away to clear land then turned S currently navigating to waypoint @ 27°000′00N 05°30.00W @ 189° T. 2 v large dolphins came and had a look at the boat then swam off. Wind picked up from N getting a bit more speed. To the east can see the top of the volcano on Tenerife sticking out through the clouds.

THE ROYAL MARINES

On Monday, 2 March 1992 I waved goodbye to my Mum and Claire at Paddington Station and boarded the train to Lympstone Commando for the second time. The previous week I'd been shopping to fastidiously complete the extensive kit list with things I'd never used before, like a three-piece razor, sewing kit known as a 'housewife' and a shaving brush and soap. I was wearing my only suit and carried my suitcase with everything I thought I needed for the next eight months. I boarded the train and found a window seat and looked through the grimy glass at Claire who returned a smile. As the train slowly pulled away from the platform, I felt I was leaving my old life behind, it was more than just a new chapter. I noticed two similarly dressed lads wearing the same nervous expression. They were sat together on the table next to me.

The one with short dark skinhead haircut, turned to me and with a distinct South London accent said, 'Are you going to Lympstone?'

'Yep, are you?'

'Yeah. I'm Sam by the way.'

The other lad was Blake who spoke with no discernible regional accent. I sat with them at their table and Sam explained that they'd been on the same PRC. As we approached Exeter St David's, the number of nervous-looking young men wearing suits steadily grew. We changed platform to catch the Exmouth-bound train, lugging our various cases and bags with us.

Suddenly we were next to the camp with the high barbed-wire fence and familiar assault course. The train seemed to be full of new recruits all looking nervously out of the window. Waiting on the platform at Lympstone Commando, was a very smart corporal with a clipboard and a light tan-coloured stick under his arm.

'Right, line up. One line.' He shouted as we got off the train. 'My name is Corporal Wickstead, you call me Corporal. I'm your DL.' He then went along the line with his clipboard and when in front of me, without looking up, asked, 'Name?'

'Spencer Corporal.' I replied.

He quickly ticked my name off his list and moved on to the next lad. When he'd finished, he looked up and said simply, 'Right, pick up your bags and follow me.'

From the platform he led us through the small gate into the camp where he formed us into three ranks and then tried to march us up a set of steps onto a road to our home for the next two weeks, Induction Block. Inside was a long rectangular room with two lines of evenly spaced large wooden lockers behind which was a single bed with a dark green plastic mattress.

'Find your bedspace, your names are on the locker,' said Corporal Wickstead.

I walked along the row of lockers and found my name 'Rct Spencer' on a small white card on the locker door. I was in the bedspace between Sam and Blake.

The next 24 hours was a blur of collecting bedding, uniforms, kit, learning how to make a bed correctly, unpacking and most notably, a lesson on how to shower with a naked Corporal Wickstead. The first couple of days' administration finished with swearing an Oath of Allegiance to the Queen and then training started. I had joined 635 Troop.

Nothing was how I imagined it. The stereotypical morning reveille of an angry corporal turning on the lights and screaming, 'Get up, you 'orrible lot' didn't happen. Instead from the very first morning we were told what time we needed to be in three ranks, waiting outside ready to go to our first detail of the day and left to get on with it. Very soon it became apparent that complying with a very simple detail like, '07:55 Outside in 3 ranks ready for Royal Marines Values lesson,' would take a serious amount of effort.

At 07:55 our uniforms and the accommodation would need to be immaculate and these required hours of effort beforehand. We had to wash our uniforms by hand and then wait for them to dry in the drying room as we had no washing machines or tumble dryers. Then they'd need to be precisely ironed, avoiding the pit fall of 'tram lines' – two creases down the front of your olive-green denims. With thirty-eight of us in 635 Troop and limited irons and sinks, this took cooperation on to a whole new level. The whole of Induction Block needed to be cleaned, dusted, mopped and the floors polished, before we stepped outside in the morning. So that simple 07:55 detail required working until one or two in the morning then getting up at five to finish everything off. We didn't know it at the time, but we were slowly being moulded into a self-motivating team.

Our PT sessions were also not what I was expecting. After the introduction and orientation, we started in the gym with Initial Military Fitness. IMF is a series of arm and leg movements, not unlike semaphore or the bloke at the airport who signals to planes with table tennis bats. It was all done in time with the PTI who stood on a large box at the front calling out movements. Other PTIs stalked along the lines ready to pounce if an elbow wasn't all the way back or a knee wasn't high enough, ensuring every movement was inch perfect. It looked and felt very 1950s National Service but was utterly exhausting.

At the end of the first week, we were introduced to rope climbing, a totally new exercise requiring new muscles and a lot of technique. The next couple of weeks would be dominated by an agonising pain in both elbows as my arms struggled to get used to this new torture.

Over the first weekend in training was the first of many exercises called First Step. Over the weekend I was introduced to the two things that would dominate my life for the next eight months, Woodbury Common and Corporal Lynch.

Woodbury Common is apparently an area of outstanding natural beauty overlooked by the brooding Iron Age hill fort, Woodbury Castle. It's covered in spiteful gorse, hills and bogs. Cpl Lynch had piercing blue eyes, mousey brown hair and a moustache you could hide a fridge freezer in. He spoke in a soft Northumbrian accent and used words I'd no comprehension of, like 'pooches' instead of pouches. I was also introduced to someone who would go on to have a lasting impression on the rest of my career, Sergeant Sid McCarthey.

Exercise First Step was a very basic introduction to 'living in the field' with our first of many 'thrashings'. Everyone partnered up with a 'bivvi partner' and mine was Sam. We'd do everything together, be it cooking, eating and sleeping.

Induction was definitely a shock to my system. I was transformed over the two weeks from civilian to something resembling almost military. I'd learned new skills, made new friends, some would last a lifetime and I was introduced to a whole new vocabulary. Toilets were heads, sinks were ablutions where you did your dhobi, food was scran and was eaten in the galley with a KFS. Waz or wazzer was good, but 'stand-by' as in 'you fuckers can stand-by' was very, very bad.

Royal Marine recruits are called Nods, the reason why became apparent when I looked behind in a lecture at a room full of nodding heads. Over the next eight months I'd also 'nod off' laying down, sat upright, sat at a desk, in an ambush, and even a few times stood up. Whilst in Induction, we were called 'Luminods' because of the orange mine tape worn on our epaulettes to signify to everyone on camp we were new and prone to mistakes.

My lifelong dream of being a Royal Marine was put to one side whilst I concentrated on just passing Induction, getting rid of the lumi tape, having my first few hours leave ashore and moving on to the next part of training in Portsmouth Company. I couldn't see beyond the next two weeks. Induction culminated with a locker inspection where my developing attention to detail saw me through with a pass.

My second weekend saw me changing block to 635 Troop's new home, B block and my first 'run ashore' in Exeter. Both were filled with more excitement than they warranted. Sam and I were in the same section under Cpl Lynch and the same room overlooking the Exe estuary. Beyond the estuary was the first of many hills cloaked in woods and forests with a patchwork of verdant green fields in between. The nearest hill had a curious ancient looking tower poking out through the trees, and behind, wooded hills climbed away into the distant slopes of southern Dartmoor.

On the seldom occasion I had a chance to look out over the stunning south Devon countryside, I found it comforting. In stark contrast was the ebb and flow of the River Exe in the muddy, brown silt-laden estuary. The cycle of the tide had a curious but tangible effect on the mood within the camp. When the tide was out, a blanket of dread would descend on the whole place. We were thrashed in the mud once and that was enough to leave an emotional scar that caused a lead weighted dread in the pit of my stomach whenever I saw the mud glistening the other side of the train tracks.

As training started in Portsmouth Company, I was filled with an almost overwhelming sense of being out of my depth. Within 635 Troop, we had a Welsh national boxer, county cross-country running champions, a national fell running champion. There were others who had experience in the military, through either the reserves or past service. And me.

Every Monday morning I'd start a new personal mission – to get to the end of the week in 635 Troop. It was made very clear to us all, that the door was always open. All we had to do was knock and say we didn't want to carry on.

Each day Cpl Lynch greeted our section with the same cheerful proclamation in his quiet northern accent. 'I do not need you. Sgt McCarthy doesn't need you. The Royal Marines do not need you. You Fookers are surplus to requirements.'

As the first few weeks passed by, I felt I was clinging onto training by my fingernails. This made it even more shocking whenever anyone gave up and dropped out. Each one, to my mind, was fitter, stronger and more experienced than me and all had the same excuse – 'It's just not for me.' I knew this was a lie, this wasn't life in the Royal Marines, it was training, it's what you had to do to be a Royal Marine. So how could they know it wasn't for them? I knew the effort it took just to get to the start line of training, so being a Royal Marine was for them at some point. And if I knew this was a lie, then surely so should they. I was baffled by their ability to lie to themselves. I knew that if I gave up, then that near constant voice whispering in my ear that I was a worthless coward would make the rest of my life a misery. I knew I couldn't lie to that voice. I knew I couldn't give in.

Day 19

I finished the last rowing session of the night expecting to see the peak of Mount Teide poking out through the clouds again. On my first row it was there every morning for three days, its presence mocking us saying 'You haven't gone that far.'

The grey light of dawn steadily grew into a grey, cloudy morning with flecks of rain spitting from a dull sky and Mount Teide was nowhere to be seen. I was now back rowing in the open ocean out of sight of land. The grey skies reflected in a grey sea with breaking waves a couple of metres high. It felt like *Hope* was surging through the water as my attention turned back towards Ralph, who was somewhere north of the Canaries chasing me down. As each two-hour rowing session came to an end, I wearily crawled back into the cabin feeling like I'd just finished a gruelling training session in the gym. I kept imagining a weather system coming between me and Ralph, pushing him back and me forwards, but for the lack of effort, I'd be on the other side of the system, getting blown backwards with Ralph.

Rowing an ocean can never be a sprint. You must row at a sustainably comfortable pace, but the thought of missing an opportunity to get away from Ralph drove me. Every rowing session I pushed myself out of the sustainably comfortable zone and pulled on the oars with an extra effort. From mid-morning it started to rain and the wind increased giving the air a chill. I was cold enough to row in my light waterproof jacket. A pod of dolphins swam past *Hope*, effortlessly breaking the surface of the waves that steadily grew bigger.

A miserable day turned into a miserable dusk and after my meal of freeze-dried Asian Noodles with Chicken, I settled into my night rowing routine. My alarm woke me for my midnight until 2am rowing shift. I donned my waterproofs and lifejacket and clambered out to a dark moonless night. The wind had increased and by the sound of the stomach-churning roar, so had the waves. I could feel the rumble of breaking waves around me. With no point of reference, it felt like *Hope* was being tossed around in a wet nothingness. After the two-hour row, I settled back into the cabin for two hours' rest. Suddenly, the alarm started beeping, as *Hope* swung round into irons. I awoke and opened my eyes filled with dread, I quickly checked the navigation system, but thankfully that wasn't the problem. In this black angry sea with big breaking waves, every second that *Hope* was side-on to the waves was dangerous. I grabbed my life jacket, fastened the straps and dived out of the cabin naked, clipping my safety line onto the deck. I grabbed the oars and pulled with all my might, quickly gaining enough forward momentum to turn *Hope* back on course. I fixed the hand steering lines in place and checked the autohelm. For some reason it had popped off the rudder and that seemed the only problem. I reattached it, waited to check that all OK, then returned to the cabin, cold and wet. This happened several more times through the night. I figured the cause was the hand steering lines were too short. In these big angry seas, the autohelm was having to work harder to keep *Hope* on course and at the extremis of the turn, the hand lines were pulling on the rudder, forcing the autohelm to pop off. It was a simple fix of just extending the hand steering lines, to allow the rudder a full range of movement. At 8am, I sat in the cabin and took my daily stats down and was disappointed with the 64 nautical miles covered in 24 hours. While it was over my 50 nautical miles daily goal, it didn't seem as far as my effort warranted.

Day 19 Logbook Entry

Position at 0800hrs on 28th Jan 2019 UTC *Distance travelled 64nm at 205°*
26° 35′ 006n 015°54.671w *Total distance 714nm*

Wind steadily grew through the night from 2300hrs. Some big breaking waves. Auto helm kept popping off and the boat going into irons because the steering lines were short. When autohelm was at full turn the lines would tighten and pull off. So extended lines which has sorted the issue. 2454nm to go.

As training progressed, the exercises got harder. After First Step came Exercise Twosome, affectionally known by Nods as 'Gruesome Twosome', where I was introduced to the 'beasting knoll' and the 'flank'. The beasting knoll is a small hillock used by training teams for correctional PT known as a beasting, and the flank was where I inevitably ended up after every morning inspection.

The whole troop paraded in section lines with our field kit uniformly laid out on our ponchos. Cpl Lynch looked through every piece of equipment with the same steely attention of an eagle scanning the ground for prey. Often I felt like prey. If you look hard enough there is always something somewhere, the tiniest piece of leaf litter that secreted itself in an unreachable corner of the firing mechanism, or the slightest smudge of camouflage cream on the back of a neck. When he'd find it, Cpl Lynch would smile and say, 'On the flank Spencer.'

I pack my kit away and trudge to the end of our line, the 'flank'.

After morning parade, came daily exercises that were a beasting, but masquerading as 'normal PT'. The whole troop would then be beasted for some collective misdemeanour, and extra beastings for those that had been flanked.

After the exercise, as I was unpacking kit, I heard Cpl Lynch scream 'Spencer. Office. Now'

I ran to the office, stood to attention, knocked on the door and then reported. 'Corporal, I am P051826 Sierra. Recruit Spencer of 635 Troop.'

'Come in, shut the door.' Corporal Lynch then berated me for failing the exercise and told me I'd now be back trooped. 'You have only yourself to blame,' He added.

Cpl Lynch was a Falklands veteran, an experienced soldier and professional Royal Marine, but he wasn't an actor.

Any niggling doubt I had about passing Twosome evaporated as I played along with his obvious attempt to wind me up with mutterings of 'Yes Corporal,' and, 'I'm sorry Corporal.'

I wasn't 'back trooped' and a few weeks after Gruesome Twosome came Exercise Hunter's Moon, where we repeated all we'd learned on Twosome, but at night.

Over the course of Hunter's Moon the morning inspection with Cpl Lynch developed into a game. One that I could never win. Cpl Lynch inspected the rest of 4 Section with the same attention to detail as the other corporals seemed to do, until he stood in front of me. He didn't move along the line until he found a microscopic bit of black fouling in a crevice on my mess tin handle. He smiled broadly and his cold, piercingly blue eyes momentarily twinkled in triumph. 'Spencer. Flank.' He said full of joy.

The beastings from Cpl Lynch also became a game, but one that I could never lose. I knew he could never break me. This game culminated on the final morning of the exercise. Cpl Lynch stood frowning in front of me with his hands on his hips. He'd just finished poking his little finger into every possible crevice of my weapon, pulling it out and inspecting it in the hope of finding the tiniest bit of dirty oil. I smiled at him and felt his frustration as his frown increased. *'Finally, I've beaten you'*, I thought.

He looked me squarely in the eye and I briefly saw his eyes widen slightly before smiling broadly. 'Clasp knife. Get your clasp knife out. All of you.' He turned to the rest of the section that had so far passed the inspection. 'Get your clasp knives out.'

My clasp knife was an issued pen knife that resided in my top right pocket of my combat jacket and was attached to the buttonhole by a lanyard. I pulled it out dreading the worst.

'Open it up then,' he said.

As I did a large bit of dirt fell out and onto the ground between my feet.

Cpl Lynch almost danced on the spot with joy. 'Spencer. Flank.'

His scrutiny of everything I did was far higher than the rest of his section and either despite this, or because of this, I still don't know which, I knew he liked me. I could joke with Cpl Lynch in a way the other members of our section couldn't and he talked to me on a level that he didn't with the rest of the section.

That morning, we had a particularly vicious beasting after our whole section somehow miraculously missed a troop 'Crash Move'. A Crash Move is where your troop is either directly attacked or you are quietly told that you must conduct an emergency move. The result is the same, packing everything away as fast as you can and the inevitable loss of precious sleep. The words 'Crash Move' were dreaded by all Nods. Sam and I had just finished sentry and laid in our sleeping bags when we both heard a sound that resembled a steam train far in the distance. 'What's that?' asked Sam.

'If we don't look it's not real.' I half joked.

Sam looked anyway. 'Fucking hell,' he said as he pulled himself out of his sleeping bag. 'It's a Crash Move.'

We packed our sleeping bags and ponchos away, threw on our kit and bergens and ran off in the direction we saw the last of the troop disappear. We took two or three steps and then crashed straight into Troll and Smudge's poncho. They were blissfully oblivious of what was happening. We woke them and then continued into another 4 Section poncho. The troop had been crash moved but no one had bothered to tell us.

Cpl Lynch was furious. Halfway through the beasting in the morning Cpl Lynch shouted, 'Fucking good effort Spencer. Go and sit down.'

I had no idea what I'd done but wasn't about to argue so sat out the rest of the beasting. After Hunter's Moon there was another berating from Cpl Lynch on failing the exercise, but he made the almost overwhelming sense of feeling out of my depth bearable. I still felt I was clinging on by my fingernails, but I had the creeping feeling that someone believed in me.

Exercise Running Man was half survival and half navigation exercise conducted on the southern slopes of Dartmoor. Before we deployed, we had lessons with the Royal Marines Mountain Leaders on all things survival, from lighting fires to setting snares. Mountain Leaders, or MLs as they're known, are the undisputed experts on mountain and arctic warfare in the British Armed Forces. They undertake and pass an extremely arduous seven-month course and are held with a reverence by all who encounter them. Their course is longer than Special Forces selection and is widely regarded as being more physically challenging. The ML section at CTC were the subject-matter experts on survival. Just before starting the exercise a few members of our section discussed the next couple of days and in particular catching rabbits. The conversation turned to myxomatosis, and someone asked if anyone knew why rabbits are susceptible to the disease and hares aren't. Troll, a tall strapping lad from the Welsh Valleys with terrible tattoos answered, 'Well I guess the hares are too fast for it.'

After the first night in the field, the troop were put in all round defence, facing outwards ready to repel an imminent attack. I was observing my arcs, desperately trying to stay awake when I heard someone clicking their fingers behind me. I turned to look and Cpl Marks, another section's corporal, gestured for me to follow. He led me out of the troop harbour, through a small wood and out into a field. As I turned into the field, I saw a Nod with a sandbag over his head being led away by another couple of corporals. I was then jumped. Struggle as I did, I soon had a sandbag over my head, then led away, stripped of all my kit and weapon. I was sat down cross legged in a stream and my hands were placed on my head.

A voice whispered in my ear, 'Keep your hands on your head and don't move.'

After what felt like hours, the troop officer, Lieutenant Ellis shouted, 'Everyone now stand up and take the bags of your heads. Do not talk.'

We all stood up and after taking the bag off my head I could see I was towards the rear of a long line of Nods in a small stream in open moorland.

'Place your right hand on the right shoulder of the man in front, do not look left or right. Do not talk. Follow me.'

We were led into another small wood where he gathered us together.

'You've all been captured but escaped. You are now in the survival phase.'

Each section was split in half into fireteams, allocated an area to build a shelter and fire, then left to get on with it.

Hours later Troll walked into the training team's tent. 'What's wrong Trollope?' one of the Corporals asked.

'I got bored,' replied Troll.

'What do you mean you got bored?'

'Well, I was sat there forever, and my arse went numb so I took the sandbag off my head and no one was there. So, I came here. I didn't know what else to do.'

Troll had been at the back of the line in the stream and had somehow not heard or realised when everybody followed Lt Ellis away. He had been sat in the stream, on his own with a sandbag on his head for hours. When he walked back into where we were all busy surviving and told us what had happened it was a well needed boost of morale at the start of what was going to be a very difficult exercise for me.

As soon as we had built our fires and inadequate shelters the navigation exercises began. After the first two, the physical exertion without any fuel began to take a its toll on my body.

Lt Ellis came into the wood and said, 'Section Commanders on me.' *'I can't do another Nav' Ex'*. I thought. Our section had been loaned Dolan, a big northern, former Coldstream Guardsman as section commander as no-one in four section was deemed suitable to lead. Dolan sat taking notes in his notebook with the other section commanders before returning to us.

'We've got quite a long Nav' Ex' to be done as a section.'

He then nominated someone to stay behind to keep both section fires going and then went through all the check points. I genuinely thought the way I was feeling, I wouldn't be able to complete it. It was quite matter of fact. I felt on the absolute edge of what was physically possible.

A few hours later we walked back into the wood and settled back around the fire. I was amazed that I'd completed it but was sure that there'd be no way I'd be able to complete the next one. I knew my own body and felt that I had absolutely nothing left to give.

Later that evening Lt Ellis returned and briefed the whole troop on the individual Nav' Ex' we'd have to complete that night.

Again, I made it back to the wood, settled around the fire, totally amazed that I'd finished. If I was sure I couldn't complete the previous Nav Ex I'd been positive that I wouldn't be able to complete the night one. But here I was.

The next morning as the sun rose, in came Lt Ellis again with another set of checkpoints for another Nav' Ex'. The same clouds of doubt resurfaced, but a few hours later I was back around the fire. At that moment I realised I didn't know what I was capable of. It was a genuine epiphany. I thought I knew where the end point of my endurance was and realising that it was nowhere in sight, completely changed the way I saw myself. I began to see myself through new eyes and in that moment, training changed for me. I'd felt totally out of my depth, always about to be kicked out and just relieved to still be with the troop at the end of each week. Every gym test, exercise or weapons test was a potential failing point to end my stint as a Royal Marine recruit. Now I believed I could make it through training.

Day 20

The sun emerged from a murky grey morning turning the sea from a dull greyish green to a vivid turquoise. Brilliant white horses trailed across the tops of the large breaking waves that steadily grew with increasingly strong north-westerly winds. With practiced timing I was catching lots of waves and as I surfed down their front, white foaming water filled the boat and filled me with exhilaration of the sea's raw power.

Late in the afternoon the AIS pinged a yacht on the same heading catching slowly from astern. It wasn't unusual, I'd seen quite a few yachts heading out across the Atlantic and I just kept an eye on her to make sure she wasn't going to come too close. The yacht drew up level about a mile to my west.

A male English voiced crackled over the airwaves. '*Hope, Hope, Hope* this is *New Destiny*. Over.'

I quickly stowed the oars, jumped in the cabin, and closed the hatch behind me. 'Hello *New Destiny*, this is *Hope*. Over.'

'Hello *Hope*, I can see you on my radar but I can't see your mast.'

'That's because I haven't got one. I'm an ocean rowing boat.'

'Wow, that's brilliant.'

I then explained who I was and what I was doing. After I had finished the voice introduced himself as John. He and his wife were sailing to the Caribbean.

'I don't suppose you've ever heard of an ocean rower called Elaine Hopley?' he asked.

I explained that Elaine had rowed the Atlantic the year after Cayle and I rowed with Row2Recovery. We'd visited La Gomera to see the rowers before the start of the 2016 race and I'd met Elaine there. She then went on to break the solo female record. In 2017, I'd sought her advice on rowing solo and she dispelled any doubts I had.

John replied that he and his wife had met Elaine in Antigua after she'd finished her row. Utterly amazed at the smallness of the world, we carried on our conversation before *New Destiny* slowly pulled away. We said our goodbyes and soon I was alone again.

Day 20 Logbook Entry

Position at 0800hrs on 29th Jan 2019 UTC *Distance travelled 78nm at 221°*
25° 36' 554n 016°51.604w *Total distance 794nm*

Distance to Cayenne 2382nm

V strong winds NW all day and night, a lot of surfing down large breaking waves and overcast most of the day. Current course 230° heading as @ approx 1540hrs yacht New Destiny transited 1.5nm to the west on similar bearing, owner John came up on the radio, he'd met Elaine Hopley in Antigua and knew the RM sailor who'd gone back into a storm to rescue someone in a race (forgot his name) Small world.

Our Troop Sergeant, Sgt Sid McCarthy, was a levelling force within the training team. There was a collective approach to punishment meted out to individual, section and troop level misdemeanours. We were almost exclusively beasted together, everyone paying the price. Sid always kept the corporals in check ensuring there was a degree of fairness not only between the different sections, but also between the punishment and crime. He would end every bollocking with 'Wrong detail centurions', before handing us over to our Corporals for a beasting. Sid's calming influence was felt even more keenly in his absence when he disappeared to get married. On the last afternoon before he left he called the troop together for a brief on the landing of our accommodation block.

'After the brief he said 'Three ranks outside ready for map reading.'

No one moved.

A look of confusion crossed his face and someone from the troop piped up, 'Err, there's another detail Sergeant.'

Sid looked to the corporals, 'I've no idea what's going on,' said Corporal Marks.

Sam piped up, 'Sorry Sergeant, we knew you're getting married so we all chipped in and bought you a present.'

Two lads brought in a newly-bought microwave oven. Sid was genuinely moved and after thanking us with a tear in his eye, we fell in three ranks ready for our map reading lesson. The next three weeks were hell.

Members of 635 Troop began to drop like flies as everything we did became a thrashing. I had no spare capacity to care about anyone who decided to leave, I felt that I was just hanging in there myself, except for 'Skids'.

During a compulsory load carry, a forced march carrying bergens with all our field kit, Skids, a member of 4 Section from the start, fell back and was told to get into the safety wagon. It seemed so unfair. The forced march was done at a pace where the whole troop was running most of the way and normally, if someone dropped back, they were given a chance to catch up. Skids went straight into the safety wagon. Having failed the march he was back-trooped. Sam and I were devastated for him. Skids had been in training for the Paras when his mother had died. He left and joined the Corps a year later.

That night, Cpl Lynch came into our room and woke up Skids. 'Listen son', he said. 'Don't give up just because you've been back-trooped. You're a good lad. You're more than capable of passing out.'

We all heard Cpl Lynch and all felt the genuine empathy and sensed he to, was gutted for him. Being back-trooped broke Skids's heart and he left training. The next day I rang Claire from one of the pay phones in the NAAFI and cried for the first time in years. I was gutted for Skids, but mostly I was crying for myself.

Within a few weeks we lost eleven members of the troop, the majority just giving up. We spent a week at Straight Point ranges near Exmouth. The ranges sit atop a cliff overlooking Sandy Bay beach and at the end of Devon Cliffs holiday park. We travelled daily from Lympstone and every morning drove through a holiday camp to get to the range. The juxtaposition of seeing normal families enjoying their holidays on the beach whilst we were thrashed daily added to our collective misery. I had a terrible week where I repeatedly failed a shooting test and only just scraped a pass on my last allowed attempt with the very real threat of being back-trooped looming over me.

On the final morning the whole troop fell in, our kit laid out ready to be inspected. Instead of returning to Lympstone after finishing shooting the night before, as we'd done previously, we'd bivvied out on the ranges as a punishment for using enough ammunition to start a medium-sized war. It was obvious that many in the troop, myself included, had been using more than the allocated number of rounds to cheat the test. In the middle of the night Cpl Marks had beasted the troop for two hours and now we were waiting for the next beasting after we all failed the inspection. At the end of Each section line the section commanders looked down the rank, facing towards the entrance to the range and the holiday camp beyond. After about ten minutes stood to attention waiting, I heard the familiar sound of a Land Rover pull-up, a couple of creaky doors opened before being slammed shut. A whisper ran through the troop 'Sid's back. Sid's back.'

A collective relief went through us all. I sensed we'd finally come through a dark tunnel and training would return to some kind of normal.

Sid walked out in front of us, 'Right Centurions, where's my troop gone?'

We were inspected and failed, then beasted again. We didn't care. Sid was back.

Although I knew I'd somehow come through a big test, there was no time to rest as we went straight into BFT blues week. The bottom field test is a massive hurdle about two-thirds of the way through training and consists of four physical tests: A 30-foot rope climb, a regain, where you hang off a horizontal rope, then pull yourself back onto it, a 200-metre fireman's carry in under 90 seconds and the assault course in under five minutes. All the bottom field tests are done carrying 22 pounds of weight plus weapon.

BFT blues week was designed to prepare recruits for the tests by having double periods every day. To compound this, we as a troop were exhausted and kept making mistakes that required corrective PT. The repeated beastings made us more exhausted that led to more mistakes. Even the bottom field performances suffered and our PTI gave us a third bottom field session one evening.

Towards the end of the week, Cpl Lynch approached me, 'Why does the troop keep fucking up Spence?'

'We're all exhausted corporal.'

'You're meant to be exhausted,' he said. 'This is training.'

'I know, Corporal. But we're spiralling down. We fuck up, get thrashed that makes us more exhausted, fuck up again and it keeps going.'

Cpl Lynch huffed and walked out. The training team then left us alone for the rest of the morning. They didn't tell us they were giving us a rest; they just didn't give us another detail to comply with.

There's a special way of laying on a military bed that all Nods learn. By keeping your feet on the floor and almost hovering over the sheets, it's possible to half lay on your back without creasing the pristine sheets. We assumed this position and did what Nods do best – slept. It was only a few of hour's rest but it made a massive difference. The constant cycle of fucking up, getting thrashed and fucking up again ended.

Although I started as one of the physically weaker recruits, I was strong on the bottom field and passed without issue. My best mate Sam, however, struggled on the ropes. The whole troop and Cpl Lynch fell in to watch his final attempt. We all screamed encouragement as he climbed two feet from the top. I could see from his face as he slid down the rope that he was devastated, but I also knew that he wouldn't give in and leave. He did get up the ropes on his first attempt with the troop behind, but by then it was too late. I'd lost my bivvy partner.

Day 21

Consistent northerly winds drove decent-sized waves. The grey, white flecked sea turned turquoise in patches as the sun broke through lowly clouds. It was a perfect rowing day.

Half an hour into my first daytime row, the navigation alarm pinged and *Hope* swung to port. I quickly grabbed the hand steering lines and pulled *Hope* back round onto her bearing. Once she'd settled, I locked the steering lines off and ungraciously clambered on my arse to the stern to investigate. Inside the stern hatch the autohelm hung limp with the piston fully extended. I removed it and tried unsuccessfully to push the piston back in. It was obvious that the gearing inside had seized. I'd kept three autohelms from *Hope*'s last trip across the Indian Ocean, and a trusted yachtsman had taken them away and assured me they were reconditioned. Of the three so called seaworthy autohelms, one hadn't worked at all and this one lasted three days. I swapped the seized autohelm over with the remaining reconditioned one and settled back into rowing. This one lasted ten minutes before it stopped working. Furious at the sheer recklessness of an experienced yachtsman sending someone out to sea with the false promise of three functioning autohelms, I replaced the last one with the autohelm I'd used in the first five days rowing before the nav' system collapsed. I now had two autohelms left – the one I'd started with and a brand new one in reserve. The first autohelm that broke had a problem with the gears, the second appeared to have an electrical problem. I hoped that between them I might be able to bastardise a third working autohelm, something I had learnt from Cayle on my first row.

I rowed through the pitch-black night with no reference point and no moon to reflect her pale blue light on the waves. Rowing in the pitch black always gave me a sense of falling into nothingness. Oars often thrashed at nothing, completely missing the sea and waves crashed over *Hope* without warning. I hated rowing with no moon.

As dawn approached, a sense of normality descended from the madness of a tiny rowing boat in the pitch-black nothingness of the open ocean.

Day 21 Logbook Entry

Position at 0800hrs on 30th Jan 2019 UTC	*Distance travelled 73nm at 230°*
24°49'352n 017°53.312w	*Total distance 867nm*
Distance to Cayenne 2311nm	

Steady winds all day, overcast for most of the day. 2 auto helms down. 1st had been going since Las Palmas (3 days) and the gearing broke down. 2nd lasted 10mins. There seems to be a problem with the drive system (electrics not gearing) so hopefully I'll be able to bastardise another. Both autohelms were 2nd hand and supposedly reconditioned. I had 3 2nd hand recon autohelms but one wouldn't work from the word go. I have 1 new autohelm left. Looks like it'll be overcast again today

The last phase of training, the commando phase, starts with a six-mile speed march. A speed march is a staple of Royal Marines training and designed to get a body of men from A to B ready to fight. It's done as a troop each man carrying 22 pounds of kit plus weapon, walking uphill, and running downhill and flats at a ten-minute mile pace.

There's a rhythm to a speed march and once found it carries you along. Much like the bottom field, speed marches were something I'd become good at and the six-miler was something I was confident I'd take in my stride. I felt strong as we set off but, within a mile, that feeling quickly evaporated. I struggled to hold my place in the troop, making life harder for those behind me as the troop began to concertina. By the time we'd reached the top of killer hill, en route to the village of Yettington, I'd dropped to the back of the troop. The rest of the speed march was a blur, desperately trying to stay with the troop. Sgt McCarthy screamed at me while grabbing my webbing, 'Get up there Spencer. Don't you dare give in.'

I only just crossed the finish line with the troop and as we stood to attention, getting a bollocking for a poor overall troop performance, my world began to spin. I felt sick and dizzy and struggled to remain upright. I was badly dehydrated and was led off to the sick bay to recover. Some people are naturally fit and others have to work hard at it and the six-miler was a reminder that I was firmly of the latter. I would never take a physical test for granted again.

Passing the six-miler meant we entered the commando phase. We ditched our blue nod berets for cap comforters, a cylindrical, olive-green woollen scarf fashioned into headgear. It's synonymous with the Commandos of WWII and worn by many before the green beret became the official commando headdress in 1942. It marked us out as a senior troop in training, but also meant that we now had to run everywhere on camp. We adopted the 'commando shuffle' to and from lectures, meals and the accommodation. Despite the blip of the six-miler, I felt strong and confident.

Out of the blue I received a letter from my Dad. That on its own was a shock. He was near written-word illiterate and would sign cards, if he sent any, in shaky, scrawling capitals with just 'From Dad'. The letter was coherent, sensitive and written by him. I could distinguish his handwriting from my nan's who often sent birthday cards in his stead. He wrote that if I wanted to give in, he wouldn't mind and that I shouldn't carry on just to prove something to him. But most shockingly of all, he wrote he loved me. That was the only time my Dad expressed any feelings for me, let alone love.

On the eve of Final Ex, Cpl Lynch called the section together to discuss who was going to be section commander. Dolan had become our permanent section commander but was going to act as the troop sergeant on the upcoming exercise.

Cpl Lynch asked, 'Who wants to be section commander then?'

We all looked at each other willing someone else to step forward. Cpl Lynch looked at us in exasperation. Being a section commander was something that he supposed we aspired to. We respected Dolan who knew what he was doing, but we all harboured a disdain for the position of recruit section commander, seeing it as a pointless voice repeating what the corporals had just said, but louder.

Dolan broke the silence. 'Spencer will do it, Corporal.'

'I ain't fucking doing it.' I said in shock.

Cpl Lynch laughed. 'Spencer, you're section commander.' And walked away.

I received my first promotion in the Royal Marines, even if it was a plastic one that I didn't want.

'Final Ex' was the culmination of everything we'd learned so far. It was something that I'd dreamed of since the first day I walked through the gates of CTC and now I was here. I loved every minute and surprisingly revelled in the responsibility of a section commander. After ten days and nights of attacks, ambushes, yomps, beach landings and helicopter rides over the whole South West, the exercise culminated with a final attack on an old Napoleonic fort overlooking Plymouth Harbour.

Having started training as one of the physically weaker members of the troop and hoping to make it to the end of each week, I finished the Final Exercise as a section commander. I could only marvel at the transformation. Only the four Commando Tests now stood between me and my Green Beret.

On cue, Cpl Lynch called me into the office to tell me that I'd failed Final Ex. 'You don't seem that bothered,' he said.

'Corporal, you've told me I've failed every single exercise since First Step. If you told me I'd passed, then I'd worry.' I said with a smile.

Day 22

I finished my final rowing session of the night and clambered into the cabin as the sun rose out of a fine mist caused by white horses atop breaking waves. It tinged the few wispy clouds that clung to the horizon in a cold, yellow light.

After recording my morning stats and eating a breakfast of porridge with blueberries, I settled in to get some sleep. The sun's heat increased as it rose from the horizon and soon turned the cabin into an uncomfortable sweatbox. Through the day a mist hung on the horizon caused by the big breaking waves but above me the sun beat down. A 20-knot wind drove waves up to 25 feet high and, as they broke, I surfed down their front.

I turned off the autohelm to save it from overworking as the huge waves and powerful surf caused *Hope* to drift. Late in the day, three huge waves broke together. The first pulled *Hope* up to almost vertical as it broke and crashed white angry foam over her stern. As *Hope* began to move down the front of the wave a second crashed over the first, then almost immediately a third. Crashing white water and foam surrounded *Hope* as she sped down the slope of the wave. The left oar bit into the water and *Hope*'s forward momentum smashed the handle back against my shin, where its stayed lodged. The oar blade bit deeper and *Hope* span round turning side on to a mass of angry foaming water. In a panic I tried to free the oar but it was stuck against my shin and I couldn't dislodge it. I felt her tip slightly as she began to roll. I pulled with all my strength and the oar handle scraped up my shin and over my knee where I let it go. The handle span past my midriff as the blade then clattered against the side of the boat. In my panic to dislodge the left oar, the right one dropped into the sea and pulled hope around to the other side. The handle this time smashed against the socket of my prosthetic leg, then span out. This happy second accident pulled her away from being dangerously side-on to a huge breaking wave. As the wave crashed around me and slowly died, the pain in my shin erupted. The oar had hit it with such a force it was badly cut and, I hoped, only bruised.

Big waves continued through the night, even as the wind died towards dawn. Again, I spent the night in the pitch black of an overcast sky. A faint green glow of bioluminescence surrounded *Hope* and drifted away in swirls from each oar stroke. The big breaking wave and almost capsizing had shaken me and I spent most of the nighttime rowing shifts, in varying states of fear. It was a long night and I was glad of the grey dawn when it came.

Day 22 Logbook Entry

Position at 0800hrs (L) (0900hrs UTC) on 31st Jan 2019
24° 01′ 572n 018°51.398w

Distance travelled 71nm at 228°
Total distance 938nm

Distance to Cayenne 2243nm

Big breaking waves with strong winds all day, @ approx 1730 3 big breaking waves picked up the boat. As she shot down the front my left oar got caught in the sea and smashed against my left knee, just cuts and bruises but very sore. Seen quite a lot of Portuguese Men of War and the 1st bit of real green Bioluminescence. Rowed on hand steering most of the day to save autohelm.

The first of the four Commando Tests is the nine-mile speed march. The nine-miler is conducted on the Friday after the end of Final Ex, with the same weight and at the same speed as the six-miler. I breezed round. We left camp as the troop in front of us prepared for their passing out parade and so returned to camp after the nine-miler as the senior troop in training – The King's Squad. We were met at the gate by a drummer, who drummed us around the camp. Everyone, from recruits to senior officers, stood to attention as we marched proudly past. Halfway around camp a recruit was ambling along with his washing bag.

Sgt McCarthy shouted, 'You there. Stand to attention for the King's Squad.'

He sprang to attention, and we all beamed with pride.

The following day was the Endurance Course, a two-mile series of tunnels, pools and a water filled tube, affectionately known as the 'sheep dip' on Woodbury Common, before a four-mile run back to camp finishing at the thirty-metre range. All done in 72 minutes, which is difficult enough, but the endurance course is followed by a shooting test. The whole way around, through all the tunnels and pools, the personal weapon must be protected so that it functions properly at the end. From the very start of the course where recruits transit through Peters Pool, I was drenched which adds to the obligatory 22 pounds of weight in my webbing. I was always quite slow on the Common but made the time up through the lanes back to camp and on the day I completed it in 64 minutes. I quickly cleaned my barrel with a pull through and then oiled the working parts, before laying down in front of my target.

Cpl Marks stood behind us and shouted 'You will receive five two second exposures. You will fire two rounds at each exposure. Target will be up on the first whistle blast and down on the second. Ready'.

I leaned to the right and with my left hand cocked my weapon then settled down ready to fire. I looked through my sight and saw nothing except a blur of fog and mist. *'Shit,'* I thought.

Before I could do anything Cpl Marks shouted, 'Watch and shoot. Watch and shoot,' then blew his whistle to indicate the targets were up. I tried desperately to clear my sight with the cuff of my combat jacket, but this just added mud to the mist and made things worse. On the second whistle blast I hadn't fired a shot. I then tried to pull the sleeve of my rugby top worn underneath and used that to smear as much of the muck away as the next whistle blast went. I pulled my weapon up into a firing position and through the sight I could just about make out the target and fired a shot as the whistle went again. I now had three more chances to get a minimum of six shots out of ten on target. Another blast of the whistle and I managed just the two shots, but as I was looking through the sight, the target was gradually disappearing as if it was walking away into a fog. On the next whistle blast I realised I wouldn't have time to clean the sight again, the gap between each set of whistle blasts was too short. The only thing I could do was to hold my aim and hope. After the last exposure, I went to get my target and my heart sank as I counted only five shots. One round had just clipped the edge of the target so I claimed that as a hit. It would have wounded the target at least.

Cpl Marks stood at the firing point with his clipboard and with his usual sneer of indifference asked, 'Name?'

'Spencer corporal.'

'How many?'

'Six corporal.'

He immediately looked up at me his face a pinched collection of suspicion and spite. Perhaps he'd seen me struggling with my sight on the firing point or maybe if I had said eight or nine, he may have not bothered, but he said, 'Show me.'

I lifted the target for him to see and counted the five shots on target and finished with the clip on the side.

'Fuck off. You're not having that one. Five.' He said as he scrawled onto his sheet. 'Fail. Patch up.'

Devastated, I walked away. I'd have to re-run the Endurance course after the 30-miler. I was annoyed at the embuggerance of re-running the endurance course, but I knew I'd pass it. I was devastated because I wanted the 30-miler to be the dream end to my training.

I hated the Tarzan assault course, the third of the four Commando tests. It's a series of zip lines, ropes and obstacles suspended high up in the trees behind the officer's mess before completing a circuit of the assault course, finishing with the scaling of a 30-foot wall. I wasn't confident on the high obstacles and it's more suited to someone who's better at quick blast cardio rather than my strength – endurance fitness. The Tarzan assault course must be completed in 13 minutes, and I had no intention of ever doing it again.

I threw my usual caution to the wind and flew round. The last obstacle is a plank that ends with a chasm and net. A recruit has to sprint across the plank to be able to jump across the chasm into the net on the other side. I ran at full pelt and then launched myself across the chasm at the net. I felt myself fly across the chasm and punched my right arm through the net.

'Bloody hell,' I heard Lt Ellis exclaim from the bottom of the obstacle. I looked down at him wondering what he meant then turned back to the net. I was right at the very top, something that should be physically impossible. I have no idea how I did it.

I passed the Tarzan with a good time and thankfully never went on it again.

That afternoon we moved to Okehampton Battle camp on the northern edge of Dartmoor ready for what was supposed to be the last of the Commando Tests, and the pinnacle of Royal Marines training – the 30-miler. Thirty miles over the rough terrain of Dartmoor, carrying 22 pounds of kit, plus weapon with the addition of a couple of safety bergens per section. We had eight hours to complete it.

Out of 38 who'd joined 635 Troop eight months before, I was one of only eleven left. We set off as a section the next morning, in the pre-dawn gloom of a cold and wet autumnal Dartmoor. The first few miles were in complete darkness then the grey dawn spread its cold light across the chestnut-brown moor with patches of purple flowering heather. We ran and walked through outbreaks of rain, and I was in my element. At some point the RSM and OC Commando Training joined us. The RSM, WO1 Perry, was a bull of a Yorkshireman and asked me about training and how I'd found it, before pulling away to chat with others. We were running along a wide muddy path beside a brooding forestry block when someone behind shouted, 'Corporal! Corporal!'

We all stopped and turned, hearing the panic in his voice. We had two Royal Navy medics who were completing their Commando Course with us and both were crouched over someone on the ground. We stood there feeling useless as the biting wind and rain lashed against us. The medics started CPR on who we now knew was the RSM with the OC, Major JJ Lear and Cpl Lynch crouched next to them.

Cpl Lynch looked up and said, 'Spence, get the lads in the tree line.'

I led us over to the forestry block and the shelter that it offered. The forestry block was like entering a completely different world. It was moss laden, green with a dreamy quietness and just the distant woosh of the wind in the treetops. The cold quickly ate into our bodies and lads started to shiver.

'Let's get a wet on.' I said and opened a ration pack from one of the safety bergens. Numb fingers made it difficult to do anything but we soon had a metal mug full of water heating up. Just as the water began to steam, Cpl Lynch shouted for us. Smudge ran out of the trees to see what he wanted, then immediately came back in.

'Quick,' he said, 'We need to join 2 Section, now.'

We ditched the water out of the mug, packed everything away and left the forestry block. Cpl Lynch, Major Lear and the medics were huddled over the RSM with Cpl Marks and 2 Section stood to the side. Cpl Marks ordered us to join the back of his section before carrying on with the march. Sgt McCarthy met us at the next checkpoint with sausage rolls and tea, worry etched across his face. As we prepared to move off, a yellow search and rescue Sea King helicopter flew ominously low over us.

We finished the 30-miler and quite rightly, to no pomp or ceremony as is the norm and quietly loaded onto the transport back to Lympstone.

It was 20 October 1992 when WO1 (RSM) L Perry RM passed away. A large granite stone sits alone next to Fernworthy Forest with open moorland stretching to the north, marking the spot where he died. All 30-milers now stop there to pay their respects.

Two days after the thirty-miler I was back up on Woodbury Common at the start line for the endurance re-run. I set off in a group of three that had to stay together until the sheep-dip, where we pushed and pulled each-other through the submerged tunnel. After the sheep-dip the other two I was running with, sped off. After a couple of minutes running on my own, I started to get an uneasy feeling that I didn't recognise the track I was running down. The further down this track I ran, the stronger the unease became. I stopped and considered my position. I knew that the group behind me had set off three minutes after my group had. If I turned back and bumped into them, I could run with them and then make up the three minutes easily through the lanes on the run back to camp. I turned and ran back the way I had just came and after a couple of minutes of not seeing anyone I realised with mounting horror I was lost. 'CORPORAL.' I shouted at the top of my voice.

'Over here you, fucking idiot,' came the worryingly faint reply.

'I'm coming!' I shouted and set off in the direction of the voice. Eventually I crashed through the undergrowth beside the tunnel where Cpl Egan and Lt Ellis waited.

'Quick, quick get through,' said Lt Ellis and I scrambled as fast as I could down into the entrance of the dark corrugated iron roofed tunnel. The tunnels on the endurance course are purposely kinked with several underground turns so that most of it is in utter darkness. As I came out of the tunnel, Lt Ellis said, 'Right Spencer, stick with me now and I'll get you back in time.'

We set off and even after the last tunnel up on the common, he stayed with me down through Red Barn Lane, then Heartbreak Lane with its famous sign in the tree that reads 'It's only pain. 500m to go.'

I sprinted over the footbridge into camp and to the finish line next to the 30-metre range. I was petrified of failing again and had run my heart out, finishing in 66 minutes despite getting lost. This time I was prepared for any fog or mist on my sight and wiped it clean before laying down at the point. The shoot was straightforward with a ten out of ten shots on target.

Afterwards, I stood to attention next to Pete 'Smudge' Smith. We had come all the way through training together in the same section. Lt Ellis walked along the short line of re-runs presenting us with our Royal Marines Commando shoulder flashes. A small black and red, fabric patch that's history goes back to the first Royal Marine Commandos in 1942 and something I had dreamed of having in my hand for as long as could remember. It was the culmination of eight months training where I had at first, just wanted to get to the end of each week believing I had no chance of passing, but now I was here. I was a Royal Marines Commando.

I looked to my left. Pete's eyes were distinctly watery. 'Don't you cry Smudge,' I said. 'Or I'm likely to go as well.'

He laughed as my eyes began to well up with sheer and utter relief of not just finishing what was at times hellish training, but the fulfilling of a lifelong dream.

Day 23

The day started grey and overcast and the wind from the previous day had almost gone, but the waves were still fairly big, though less angry.

After completing my daily stats, I called Leven.

'Hello, Captain,' he said over the faint line of the satphone. 'Stay close to a heading of 220°, it's best to get the south in now while we can. The winds will be mainly from the east later.' He ended with his second mantra, 'Speed over course. Keep the boat moving, Captain.'

I moved *Hope* round on to her new course, but the more oblique angle of the waves put the autohelm under a lot of strain. I decided to rest it and steered on handlines for most of the day. A lone white bird that looked like a tern followed me for four hours during the middle of the day. Its pure white body and wings were perfectly framed by the grey cloudy sky as it gracefully swooped and glided on the gentle breeze. It reminded me of a poem a good friend called Richy had written for me before the start of the row. I'd copied it in marker pen on the inside of the cabin wall, right next to where I laid my head.

Of all our great fury's
And Tempest roar
One sonnet,
Soars above my journey
Like a Turn.
Broad as the air and
Holding the bowl of the Ocean
Breathless without need
All drift flows gently beneath me.
Little wings, ever present,
Ever striving
And guiding me home.

In the afternoon between rowing shifts, I called Claire.

'Ralph has called into the Canaries to get repairs,' she said.

'Really? What's wrong?'

'Something's wrong with his batteries.'

I thought it would be a very quick fix of removing his old batteries and fitting new ones and soon he'd be rowing. But I was happy for small mercies. The thought of Ralph overtaking me and getting the record continued to drive my effort on every rowing shift. Late in the afternoon a very big container ship went past heading north. It hadn't alerted on the AIS system and that worried me. The rest of the Nav' systems all seemed to be working OK but I still noted the ship passing in the logbook in case there was a problem with the AIS system.

Day 23 Logbook Entry

Position at 0800hrs (L) (0900hrs UTC) on 1st Feb 2019	*Distance travelled 60nm at 220°*
23° 15' 982n 019°33.444w	*Total distance 998nm*

2189nm to Cayenne.

Winds dropped considerably overcast all day. No autohelm all night and majority of day, tried to stay with the wind heading more south than west under instruction from Leven. Better to get the south in now than later. When the winds are more likely to be predominantly easterly. Had one very large cargo ship go past approx 5-10nm to the east heading north that didn't show up on the AIS. Noted and I will continue to monitor in case there's a problem with AIS.

As soon as I finished the endurance course, I called my grandad Spencer. 'I've done it grandad. I've got my green beret.' I said, beaming with pride.

'Oh well done son,' he replied. I could tell from his voice that he was smiling.

I was never close with my grandad Spencer, I found him distant and emotionally cold, but I always associated him with his service in WWII as a Royal Navy stoker. He'd always kept those links with his past service through the British Legion club and his associations of the various ships he'd served on. Like so many of the war generation, his brief wartime service defined him and I was now the first in his family to follow him into military service.

When I was about seven, my grandad Spencer gave me a small metal lapel badge with the Royal Navy's anchor insignia and 'OPPO's' along the bottom. He explained that it was a Royal Navy OPPO's badge, OPPO standing for 'Opposite Number' and that your Oppo was your best friend. As he gave it to me, he said that I was now his opposite number, his best friend. It was the only time that I ever saw him express any affection towards anyone, let alone me. Passing the commando course would resonate with him more than anyone else I knew. I called Claire, who'd been with me through training from the very start and was more relieved than anyone at me passing.

635 Troop moved onto a week of constant drill to get ourselves ready for our passing out parade on the following Friday, but first, on the Saturday, we had our King's Squad piss-up to celebrate getting to the end of training. We took a coach to Okehampton Battle Camp and got drunk with the training team. I was awoken in the morning by the duty officer, who leaning over me asked, 'Recruit Spencer?'

'Yes, sir.' I replied, slowly coming out of a deep alcohol induced sleep.

'I'm afraid of got some bad news. Your grandad has died.'

'Oh. OK', I said, not really taking in what he was saying.

'Are you OK?' he asked.

'Err, yes, Sir.' I said.

He turned and walked out of the room. I laid there for a couple of seconds digesting what he'd just said. The room was silent, everyone else still fast asleep. And then I thought, *'Which grandad?'*

My grandad Spencer died of a heart attack in Yorkshire at the reunion of a ship he'd served on during the war. He was surrounded by his oppos, his true friends whose bonds were forged in the hell of the Battle of the North Atlantic. It was the day after I told him I'd earned my coveted green beret.

My passing-out parade went by in a blur and then I had a long weekend off where my uncle graciously gave me a bottle of champagne, admitting he was wrong. After the two weeks' guard duties at Lympstone, I was drafted to 42 Commando, based next to the village of Bickleigh on the southern slopes of Dartmoor. I joined 1 Troop K Company and after reporting to the Company Sergeant Major, I introduced myself to the acting troop Sergeant, Shep.

'Corporal, I am P zero five one,' as I had reported to corporals in training.

'Yeah, yeah you don't need to start with all that.' He interrupted. 'I'm Shep.'

Shep was a small, fit-looking Corporal, with short curly hair and a quick smile. I fell in with my new troop and Shep called out the nominal, stopping at my name. He looked up and asked, 'What's your name Spence?'

'Lee, Corporal,'

'Call me Shep.' He reminded before pausing. 'Frank. Frank Spencer. We'll call you Frank.' As is Royal Marines lore should you share a surname with a famous person you will often adopt their first name, and so I became Frank, after the hapless character played by Michael Crawford in a 1970's sitcom.

If I thought passing out and fulfilling my dream of being a Royal Marines Commando would be the end of wanting to being someone I could be proud of, the next hour would prove me wrong. After the first parade and nominal, 1 troop went for a seven-mile run led by Shep. Within minutes I was struggling up a huge hill to the village of Shaugh Prior and to my utter horror, slowly dropped back. This was not the way I wanted to introduce myself to my new troop. As I dropped back, Shep called the troop, 'About turn.' The troop then turned and ran back down the way they had just come to the stragglers, one of whom was me. Shep 'about turned' the troop again and they started to run back up the hill. I tried and failed to latch onto the back of the troop as they passed me. At the top of the hill, I caught up and then dropped off the back of the troop again as they climbed up the last hill on the run, aptly known as killer hill. I was devastated. After all my hard work through training and finally gaining confidence in myself, I was thrust right to the bottom of the pack again. As I struggled exhausted through the camp gates, I swore I'd never drop back on a troop run again. But

I did drop back on most morning runs. I started to run in the evenings around Bickleigh in a desperate attempt to get running fit and not drop back on troop runs. In hindsight I was grossly overtraining, but Royal Marines judged themselves by military professionalism and physical robustness. I began to realise that although I'd passed the Commando Tests and passed out of training, earning my green beret was now a daily task. Every time I dropped back on a run it devastated me. The confidence that I'd worked so hard to gain through training, slowly but surely ebbed away. As the months passed, my running fitness slowly got better. One morning, I was out on a troop run led by Shep and he took off up a series of hills on the other side of Bickleigh vale called the 'roller coaster'. At the top of the last hill, he stopped. There was just four of us with him with the rest of the troop strung out behind us. As they slowly ran in one by one, I thought '*That's it. I've done it.*' I'd stopped dropping back on morning runs, but by then any confidence I had in myself had gone. I'd dreamed of being a Royal Marines Commando for the majority of my life, but now that I was one, the new normal; those who I judged myself against – other Royal Marine Commandos – I felt I was firmly at the bottom of the pile.

Almost a year after passing out, Claire and I were married in old Dagenham Church. Claire had meticulously planned a frugal wedding as late as possible in the day so we could have a buffet instead of a sit-down meal and then go straight into the evening do. It was the best wedding we could afford. I can't remember much of the day; it was the first time both sides of my family had been in the same place at the same time and I was worried that there would be a fight. There wasn't and Claire and I headed off to our honeymoon in Scotland.

Back at work, Shep was promoted to substantive Sergeant and moved on to another job within the Corps. If life as a Royal Marine in 1 Troop, K Company was physically demanding under Shep, under Phil, Burt and Tweety, the corporals, it only got harder. Deep down I felt as out of place as I did when I started training, but after the wedding how I related to that feeling had changed. I still desperately wanted to be someone I was proud of, but now I was a husband and presumed that I would soon also be a father, I had to be someone they could be proud of as well. Just being a Royal Marine wasn't good enough, what drove me now was the dream of being an average Bootneck.

Day 24

Throughout the day, a fresh blustery wind blew from the north pushing me further south than I wanted. During my call with Leven, he'd warned me of a strong northerly wind and try not to go further south than 213°.

I struggled throughout the day to maintain the 213° heading. I was pushing just to the west of the Cape Verde Islands where I'd start to pick up the trade winds west, but this predominantly southerly course would take me too close to the African coast. The brisk wind was whipping up short, angry waves that were nigh on impossible to row at an oblique angle. Nearly every wave top was crested with breaking white horses. I had little option other than to run with the wind and the waves. The sun set over my left shoulder into a yellowing horizon as I finished my last daytime rowing session and, almost on cue, the wind suddenly picked up. As I ate my evening meal in the cabin, I could feel *Hope* being battered by larger waves kicked up by stronger winds.

At 8pm I readied myself for the first of my nighttime rowing shifts and clambered out of the cabin into a pitch-black cauldron of crashing waves. I could feel the rumble of the breaking waves in the pit of my stomach, a deep almost carnal growl that stirred a primitive unease deep within me. Only the billions of stars overhead in the moonless sky gave me any reference of where I was in space. Through the night the wind and waves pushed me too far south of the line I should've been travelling on. The distance between me and that imaginary navigational line is called the Cross Track Error (XTE) and by sunrise, mine was just over ten miles. I was ten miles off course. As the sky lightened in the east the wind thankfully dropped and moved into a north-easterly. The waves calmed enabling me to change my course westerly as I began to claw back those 10 miles.

Day 24 Logbook Entry

Position at 0800hrs (L) (0900hrs UTC) on 2nd Feb 2019
22°16' 551n 020°21.793w

Distance travelled 74.5nm at 217°
Total distance 1072.5nm

2123nm to Cayenne

10-15kts winds throughout the day predominantly NNE. Wind picked up to 20-25 kts at sunset settling back down to 15-20kts at sunrise. Wind turned more NE at sunrise as well. New course of 231°t, currently 230°-235°t to claw back 10nm XTE. Good sun throughout afternoon, good for solar power.

Sniping in the British Army went out of fashion after the Second World War as large infantry and armoured divisions became the focus to counter the Warsaw Pact threat. The Royal Marines had kept sniping alive and Royal Marine snipers retained an envious mystique. 42 Commando ran a sniper selection in early 1994 for an upcoming sniper course at Lympstone. I immediately applied. The two-week selection concentrated on the core sniper skills of shooting, observation, judging distance, stalking and map reading as well as more advanced military skills like memory retention, advanced navigation and military knowledge. As usual I felt way out of my depth, but miraculously passed. I was elated and couldn't wait for the course. Almost immediately, the more senior members of K Company came up and congratulated me. I soon realised that just passing the sniper course selection was an achievement in itself.

Being completely out of my depth was by now something I was used to and the sniper's course at Lympstone would take that feeling to a whole new level, yet I loved every minute.

By its very nature sniping is very individualistic and instead of learning new drills and procedures, we were presented with a set of problems to solve and left to get on with it. I learned so much, not only from the course instructors, but also from the experienced and senior marines who were also on the course. As the course progressed, I was continuously just behind the learning curve and hadn't passed a single stalk. However, my marksmanship improved dramatically. I really excelled in map reading and navigation. The sniper course culminated with the five 'badge tests', all of which needed to be passed in-order to qualify as a Royal Marines sniper. We were permitted two attempts at each. I passed the shoot with a marksman score on my second attempt and got a very commendable 100 per cent on the map reading test. On my final stalk I came within a whisker of passing, it all clicked into place right at the very end. But by then it was too late, I'd failed both observation and judging distance tests. Failing anything is never pleasant, but I was strangely content with not passing the course. I thought the prospects of me being a Royal Marine sniper was such a long shot when I first applied, that I was just happy to be there. But my general soldiering skills had improved dramatically, so by the end of the course I felt I had a fair shot at passing. This was reflected in the course report that I took back to K Company. I'd displayed bags of enthusiasm and effort, but ultimately my lack of experience had let me down. I returned to K Company with my head held high and with a newfound confidence, just as 42 Commando started to gear up ready for the upcoming six-month tour of 'Bandit Country', South Armagh, Northern Ireland.

K Company was split down from the conventional warfighting 28-man troops to 12-man multiples to patrol the urban and rural areas of Northern Ireland and I was placed in the specialist sniper multiple.

Unusually for a multiple we had both a sergeant and officer. Nick the sergeant was a tall good-looking PW weapons specialist and a sniper. He had a calm unflustered character and exuded confidence. Gav the officer had been a marine in K Company before going through officer training. He was tall well-built South African with a reputation for being both a good bloke and a wretch on the beer. The rest of the multiple was made up of marines who'd just finished 40 Commando's tour of West Belfast. It was a hugely experienced multiple and I felt lucky to be a part of it.

We deployed to Bessbrook Mill, an imposing Victorian linen mill on the outskirts of mainly Catholic Newry. Gav had been sent out as part of the advance party to ensure a smooth handover with the previous army unit and met us from the helicopter. He led us straight into a classroom where a short, stocky, long-haired bloke wearing a denim shirt and jeans was stood at the front next to a lectern.

'Right lads,' he said in a London accent, 'Leave your kit at the back of the room and sit down.'

'Who's this civvy ordering us about?' I thought.

This 'civvy' was Berny, a legendary Royal Marines colour sergeant PTI. He was renowned as a fighter and had written the unarmed combat handbook for the Corps.

'Instead of me waffling on I'll just put on this short video and then I'll talk a little about what we'll be doing.'

He then pressed play a VHS machine and the small TV next to it flashed into life. The video was a recruitment film for the Joint Support Group (JSG), a clandestine unit whose role was to infiltrate and gain intelligence on the various terrorist groupings in Northern Ireland by the running of agents. Berny explained we were now JSG's multiple and would be working solely with them. Weeks before we deployed to Ireland, the Provisional Irish Republican Army (PIRA) declared a ceasefire and the next six months would be known as the first peace tour. As with all terrorist organisations, PIRA was split between moderates and hardliners, the latter being dragged to the negotiating table against their will. An uneasy quiet descended on South Armagh, everyone believed that the peace wouldn't last and when it did breakdown, it would be here, in the hard-line bandit country of South Armagh.

Op Banner, the official name for military operations in Northern Ireland, was typified by long hours of physical and mental strain, patrolling in awful weather carrying heavy electronic counter measure (ECM) equipment, long periods of mind-numbing monotony in sentry positions and sangars and occasional fleeting moments of terror. As

JSG's multiple, the mind-numbing monotony of sangar duties passed us by and peace held, so there were no moments of fleeting terror. I didn't see a shot fired in anger. But we patrolled. A lot. We covered the whole of South Armagh, from the border towns of Jonesborough and Crossmaglen to Newtownhamilton. We often strayed into nearby counties of Tyrone and Fermanagh.

The South Armagh countryside is dominated by the extraordinarily beautiful mountain Slieve Gullion and the Ring of Gullion that encircles it. It has a unique beauty and felt in parts strangely small and intimate, the small folds in the land forming tiny glens and small intricate dells. Across the border areas, small steep sided hillocks were topped by satanic-looking Golf towers, named after their codename and overlooked the surrounding countryside.

In our multiple I had the Antler, the largest of the ECM suite. It was like carrying a small fridge on my back. Northern Ireland's inclement weather and wet boggy ground means that the rural landscape is crisscrossed by deep drainage ditches with thick thorn-laden hedges and the inevitable strands of barbed wire. Any natural route from field to field becomes a choke point targeted by the PIRA with booby traps and bombs, forcing us to battle through the almost impenetrable hedges, then jumping across the ditches. Patrolling through the green patchwork of small pasture fields was very slow and hard work. JSG's work was highly secret but we were given as much insight to why we were on a certain patrol as possible. Having a definite purpose and knowing exactly why we were cold, wet and often exhausted made a massive difference to how we felt on each patrol. My six months in South Armagh working closely with JSG opened the door into a world that I didn't know existed.

Day 25

Another pitch-black, moonless night with only stars for company slowly gave way to a stunning sunrise near the end of my last nighttime rowing shift. An orange-yellow glow flecked across the bottom of a few scattered wispy clouds that hung near the horizon heralding the coming sun. It then burst into a billion diamonds of yellow light across the countless waves.

Once in the cabin I wrote down my stats for the last 24hrs and filled out the logbook. I then called Claire to ask her about Ralph.

'He's still in the Canaries,' she said.

'Why?' I asked. 'Has he posted anything? What's the weather like?'

'Nothing,' she replied. 'Maybe he's stuck waiting for a weather window?'

Ralph's head start of five days caused by my stopover in Gran Canaria, was now cut to three days, two if he didn't get out today.

As I made breakfast the sun started to cook the cabin interior. On the inside of the clear Perspex hatch door was an old car windscreen sun reflector that I'd cut to shape to help keep the temperature down during the day. Resting with the hatch slightly ajar would be catastrophic if a rogue wave capsized her. Sea water would uncontrollably rush in, shorting all the electronics and worse, stop her from righting. I religiously kept the hatch door shut with the only exception of entering and exiting the cabin. The further south I rowed the bluer the sky became and the hotter the sun shone. The cabin became unbearable during the late morning and early afternoon.

At the hottest part of the day, three small silvery flying fish, darted out of the water in front of *Hope*'s bow and skimmed majestically inches just above the waves away to my right. They were the first flying fish I'd seen and a welcome sign that I was progressing south in the otherwise daily featureless seascape.

It was perfect rowing conditions and with the ever-growing sense of progress and Ralph held up in the Canaries, I felt good. In the late afternoon a ship showed up on the AIS system demonstrating that it was functioning OK and that the ship on 1 February that didn't alert on the AIS was most likely down to them not broadcasting their position properly. Knowing that my AIS system was functioning properly was a big relief.

At 8pm I started the first of my nighttime rowing shifts. The wind picked up and the waves started to build. High clouds covered the first stars and again I rowed in black nothingness with no sense of where I was. The rest of the night was spent rowing in uncomfortably big seas. The roar of the crashing waves engulfed me and with no reference of space, I repeatedly missed the sea with my oar strokes.

Day 25 Logbook Entry

Position at 0800hrs (L) (0900hrs UTC) on 3rd Feb 2019
21°34′460n 021°31.402w

Distance travelled 77nm at 237°
Total distance 1149.5nm

2047nm to Cayenne

Excellent days rowing with lots of sun all day and mostly clear through the night. Wind dropped off slightly at 20.00hrs but picked up to a v. brisk NW before sunrise. Saw first flying fish, other ships showing up on AIS, so ship that wasn't showing on AIS on 1st Feb appears to be their problem.

I returned home from Northern Ireland to a lot of changes. Before I'd deployed to South Armagh, Claire and I had moved into a married quarter in a village on the western slopes of Dartmoor. It was a million miles away from Dagenham and literally a dream come true for both of us. Now I was returning to my home on Dartmoor and to a pregnant wife. Claire had fallen pregnant whilst I was on RnR. Also, my time at 42 Commando would soon be coming to an end. Royal Marines change jobs every two years and I'd overstayed my welcome at 42 Commando. I applied for a Heavy Weapons Anti-Tank course as it would at least keep me in commando units and away from the dreaded, chefs, clerks and signals branches.

Whilst I was in Ireland I had formerly applied for promotion and would now be expected to start taking more responsibility in whatever troop and unit I ended up in. After my post-Ireland leave, I was drafted back to the Commando Training Centre at Lympstone awaiting the next available Anti-Tank course. Lympstone had a permanent troop whose sole job was guarding the camp and were split into three different watches. Most of the troop were waiting to leave the Marines and for those men the guard room offered some stability and a good amount of time off to plan a future outside the Corps. I joined one of the watches in the guard room and started rotating through a week of day shifts, a week of night shifts then a week off. Each of the watches was commanded by a corporal and mine was Scotty Mills. Money was extremely short, especially as Claire had to give up work towards the end of her pregnancy. No one likes being on duty and often the younger single Marines would sell theirs to go out on the town. I was able to earn the much-needed extra money doing their duties. In September 1995, Claire gave birth to our daughter Harriet and because I was at Lympstone, I was able to be with her, something that is all too often a luxury within service families.

It soon became apparent that I had been forgotten about and had slipped through the cracks of the drafting system as Anti-Tank courses came and went without me. I took the opportunity to spend quality time with my new family and kept my head down. Claire fell pregnant again and I changed jobs at Lympstone. I moved from the guard room to Field Training Staff with Scotty. We acted as enemy for all the courses that were run from Lympstone. My working day would often be, walk along a track, get shot, die, get searched then go home.

Billy was born in June 1997 just as my Anti-Tank course finally arrived. But the Royal Marines were extremely short of manpower and had effectively gone down to two units. I realised that as an anti-tanker I would be on a continued cycle of 42 Commando in Devon, 40 Commando in Somerset and 45 Commando in Arbroath. Air Defence Troop were based in Plymouth but had a reputation for being a hard place to gain promotion and was full of very senior marines. Because of this it wasn't a popular specialisation. With the birth of our kids, my priorities changed and although we were skint, I decided to forego promotion in place of a more stable home life. I went to see the Heavy Weapons branch sponsor and asked to change from Anti-Tank to Air Defence. I think he was just happy to have a volunteer for Air Def' and readily agreed.

A month later I joined my Heavy Weapons Air Defence course at the Royal School of Artillery at Larkhill in the middle of Salisbury plain. I was one of twelve other Bootnecks on the course with twelve ranks from the Royal Artillery. Also on the course was my best friend from my time at 42 Commando, Doch. He was recently married and we lived in the same married quarters estate. We travelled to and from Larkhill every weekend together.

The course was run by Sergeant Major Instructor Gunnery, or SMIGs. SMIGs wear a stupid white hat reminiscent of a cornetto salesman, carry a pointless big stick and with Larkhill's deserved reputation as the embodiment of inane army regimentation, it was an ill fit for Royal Marines. As the course progressed, a few of us marines noticed that one of the Artillery lads had been singled out for bullying. Doch took the lead in ensuring the bullying stopped and put a friendly arm around the young gunner. In one of the lessons as we were sat waiting for the instructor, the bullying started up again.

I stood at the front of the class and shouted, 'Oi! Fucking leave him alone.'

As I turned back, I saw that the instructor had entered the room and seen the whole incident. That weekend the bullied young gunner put a formal complaint into the hierarchy causing a lot of trouble for the instructors. The SMIGs assumed that I was the one helping him and because of this one incident, I came top of the course. I joined Air Defence Troop with a very good course report, just as they were gearing up for a winter deployment to Norway.

Day 26

The big seas continued through the night and as light grew, I could see the waves were not only big and angry, but the sea was also very messy. Waves mostly come in a set pattern from the same direction. These waves didn't, and rowing became very difficult.

I noticed a change in the storm petrels that gracefully swooped around *Hope*. On my first row, Cayle and I nicknamed them the Hamish bird – solitary figures that darted past our boat with the merest glance of indifference before swooping away millimetres above the waves. Now they appeared curious and flew around *Hope*. They swooped past her repeatedly to get a better look. More significantly, they were now rarely alone. I'd see them as a solitary figure gliding past *Hope*, but over the last few days they seemed to be in twos or threes flying together and once, two sat on the surface of the sea like a pair of odd-looking ducks.

Storm petrels spend their lives out in the ocean only returning to land to breed, many to Northern Europe and some even to the UK. My last row started in December, so thought the difference in behaviour was due to the slight difference in season. I realised I was seeing the first stirrings of spring in Northern Europe. It appeared that the Hamish birds knew there was more to life than just sea, gusts of wind and crashing waves. I imagined the pair I saw making their way to the cliffs around Devon to nest and start a new generation of Hamish birds to buzz past small boats in the middle of the Ocean. It suddenly occurred to me that we still live in a very connected world.

As the sun set, the dark enveloped *Hope*. I was soon rowing in pitch black nothingness. Despite the earlier drop in wind, the waves, if anything, seemed bigger and more confused. Fear gripped me throughout the night and my utter isolation nagged at me. It was a horrible night's rowing.

During my morning stats I calculated I had less than 2,000nm to go. The next big milestone would be passing the halfway point, which I estimated could be as little as a week away. Then with 1,000nm to go I knew I'd soon be counting down miles to the finish line.

Day 26 Logbook Entry

Position at 0800hrs (L) (0900hrs UTC) on 4th Feb 2019	*Distance travelled 62nm at 242t°*
21°06' 051n 022°30.289w	*Total distance 1211.5nm*

Distance to Cayenne 1985nm

Less than 2000nm to go!

Day of very different weather patterns, morning up to approx 1600 was v big angry waves coming from what seemed multiple directions. At approx 1600hrs wind dropped considerably and turned from NE to NNE. Nothing of significance happened partially cloudy most of the day.

My first day with Air Defence Troop started with thirty of us parading for our morning nominal, called out by George, a legendary Geordie sergeant with a fearsome reputation. He'd fought in the Falklands War and looked like his reputation, with a completely bald head atop muscular shoulders and a disconcerting scar around his neck.

After the nominal, George said, 'Back here at 0945 in phys kit ready for a smally run.'

I wandered back to the troop lines with Doch expecting to see the whole troop ready for phys. Instead, there was just us twelve who'd just finished the course. And George, looking ridiculous, his huge frame hideously bursting out of a purple lycra running suit.

'Where's the other lads?' he asked.

We all looked at each other nonplussed and shrugged in response.

'For fuck's sake,' He muttered. 'OK, just us then, follow me.' And off he sped.

Despite his huge bulk, George could run like the wind. As for the rest of Air Defence Troop, they'd gone en masse to El Veras café around the corner. Air Def' was full of very senior marines and corporals who all marched to their own tune.

During the Cold War, 3 Commando Brigade's primary role was to deny Russia deep-water ports through hit and run tactics in the mountains along the Norwegian coast. Royal Marines would end the year mountain training either in the Scottish Highlands or in Snowdonia in North Wales and start the new year with a three-month deployment to Norway.

Mountain training is extremely arduous, with long days load carrying heavy weight up and down mountains and our training package in Wales was no different, but I loved it. After Christmas leave, Air Defence Troop deployed to Norway with 20 Battery Royal Artillery.

Every unit location had a bar that sold Norwegian beer considerably cheaper than the local bars, and Royal Marines bars had a reputation as a den of wretchedness. I woke up to start my novice ski and survival course with a hangover, wearing makeup. The night before I'd taken my guitar to the bar to perform a Ginger Spice concert complete with Union Jack mini dress. As I shaved, I noticed that I couldn't remove the makeup no matter how hard I scrubbed. I had little option but to fall in wearing makeup. The course started with an inspection to ensure everyone had deployed with correct kit.

Kenny, our Glaswegian troop boss wore the haunted look of someone in charge of the most feral troop in the Corps, stood looking at me. 'Marine Spencer, have you showered this morning?'

'Ah, that'll be the make-up sir. I couldn't get it off.' I replied.

'Did you no bring any make-up remover?'

'Er, no sir. I didn't think I'd need it.'

Kenny shrugged and walked along the line. I noticed Craig, the Mountain Leader (ML), running the course, smirk as he was inspecting someone else's kit. We set off, hungover, to the Trondheim hills for two weeks learning how to survive in the arctic and skiing around on military cross-country skis lovingly called pussers planks. 20 Battery was the larger unit and commanded by a Major, whereas we were just a troop commanded by Kenny, a Captain. It soon became apparent that the Royal Marines were thought of as the junior partner on this deployment, but on the novices, Craig the ML was in charge. 20 Battery was useless. I've never come across a more inept and unfit for purpose unit in my entire career. It wasn't a cap-badge thing as I've worked with the Royal Artillery many times, even in Norway and found them thoroughly decent soldiers. But 20 Battery were so awful, it's difficult to quantify why. Their hierarchy were appalling, from Lance Bombardier to Major. I, on the other hand, thrived. I had dreaded Norway, with its reputation for being physically arduous and believing that I wouldn't be fit enough. Falling back on morning runs with K company still haunted me, but Norway was perfect for me. It required a deep endurance fitness and I relished the hard graft required to not only survive, but to fight. Also, the abject buffoonery from 20 Battery made me feel and look good.

The novices course ended with a ski march out of the training area. Although only a few kilometres, the course was strung out like a retreat from Moscow. I was in the HQ tent group and because no one else could, carried the radio and ended up pulling the pulk, a sledge like contraption that contained all the troops heavy stores. The yomp ended in a long hill, I put my head down and pulled, expecting the person behind me to be pushing the pulk with their ski poles.

When at the top, the sergeant major asked, 'Frank, where's the rest of your section?'

I stopped and looked behind me, they were nowhere to be seen.

'I thought they were pushing.' I replied.

He noticed I also had the radio. 'Why have you got the radio?'

'No one else could carry it.'

'OK. Go and take your kit of over there and wait for the rest.'

It had been the same with the other Bootnecks on the course. We'd carried the few remaining 20 Battery lads through the exercise, just the ones I was with required more carrying. I was awarded the Top Novice prize, nothing of any real significance, especially amongst a course predominantly made up of 20 Battery, but it was a nice thing to happen.

After Norway, Air Defence Troop sailed to France to train with a French Marines Air Defence unit, near Lens. Upon arrival it became apparent that we were either not expected, or the French didn't much care. We spent two days looking at half-hearted demonstrations of their air defence kit and we reciprocated with one of ours conducted by Danny, a senior marine who for some reason started to speak like the policeman from *'Allo 'Allo*. The rest of the time we spent drinking in Lens. Every morning at 05:30 a French NCO would burst into our room blowing a whistle to wake us up. A voice from the room would offer a derisory response then close the door and turn the lights off. We'd rise at the more reasonable hour of 08:00, shower and fall in with the French unit ready for them to sing their national anthem. On our penultimate night, I went out with a few others and at some point in the night, peed all over Doch whilst he was asleep, and got in bed with him. When the usual blasts of whistles signalled the start of the French marine's day, the bloke who came to wake us up stood over me and Doch happily snoring away, and asked Mozzy in the next bed to us if this was normal.

'Never seen it before in my life,' he replied before turning over and going back to sleep.

Doch was later given 100 press-ups by the Sergeant Major for 'being beef in front of the French'.

I was called into the Sergeant Major's makeshift office along with Ads, another lad from my air def' course. Inside was George, Kenny and Shaun, who started to tell Ads that he'd been picked up for his Junior Command Course (JCC), the course required for promotion to corporal. Ads was a senior marine, so I wasn't at all surprised. He had a razor-sharp intellect that he hid behind a Mancunian swagger. He'd also been my Military Skiing Instructor on the novices' course, something he had a flare for. I stood listening as they explained the process including the Pre Juniors that would be run in the unit before the course proper at CTC.

Shaun finished talking to Ads before turning to me. 'Oh and Frank, you're first reserve'.

I looked around the room in utter shock. It was the last thing I was expecting.

Shaun added, 'You'll almost certainly be called up for the course so you'll do the Pre.'

I walked out of the office dumbstruck.

After a stop-off in Spain where one of the lads swapped all our pornography for cigarettes with a bemused Spanish soldier, we sailed home. I'd been away since the start of January and now it was April and a rare, beautiful spring day on Dartmoor.

I knocked at the door and Claire answered holding Billy on her hip. He'd been a baby when I left and had grown so much in my absence. Billy was ten months old and unsure who I was. Harriet was now old enough to be in playschool and ran from behind her Mum to give me a hug. Within hours Billy was sure who I was and spent the next couple of weeks following me like a shadow. I'd decided to change my draft to Air Defence because I wanted to have as stable a family life as possible. I'd reconciled that it would probably be at the expense of my career and promotion prospects, but family was the most important thing in my life.

After news spread within Air Def' that I was first reserve on the Juniors, I felt some resentment. I certainly thought I wasn't ready for promotion, so why would anyone else think I was? I believed that I'd been selected due to a mistaken assumption that I was stopping bullying at Larkhill and being made to look good in Norway by the inept buffoons of 20 Battery. Money was extremely tight. I wouldn't attend the JCC to prove anything to myself, I had to do it for my family. I now had my toe on the first run of the promotion ladder.

Day 27

The wind dropped considerably as the sun rose into a cloudless sky and the sea settled, which was a blessed relief after the last 24 hours. The light breeze shifted to a more northerly direction pushing *Hope* further south than I liked.

Then about noon I noticed some dolphins jumping out of the water 200 metres behind *Hope* heading towards her. Within seconds I was surrounded by what seemed like hundreds of dolphins. Calves swam with mothers and adults jumped in twos and threes. I scrambled to get the GoPro to video them zipping past under *Hope*'s hull or jumping clear of the water right next to me and then spectacularly splashing back into the waves. They swam round *Hope* and seemed to disappear south with more dolphins coming to take their place like a long conveyor belt of dolphins going from north to south. They kept coming in waves that made me think they couldn't possibly be a single pod stretched out over a couple of miles. After about an hour, the last of them swam away south to wherever they were going and left me on my own.

The nighttime rowing shifts went without incident and after the sun rose into another blue sky, I sat in the cabin and called Claire. 'Is there any news on Ralph?'

'No. Nothing. He's just gone quiet on social media.'

If Ralph was still in the Canaries, he'd lost his five-day advantage. The thought of almost three years in planning the row to beat the able-bodied record, only to give the record away days after getting it, still haunted my every rowing shift. It drove me and I continued to row my heart out.

Day 27 Logbook Entry

Position at 0800hrs (L) (0900hrs UTC) on 5th Feb 2019
20°31′779n 023°19.777w

Distance travelled 57.5nm at 233°t
Total distance 1207nm

Distant to Cayenne 1929nm

Sunny hot day and cloudless (mostly) night. Light winds all day and night. Massive pod of dolphins came round the boat for about an hour. Either that or it was one massive pod stretched out and they had a nose as they swam past. Had autohelm off from 16.00hrs trying to keep a good westerly heading against a more northerly wind.

The crux of the Junior Command Course is passing orders and section attacks, both underpinned by good navigation, something I excelled at. The Section is the fundamental building block of the British Military and section attacks are the basis of every battle ever fought since probably WWII. During the Pre course, I was given some valuable advice. *As soon as you come under fire from the enemy, take a 'Condor moment'. Get into cover, sit, do nothing for a couple of seconds, then look at the ground, the enemy position and then the plan will become magically obvious.*

To stop and do nothing seems counter intuitive when coming under attack, but the section's immediate drills will ensure they'll be getting the rounds down on the enemy. Making a wrong decision in the heat of the moment is catastrophic and the 'Condor moment' stops that. It really worked for me, and I found section attacks on the Juniors easy.

The orders process is nothing more than the standardised NATO way of getting your plan over to those executing it. It was tested over the two gruelling exercises that worked on a non-stop eight-hour rolling routine of two hours to prepare your orders, two hours to deliver them and then four hours to carry out the subsequent patrol. I found the Orders process quite easy. If you didn't lose yourself and ensured that the right amount of detail was delivered in the right place, it was hard to get wrong. Unless of course, you hadn't slept for five days and nights and that was the hard part of the exercise.

The remit of both exercises was to test prospective corporals in decision making under conditions of extreme sleep deprivation. On

Another hard goodbye to Claire before leaving on a long journey. This time it was on the ramp down to the pontoon in Portimão, just before getting into the boat.

Rowing out into the Atlantic Ocean from Portugal just after midday on 9 January 2019.

Hannah the Afghan puppy days after rescuing her in Lashkar Gah. This photo is taken at the back of our compound where we built her a pen.

Hannah on Dartmoor after making the long journey from Afghanistan. Little did I know that the simple act of rescuing her would give me purpose after losing my leg.

Finishing the Dartmoor Double Marathon in my home village. Six months later I would be lying in a hospital bed having lost my leg.

The crash site on the M3 with the engine and gearbox that hit me and sent me flying over the barrier and onto the grass verge beyond on the night of 5 January 2014.

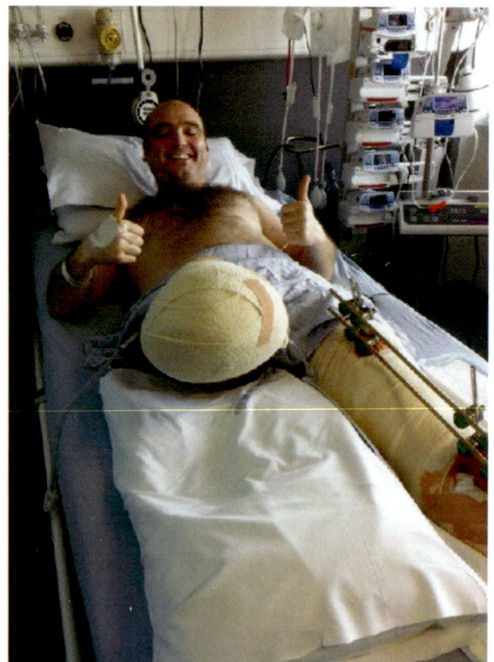

St George's Hospital, Tooting, London. Bruised, battered and missing a leg, but elated to be alive.

Me rowing somewhere in the mid-Atlantic on my first row with Row2Recovery. Rowing the Atlantic changed my life as significantly as losing my leg.

Rowing into English Harbour in Antigua on 4 February 2016 after 46 days, 6 hours and 49 minutes at sea.

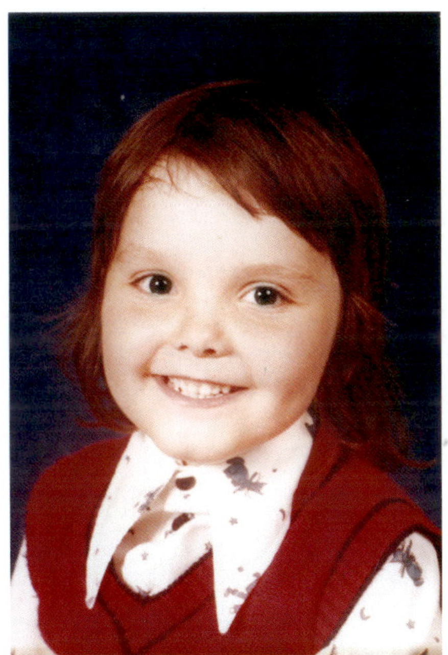

Aged 5 in 1974. I had just started infants school in Dagenham and I can still remember the 'Hey diddle diddle the cat and the fiddle' shirt I'm wearing.

Jiwi Rock, perhaps the worst breakdancer in Dagenham. Me sporting a perm circa 1984 aged 14 or 15.

Claire and me on a Church Holiday near Bournemouth in 1987. It's no wonder she couldn't resist me in my speedos, mullet haircut and earring.

The summit of Cadair Idris after accidently spending the night in the mountain refuge shelter. According to the legend, if you sleep on Cadair Idris, you either go mad, become a poet or die.

My bivvy partner and best friend Sam and me at RNAS Yeovilton undertaking helicopter drills. A rare highlight early on in Royal Marines training.

Back in our grot at CTCRM having passed 'Bottom Field', a big hurdle in Royal Marines training, the relief etched on our faces. I'm stood with Jim Gleddhill

Dartmoor on the Final Exercise, October 1992. I'm wearing a PRC 349 radio after my reluctant (and unwarranted) promotion to section commander.

635 Troop Royal Marines. Passed for Duty 30 October 1992. I was one of only eleven who started with 635 Troop to pass out as an original.

Cpl Lynch, my section Cpl throughout training after my passing-out parade on 30 October 1992. Photo taken on the Bottom Field with the 30ft ropes in the background.

Sgt Sid McCarthy, Lympstone, 30 October 1992. The Sergeant I always aspired to be. He's smiling because my mum had just called him 'Sid' instead of 'Sergeant.' My Grandad Horder is in the foreground.

Sat in a hedge in Silverbridge, South Armagh, winter 1994. We had been re-tasked during a patrol and had to spend the night freezing in a hedge.

My section and the building we captured on the first night of the invasion of Iraq, 22 March 2003. The Manifold and Metering Station just outside the town of Al Faw in Southern Iraq. We were in the first wave of troops to go in.

In my element as a Military Ski Teacher in Harstad, Norway, February 2004

Scotty and me in Newcastle sometime in the summer of 2004 during Commando Display Team season. Scotty had this photo on his desk for years.

Finally passing the shooting test on the Security and Survival training part of my DHU Course. I'm squinting, a technique shown to me by Tommy the pistol instructor. Counterintuitive but effective.

Taking a well-earned break during a clearance operation with 40 Commando, south of Sangin, summer 2010. I was trying to recruit an agent and went out on every patrol and operation I could.

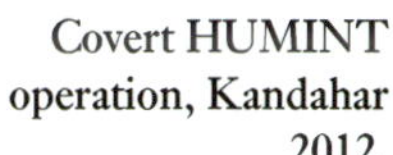

Covert HUMINT operation, Kandahar 2012.

Crossing the finish line into the Mahury River in Cayenne, French Guyana early in the morning of 11 March 2019. Photo by Ant Upton.

The photo that went around the world. I set out to prove that no one should be defined by disability and news of my record breaking row reached twenty-two different countries' newsfeeds. Photo by Ant Upton.

My four Guinness World Records.

Finding out I was in the *Guinness Book of Records* was amazing. It changed how I felt about the row.

Frank, Zanele and me receiving our Chief Constable commendations from Surrey Police.

My mum and me at a fundraiser for the Rowing Marine shortly before she died. We both had a very difficult time when she was married to my dad and that impacted our relationship. I know she was worried about my row and I wish she could have seen me finish. She would have been so proud.

both exercises, I was carried through by adrenalin of my moment in the spotlight and managed to get through my orders with few hiccups. The sergeant who was overseeing my section through the JCC was a stocky Londoner called Pete. He'd coincidently been my section corporal on my Potential Recruits Course.

At the end of the course I half-jokingly said to him, 'That's twice now you've let me slip through the net.'

After twelve weeks, I passed my Junior Command Course ranking a credible 14th out of 48. But having a credible pass on the JCC and being a credible corporal are two very different things, as I was about to find out.

Sergeants and corporals screaming orders at young soldiers springing to attention shouting 'Yes Corporal', is about as far from the reality of leadership within the Royal Marines as it possibly gets. Leadership is a skill, not an appointment. I knew that the two stripes I now had on my arm meant very little and on returning to Air Defence Troop, it was apparent I'd have to work extremely hard to gain any form of credibility.

Air Defence Troop worked in three-man detachments. On my first exercises taking charge, I called the det' together at the start and explained how I saw the situation. 'Look lads, I know I've got no experience in air def. I'll obviously listen to your advice.'

By day two, I got the detachment together again. I'd received a constant barrage of 'that's not how we usually do it' and 'I think we should do it this way'.

Although air defence involves firing surface-to-air missiles, it really isn't rocket science. It's a fairly straightforward job and I knew what I was doing.

'Right lads this isn't working,' I said. 'From now on, I'll listen to your advice, but the decisions will be mine. If it's wrong, then it's my wrong and I'll take the blame. Just do it and stop fucking moaning.'

The other corporals in the troop were of a different peer group and it was clear I wasn't 'one of them' and at the same time, I felt I was no longer part of the same group who I'd done my Air Def' course with. Apart from Doch, I didn't really fit in with anyone. There was an undeniable resentment throughout the troop to my promotion. I'd come to the troop with a couple of good reports and grades that had immediately placed me above my new contemporaries, all of whom had been in Air Def' for years accumulating, at best, average grades. Air Defence Troop's reputation as an unmanageable rabble of senior and experienced marines had ensured that the higher grades within the unit, went to the other troops. This was the underlying reason behind Air Def's reputation for slow promotion. Through nothing other than circumstance, I had bucked that trend.

I knew that I was generally considered to be a bit of a wally and it's probably not a coincidence that's exactly how I believed my Dad thought of me as a kid. I not only felt extremely lonely, I was also extremely unhappy. It was the most unhappy I'd been since I was a child.

Air Defence Troop were about to be issued new vehicles that required both C plus E categories on a licence. I've always hated driving and the thought of spending six weeks with the Royal Logistic Corps instructors at Leconfield didn't fill me with enthusiasm.

I banged on the Sergeant Major's door and walked in. 'Sir, I've lost the paper part to my driving licence.' I lied. 'I've already requested a new one at the post office, but it's gonna take six weeks'.

'Well, that rules you out of the driving course.'

'I know I'm gutted.' I again lied.

'OK then,' he said, signalling the end to the conversation.

'Errm. If I'm not going on the drives, can I go on the next MSI's?' I asked.

The Military Skiing Instructors course was widely regarded as a month-long skiing and drinking holiday in Rukan, Norway.

The Sergeant Major's eyes narrowed with suspicion 'Aye, go on then,' He smirked.

The MSI course was everything I thought it would be, four weeks of drinking and skiing. I passed the course and returned to a lot of changes within Air Def'. Shaun the Sergeant Major was replaced by a huge man called Daz with a reputation as a 'hard man' and Kenny the troop boss was replaced by Jez. Several other marines from my peer group had been called through for their promotion courses, including Doch, which meant I no longer felt isolated.

Day 28

The sun rose again into a cloudless blue sky and after completing my stats for the last 24 hours, I exited the cabin to start my daytime rowing shifts. The sun beat down relentlessly through a scorching hot morning's rowing.

There was still no news on Ralph and today would mean I had a 24-hour advantage over him, but I still pulled hard on the oars. *Hope* would surge forward at four knots, then for no apparent reason stop dead in the water. I'd then have to pull my heart out to plod along at a meagre two knots. There was no change in the sea conditions, wind, or anything that I could see. One minute I was flying then the next I was rowing through treacle. At noon, I collapsed into the stiflingly hot cabin, every inch of my body in pain, especially my lower back.

On my first row, I'd come to terms with pain. Every time I'd go on the oars, I'd say to myself, *'For the next two hours, pain is now part of my life.'* By acknowledging the pain, I could process it and put it to the back of my mind. On this row I'd become so practiced at it, I was only reminded of the pain when I would lay, stretching my back out in the cabin.

Since leaving the Canaries, I'd been rowing hard every shift, silently shadowed by the spectre of Ralph Tuijn, somewhere beyond the horizon chasing me down. Between each two-hour rowing shift, added to the usual pain in my bum, lower back and neck, were aches in every muscle. Now the small jobs that regularly needed attention, like checking the water maker for leaks, took on a new urgency as I rushed to get them done so I could rest for as long as possible between rowing shifts.

Through the afternoon the sun continued to beat down and as it slowly made its way towards the western horizon, I could just make out the thinnest sliver of a crescent moon, high in the sky. I hated the nighttime rowing shifts in pitch-black nothingness, especially in big seas. I smiled to myself, knowing for the next few weeks the moon would be a welcome companion for at least part of the night. This tiny crescent moon; however, set only a few hours after sunset leaving a sky filled with a billion stars. The water around *Hope* glowed. Where my oars splashed, clouds of green, glowing luminescence swirled behind. It reminded me of the aurora borealis as if it was reflected in the sea from a Norway sky.

From 1am, a lone white seabird followed me for about an hour, swooping in and out of *Hope*'s light, before disappearing on its own journey. It was a sure sign that I was close the Cape Verde Islands and the bioluminescence another reminder that I was pushing ever south.

Day 28 Logbook Entry

Position at 0800hrs (L) (0900hrs UTC)	*Distance travelled 57.5nm*
on 6th Feb 2019	*at 232°t*
19°56' 191n 024°07: 849w	*Total distance 1264.5nm*

Distance to Cayenne 1873nm

Another scorching hot day with intermittent periods of flying @ 3.5-4kts to slogging to get 2knts. Fairly light wind (10-15kts) consistently from NNE. At around midnight a white bird kept circling the boat. Kept catching glimpses of it as it flew past the lights.

The difficult year I'd endured since becoming a corporal soon came to an end. Two separate incidents really changed how the rest of the troop saw me and more importantly, how I saw myself as a corporal.

In late 1999, Air Defence Troop deployed with the rest of HQ & Sigs Squadron to Egypt on the most pointless deployment I've ever done. Having never been to the desert before, I volunteered to go out two weeks early in charge of an advance party of three and instantly remembered the Marines mantra, 'never volunteer'. We spent two weeks putting out a barbed-wire entanglement around the desert camp and digging desert roses, a type of field urinal consisting of a big rock filled trench with a pipe sticking out. We dug one and a half meter deep by three-meter-long trenches and then scavenged the desert with a sandbag for rocks to fill the trench before covering it over. It was long, backbreaking, thankless work in extremely hot, dusty and miserable conditions.

The rest of the troop rocked up and it became apparent there was no plan for the exercise or timetable for training. We just sat in the desert. Daz, the new Sergeant Major, seemed to be in his element doing nothing and Jez the new boss and the sergeants followed. Air Def' Troop's inactivity soon became conspicuous, and something must have been said as the sergeants were soon in a frenzy of cobbling together some training out of thin air.

The rest of HQ & Sig's Squadron had found a beachfront resort about an hour's drive away and were taking it in turns going there for the day. I asked one of the senior corporals to speak to the grown-ups, our collective name for the sergeants, sergeant major and boss, to see if we could go. Two days later we were sat ready to go in a 4-tonne lorry. Daz, Jez and the rest of the grown-ups led off in a Land Rover with a young marine called Steve navigating. Steve was a good Marine and the only one in the troop who'd been to the resort. After about half an hour of trundling through the desert on rough Egyptian roads, we suddenly stopped, turned around and headed back to the desert camp leaving us all confused. Back at camp, the driver came round and let down the tailgate of the 4-tonner. As we got out the Land Rover with the grown-ups sped off. Steve wandered over to us and explained what had happened.

On the way there he'd gone past a turning and unsure whether it was the correct one said, 'I think we should've taken that left turn.'

Daz asked in annoyance, 'Well, was it or not?'

Steve said, 'Let's go a bit further.' Then realising that it was the turning, said. 'No, I think it was the turning. I think we should go back.'

Daz started shouting at him and said 'Right, fuck it. We're going back.'

Steve led the rest of us back to the camp and the grown-ups pissed off to the resort on their own. Later that night the Land Rover pulled up and out they all got, very drunk. It is the most appalling lack of leadership I've ever experienced in the Marines.

A week or so later, the troop were sat in the tent talking, telling jokes and generally doing nothing when Jez came in and asked all the corporals to step outside for a chat.

'What's wrong with the troop?' he said. 'The lads seem threaders. Is everything OK?'

I couldn't believe what he was asking. I looked at the senior corporals, waiting for them to say something. A couple gazed at the floor, kicking the sand around.

'I mean if something isn't right then I need to know,' said Jez earnestly.

I was dumbstruck at his apparent ignorance of what had gone on. But was even more shocked when I realised that none of the senior corporals were going to say something. I knew that he'd seen what we had seen. He knew exactly what had been going on. This farce was nothing more than him doing his duty and hoping that the corporals would say that the lads were fine and it's just a blip and he could go back vindicated. But I knew that this was a lie and I also knew that one of us had to say something.

'You are joking, aren't you?' I asked.

Jez looked round at me irritated. I looked round at the senior corporals, earnestly willing one of them to jump in and help me. They all avoided my gaze.

'Well to be honest, I'm shocked you don't know and need to ask.' I then as accurately as I could, listed all the grievances the troop had with the so-called command element.

Jez stood listening, his frown slowly turning to a sneer of contempt as I continued with a growing sense of isolation. Then to my utter relief, Tommo started in with his list of grievances and a few that I had missed. Tommo was one of the new corporals but had been in Air Defence Troop for years. He was a short, stocky cockney, popular and was widely respected, unlike me. He suddenly gave what I was saying credence. Jez muttered something about respect and the chain of command and wandered off.

'I can't believe none of you said anything.' I said accusingly at the senior corporals.

Later that night, I began to mull over what had happened. I knew I was still learning as a corporal and that I was prone to mistakes. But I now knew that I possessed moral courage. I had the strength of character to do and say the right thing. In that moment I believed I was a better corporal than any of the senior corporals. For the first time since I was promoted, I felt like I deserved my stripes.

Air Defence Troop conducted a joint exercise with 20 Battery, Royal Artillery on their base in Kirton Lindsey in north Lincolnshire. Daz, the Sergeant Major, was regarded as being lazy and useless and his sergeants as spineless weaklings. As a new group of corporals we were quite militant and our respect for the new troop command element was now zero.

The exercise surpassed our expectations of being a shambolic waste of time. It was conducted on the base, with the 20 Battery sergeants and officers wanting us to camouflage ourselves, pretending that we were out in the countryside, instead of on the base. After the exercise all the corporals went into the nearest town, Scunthorpe for a drink. The night ended in a huge town centre brawl with several of corporals arrested, including me. The incident made the local news with the headline, 'Marines Run Rampant in Town Centre.' In the morning Daz came and bailed us out, the locals who we were fighting wouldn't press charges and I think the police just wanted rid of us. But they also gave Daz the CCTV footage of the whole fight. We went straight from police cells to the waiting coach ready to drive us back to Plymouth, but frustratingly the coach's video player wasn't working. As soon as we got back to Stonehouse barracks we ran to the nearest large room and gathered around the TV. As soon as the fight erupted, the camera zoomed into me and the CCTV operator followed me throughout the whole incident. On the TV, I get into a scrap with one local who I drag to the ground and try to punch. I could remember punching the floor and cutting my knuckle bad enough for it to require stitches. I then tried to punch him again but drunkenly miss and hit the pavement instead. After several attempts to hit him, all of which missed, I gave up and he got up unharmed to carry on fighting somewhere else in the brawl.

On the TV it looked awful. I flinched at the apparent viciousness of what looked like me repeatedly hitting someone. But that moment changed the way everyone in the troop saw me. Before they pressed play on the VHS player, I was a bit of a wally. Afterwards I was OK. It was that ridiculous, because I had drunkenly failed to punch someone, I was suddenly OK.

Collective opinions of people are fickle and almost always wrong.

Day 29

I finished my last rowing shift as dawn approached and *Hope* was covered in a fine red dust. The cloudless sky appeared murky brown as the first rays of sunlight danced across the sea.

After my usual morning routine of filling out the logbook then calling Claire and Izzy, I made myself breakfast. Every inch of my body ached, and I tried to rest as much as possible before rowing again. After every rowing shift, I wiped my body down with wet wipes to clean the salt from my skin. I'd rationed seven wet wipes per four hours for 90 days and religiously used all seven. If I didn't wipe the salt away, it would quickly form tiny crystals that would cut into my skin causing sores that had the potential to become infected. As I collapsed exhausted into the cabin after each rowing shift, wiping myself down became a chore and took considerable mental discipline to complete. However, I knew that if I didn't, rowing with infected sores all over my skin would be a misery.

Ralph still hadn't set off from the Canaries, but I didn't let up in my effort to put as much distance between me and him. The sun beat down relentlessly through the day. I pulled as hard as I could on the oars, struggling to gain a meagre two knots. Every stroke felt like the oars had plunged into concrete.

Late in the afternoon, I passed a clump of rubbish. There were ropes, plastic bottles, fishing nets and I wondered if something had become tangled in the rudder and slowing me down. The autohelm sounded OK, so I got a GoPro out and videoed under *Hope*. The rudder was perfectly fine so assumed the slow, hard rowing must be down to currents.

The backbreaking rowing conditions continued through the night. I had mentally set a goal of rowing at least 50 nautical miles every 24 hours and by dawn I was slightly relieved that I managed it. Just.

Day 29 Logbook Entry

Position at 0800hrs (L) (0900hrs UTC) on 7th Feb 2019	*Distance travelled 50nm at 244°t*
19°33' 755n 024°56: 512w	*Total distance 1314nm*

1822nm to Cayenne

Hard days rowing through sometimes treacle, early evening rowed through loads of rubbish, plastic bottles, ropes, string and general plastics. First flying fish on board.

After Egypt, I was called into the office to see Jez to get my yearly report, my first as a corporal. It was awful.

'That's not very good.' I said.

'You know you are signing it to say that you have read it and not that you agree with it.'

I walked out of his office filled with rage but knew that a screaming match wouldn't achieve anything. Before I forgot, I wrote down everything that was factually incorrect in the report and waited a couple of days, then knocked on his door.

'Have you got a couple of minutes please Sir.'

Jez beckoned me in and I then went through my list point by point. He had omitted to mention that within the reporting period, I had come top of my Air Def' corporals' course, passed an MSI's and even got a very credible pass on my juniors. All important career courses and written in stone, not a matter of opinion. When I finished, Jez looked crestfallen. He'd have to go back to the Company Commander, who signed off on the report and explain that he'd got it wrong.

'OK, what do you want to do about it?' he'd asked.

I told him that I thought it sometimes worse to get a name as a troublemaker, but he'd better not forget that for my next report. It was the single worst career decision I've ever made and regretted it ever since.

I finally had the confidence to apply for Special Forces (UKSF) selection and the Special Boat Service (SBS). There are two selections a year, a summer and a winter course, and I hoped to get on the summer course in June 2000. I had an interview with Jez, who forwarded my application. Or at least he said he did. As the summer approached, I wasn't on the list to attend the aptitude, the pre-course for UKSF selection for that summer. I re-applied but again, I wasn't on the list for the winter selection. When I chased up my application, I was told that there was no record of me applying. I again applied, resubmitting my paperwork to the boss hoping for a summer course in 2001 and yet again, I wasn't called forward for the aptitude. Instead, I was drafted out of Air Defence Troop to 40 Commando in Taunton and the Provy Section.

In the late summer of 2001, 40 Commando embarked on HMS *Ocean* and sailed towards the Middle East on Exercise Saif Sareea. The Provy section consisted of Bob, the Provy Sergeant who was in charge of disciple on camp, myself and Proko, a Mancunian with an easy smile, good sense of humour and piercing blue eyes.

On the way to Oman we stopped at Lisbon for a couple of days' heavy drinking and then Cyprus where 40 Commando undertook series of military exercises. Before the troop-level training, I received a series of texts from Claire about a skyscraper in New York that had fallen down. Then Claire texted that it was believed to be a terrorist attack and that thousands had died. I didn't call Claire back to get any more details as it was too expensive to use a mobile abroad. Instead, I found Bob and showed him the texts I'd received.

'Nah that's nonsense mate.' He replied handing back the phone. 'There's no way anyone could pull that off.'

I shrugged and walked off to get Proko to go to the bar on the camp next to our accommodation. Inside it was empty except for a couple of marines. They stared in disbelief at an old TV in the corner replaying the now infamous footage of the attacks in New York. The date was 11 September. We didn't know it at the time, but the whole world had changed.

As we stood and watched, more people came into the bar and like us, just stood there gawping at the screen, barely able to comprehend what we were seeing. Bob came and stood with me and Proko, 'See, I told you so,' didn't seem appropriate.

Later that afternoon I bumped into the Ben, the Company Sergeant Major for Charlie Company. Ben always had an air of confident professionalism and his reputation for being a popular CSM, proceeded him.

'Frank, I was hoping to see you.' he said. 'Have you swapped with Chris and coming to Charlie Company?'

'I don't know anything about it,' I replied, a bit confused. 'Why?'

'Apparently you and him have agreed to him taking your job in the Provy and you swapping with him as a section commander with me in Charlie.'

'This is the first I've heard of it, but if Bob is OK with me swapping, then I'd bite your arm off to get into Charlie Company.'

'Leave it with me.' Ben said then walked off.

Twenty minutes later Bob came and found me, 'Mate are you happy going to Charlie?'

'More than happy Bob,' I said, 'If it's OK with you?'

'Crack on mate, pack up and move over now to their accom.'

I was now a section commander in Charlie Company. My new troop sergeant was my old mate John and Scotty Mills was one of the other troop sergeants. Almost immediately I was packing my field kit, ready to deploy on a short exercise in the Cypriot countryside where I properly met the other members of the troop. They were all very young lads but super keen.

After the exercise we headed back onboard HMS *Ocean*. After the New York attacks, the mood surrounding the deployment changed. 40 Commando now had a sense of purpose. We sailed through the Suez Canal in an unbearably hot ship. The only relief from the heat was the forecastle, an open area at the very front of the ship, below the flight deck. Most weekend evenings the forecastle would be busy with lads chilling with a few beers and I'd often take my guitar to instigate a drunken singalong. Soon the ship transited the Red Sea, through the Gulf of Aden and finally into the Arabian Sea where we prepared to disembark.

Day 30

The day started with a cold yellow light on the eastern horizon as the sun struggled to break through a thick sea mist.

I finished my morning routine and started my first daytime rowing shift. The conditions were good, and I felt I was clawing the miles away. With no reference point, movement across open ocean is hard to ascertain, but today as I rowed, I sensed clear movement. The greying sky heralded the coming night. A very welcome thin crescent moon hung high in the sky that I knew would light the sea around me for my early nighttime rowing sessions. Before the sun set, I was averaging three to three and a half knots, then as it darkened, I struggled to get two knots. I pulled hard on the oars through the night and was very disappointed when I totalled the milage up in the morning. I scraped over the 50-mile minimum goal that I'd set myself. For how exhausted I felt, 54.5 nautical miles seemed way too low. On a positive, I used a calculator to check the total distance rowed and found I'd lost 100 nautical miles by adding up in my head. It hadn't changed the distance to Cayenne, but it brought the halfway point closer.

Day 30 Logbook Entry

Position at 0800hrs (L) (0900hrs UTC)	*Distance travelled 54.5nm*
on 8th Feb 2019	*at 246°t*
19°11′464N 024°49: 027W	*Total distance 1481nm*

1768nm to Cayenne

Total 1481.5nm increase because of poor maths checked with calculator.

Misty/foggy day with sun coming through @ approx 10.30. Good rowing in daylight hours then slowed right down through the night, disappointed with only 54.5nm.

Auto helm sounding OK, gave it a couple of hours off.

We packed up all our belongings and cross-decked from HMS *Ocean* onto landing craft that took us the short distance to the Omani coast where I struggled up the beach carrying a large bergen, a huge holdall and my guitar. Awaiting transport took us straight into the Omani desert, one of the hottest places on earth and our home for the next couple of months. We'd be living in old military 12-foot square tents forming a small, tented town that housed the whole of 40 Commando. Luxury it wasn't.

Living in the desert was misery. There was no escape from the heat during the day and at night, just before sunset a stiff desert breeze would build, blowing a fine dust into the air. We slept with scarfs covering our faces and had constant grit in our mouths and eyes. The next few weeks consisted of various exercises in the heart of the desert, building from section level, up to troop, company then a final unit exercise. The exercises were a relief from the misery of the tented camp where constant movement of vehicles around the tents had broken through a hard crust on the ground creating fine dust. In comparison, out in the desert, during the day the heat was unbearable, but all movement would stop between 11am and 2pm. We would put up a poncho as shade and lie down trying to stay as cool as possible.

The desert can be the most beautiful place on earth just before sunset and sunrise. At night, without the constant dust cloud around the tented camp, the desert breeze was a blessed relief from the heat of the day.

Oman is memorable to me for three reasons.

A now legendary concert in the desert was organised. Both 40 Commando and 45 Commando were marched across the desert to a makeshift stage to watch Les Dennis, who was hilarious, Gerri Halliwell, who was rubbish, and Steps, who were brilliant. A load of support company lads had somehow managed to make a ginormous banner that read 'H SHOW US YOUR STARFISH'. Whenever H, from Steps would come to the front of the stage a massive cheer would erupt.

Secondly a tornado. One day between exercises when I was chilling in my tent, I heard cheers and rushed out to see what was happening. Across the desert a tornado was tearing through the tents of 45 Commando who were camped a mile away. Tents like ours were being ripped up and thrown about to the collective amusement of everyone at 40 Commando.

Thirdly and something that sticks with me to this day was a can of Coke. The unit Quarter Master had been somewhere near civilisation and bought the whole unit a can of Coke each. I queued up, grabbed my unbelievably cold can and walked back to my tent with a massive smile on my face. I thought that all my birthdays had come at once as I sipped the cold bubbly liquid and then suddenly thought, *'How shit is my life at the moment, where a single can of Coke can make me feel this great.'* That single can of Coke taught me the invaluable lesson that it's impossible to be happy all the time. If you get everything that you want, that will soon become normal and you will need to get something more or better to continue being happy. The search for happiness is an ongoing, never-ending, impossible task and therefore pointless. Happy is only in comparison to not being happy, like my can of Coke in the desert, the best thing to happen to me in comparison to life there.

Shortly after the concert in the desert, Ben came and found me to tell me that my SBS selection date had finally come through.

'I can get you on a plane back to the UK in a couple of days. If you want to go. You know what's coming up and what could happen.'

Ben was referring to the growing sense that war was brewing. Since the 9/11 attacks, Osama Bin Laden had been identified as the prime suspect and the finger was pointing at the Taliban regime in Afghanistan for hiding him. There was an edge to our desert training along with rumours of task forces assembling and that the Corps was in the middle of it all. It would be typical of my luck. The first proper action the Corps had been involved in since the Falklands and I'd miss all the action and fail selection.

I was 31 and would be 32 during selection, the upper age limit, and I'd already applied for special dispensation to attend. To delay selection would push me over the age limit.

'I've gotta give selection a shot,' I said. 'If I don't, I'll forever wonder what if.'

'I totally understand, mate.'

A couple of days later I was on a flight back to the UK to attend the Briefing Course at Royal Marines Poole, the home of the SBS.

Day 31

The sun rose as a perfect orange disc, light scattering across infinite small waves and ripples.

As I ate breakfast, I decided to make today Morale Saturday. In planning the row, I'd known that I'd need something to look forward to and much like the can of Coke in the desert, the smallest morsal of morale takes on enormous significance in adversity. By the time I'd finished eating, I had 'Morale Saturday' planned. I checked how many clean pairs of pants I had left and happily realised I had enough spare to change my underwear every Saturday from now on. I took a new pair out of the sealed canoe bag I kept them in and savoured the fresh smell of clean washing. I binned the old pair with the packaging from my breakfast and the used wet wipes. I made sure I kept every scrap of rubbish and only organic matter ended up in the sea.

The day was hot and the light north-westerly breeze gave little relief from the heat as I rowed, but rowing in fresh pants felt remarkably better. After I finished my last daytime rowing shift, I dug around inside the hatches looking for my favourite main meal, pasta carbonara, and then dug deeper looking for one of the few chorizo sausages I'd hidden about the boat. Once I found both, I settled myself on deck with my back against the cabin door and the setting sun over my left shoulder and prepared Morale Saturday's dinner – pasta carbonara with fried chorizo. I used the knife on my Leatherman to chop up the chorizo and fried it on the small frying pan I'd brought for just this reason, as the carbonara rehydrated in its pack. After a large dash of tabasco I tucked in. It tasted amazing. It started me thinking about my wet rations. I'd rationed 90 days of 6,000 calories a day split between 69 days of freeze-dried high energy meals and 21 days of wet boil-in-the-bag military rations. The wet rations were for an emergency in case the water maker packed up as the freeze-dried rations took a lot of water to rehydrate. Wet rations day was a key marker on the last row. It not only signified that we had just three weeks to go and could therefore start eating the emergency rations, but it was also a change in diet. I still reckoned I was a couple of weeks away from wet rations day on this row, but it was another marker that I was slowly closing in on.

The night was clear with no clouds to obscure the thin crescent moon and once it set, the billions of stars dazzled in the black sky from the horizon to the Milky Way overhead. At 1am, I briefly stopped rowing for the final part of Morale Saturday, and took a large glug of Glenfiddich whiskey. I looked up at the stars as the warming liquid coursed through me. Morale Saturday had been a roaring success and I was already looking forward to the next one.

Day 31 Logbook Entry

Position at 0800hrs (L) (0900hrs UTC) on 9th Feb 2019	*Distance travelled 53nm at 238°t*
18°43′ 424N 026°36: 761W	*Total distance 1534.5nm*

1715nm to Cayenne

Hard day rowing with gentle NW breeze @ approx NW turning N occasionally.
Wind picked up during the night.
Clear night with no clouds and good sun rise.

I passed the Briefing Course then waited to attend the next selection starting in January 2002. I threw myself into training for 'The Hills', the first big hurdle of selection with a determination brought about by a sharpened focus that the impending selection had given me. I knew exactly what I wanted to do and what I had to do to achieve it although I didn't have much time.

'The Hills' is the first four-week phase of selection and consists of a series of yomps or marches against the clock over the Brecon Beacons and vast empty hills of Mid-Wales. On the first march I bruised my heel and as the first week progressed the pain worsened. The first week finishes with the Fan Dance – a 24-km yomp over Pen Y Fan, the highest peak in the Brecon Beacons. The route then heads down to the halfway point near Pentwyn Reservoir, then returns over Pen Y Fan finishing to the start point. You have just four hours to completed it. If I could get to the weekend and rest my heel, I might give it a chance to recover, but as the weekend and the infamous Fan Dance got closer, my hope of passing selection began to fade. I tried my hardest to stay with the group over the top of the fan but by the time I had hobbled down to the halfway check point, at least three other groups had passed me. I gave my name to the DS at the check point who scanned up and down the sheet looking without success for my name,

'What group are you?' he asked.

'Group three.'

'Group three?' he said with surprise, flicking over the sheet to the previous page and ticking my name off. 'You haven't got a hope of passing now. Go jump in the wagon.' He gestured back towards a couple of 4-tonne lorries full of other failures.

'I can't wrap.' I said. 'If I fail, I fail, but I can't wrap.' It was far from a pointless heroic gesture, I could forgive myself for not passing, but I would never forgive myself for giving up.

'Alright it's up to you.' The DS said. 'Fucking pointless though.'

I trudged back up the long rocky path to Pen Y Fan. Going back over the Fan was torturous. I knew it was pointless and I was genuinely in agony with my heel, but afterwards, I was able to look at it with a tiny amount of pride. Not giving up at the halfway point was a tiny positive that I clung to out of the utter failure of selection. I sat in the awful showers at Sennybridge that fluctuate between scolding hot and ice cold for what felt like hours. The rules for SF selection state that any person can only have two attempts and because of my age, I had no choice but to go on the upcoming summer selection.

Initially my heel was too painful to walk on, let alone run, so I started cycling. I rested my heel as much as possible and cycled everywhere, then as winter turned to spring, my heel improved and I was able to start running again. I then trained as often as possible over the hills of Mid-Wales and the Brecon Beacons. I found I was so much stronger going over the rough terrain of the Welsh hills than before and attributed this improvement to cycling, though probably it was just the ability to train instead of going straight on selection from the desert.

Throughout my career as a Royal Marine, I'd constantly trained through necessity. I'd known I wasn't a naturally gifted athlete and took pride in working harder to maintain basic Royal Marine fitness. In school, I'd clung to the belief that I might be good at long distance running, because I was terrible at sprinting. But this hope was shattered when I tried to get in the cross-country team but came a miserable 53rd in my year at the trial run.

I carried on training with the odd trip to Norton Manor camp and watched the news with interest as 40 Commando were held in readiness to support the operations in Afghanistan. Op Jacana, the mopping up operation to clear the remaining Al-Qaida and Taliban forces from the Tora Bora and Shah-i-Kot mountains was headed up by 45 Commando but elements of 40 Commando were also deployed into Afghanistan. After the failure on the Fan Dance, my confidence began to grow as my training progressed through the early summer.

Two years earlier in 2000, Claire had been working in the music department at Plymouth city library. One of the regular music lenders who was normally very shy and quiet, came to the desk clutching David Bowie's entire back catalogue. He enthusiastically told Claire about how he'd just seen Bowie at Glastonbury and what an amazing experience the festival had been. She was so moved by the dramatic change and the way he spoke about Glastonbury, she decided we would go to the next festival.

In late June, just before selection, we travelled to Glastonbury with a Norway four-man tent from the store, a couple of rucksacks and little idea of what to expect. I was as prepared as I could be for selection and thought the festival a good way to relax. We arrived late on Friday afternoon and parked in a massive field full of cars, then trudged through more fields of cars then fields of campervans. They led to a small plateau at the top of a hill that led down to the entrance. From the top the entire festival filled the vale below. The brand-new white fence enclosed a huge sprawling metropolis of vivid colours, flags, tents and huge marquees, with Glastonbury Tor shimmering in the distance. The Dandy Warhols played 'Bohemian Like You' on the legendary pyramid stage. We both stared with our jaws dropped open in sheer amazement at the magnitude of what we were seeing. In that moment, Glastonbury Festival became part of our lives.

Day 32

The hard rowing continued as the sun beat down relentlessly and the currents and gentle breeze conspired to make every nautical mile gained an effort.

Throughout the daytime rowing shifts I struggled to get more than two knots and knew that my daily target of 50 nautical miles was under threat. I'd stopped thinking about Ralph, assuming he'd given up, but I continued the punishing pace I'd set rowing out of the Canaries. It was partly out of habit, but as I closed in on the halfway point, I could see that not just beating the able-bodied record but smashing it out of the park, was becoming a distinct possibility. There was still a lot of ocean between me and Cayenne and I knew that I was only ever one bad wave from utter disaster, but from halfway, I'd be on the metaphorical downward slope to the finish. The rest periods between the two-hour rowing shifts were taking on an importance of their own as I desperately tried recover enough before the next back-breaking rowing shift.

Day 32 Logbook Entry

Position at 0800hrs (L) (0900hrs UTC) on 10th Feb 2019 18°22' 228N 027°26: 459W	*Distance travelled 51.5nm at 246°t Total distance 1586nm*

1663nm to go

Virtually the same as yesterday. Same weather pattern for the next few days, few more clouds and a bit hazy

All too soon after Glastonbury I was back in South Wales on selection. The first few days went by much like last time, but I felt a lot stronger, a lot fitter and a lot more confident when the morning of the Fan Dance came around again. Everything was the same except for the weather and how I felt. Whereas before I was dreading the Fan and almost inevitable failure, this time I was looking forward to exorcizing the demon that had sat on my shoulder for the past six months.

After checking bergens and weights, we set off under blue sky and I positioned myself at the back of the group. Almost immediately it strung out and I started passing the stragglers, each one a boost to my growing confidence. As we approached the summit of Pen Y Fan I was still on the back of the now much smaller pack with the DS. The DS was much faster than me down the steep slope of Jacobs Ladder and as I cautiously descended, two stragglers hurtled past. I held myself back not wanting to trip and injure myself and as we approached the halfway point, I was a couple of minutes behind the pack. I felt strong and confident that I'd be able to make up the time going back uphill. As I progressed back up the long slog up from the half-way point, I began to feel myself slow. I was pushing myself as hard as I could, but my legs just wouldn't respond. With a sense of impending doom, I recognised the onset of heat exhaustion and as I did, the group behind me came past. I kept pushing myself as hard as I could and concentrated on ensuring that I stopped regularly to drink. I tried desperately to stay with the group that had come past me, but I had nothing to respond with as they slowly pulled away from me. As I climbed back up Jacob's Ladder to the summit of Pen Y Fan, with each step my legs were going into a spasm of cramp. At the top I replenished my water bottle and with a shout of 'You'd better get a shift on' from the DS I headed back down to the finish line. Just over a kilometre from the finish, the path crosses over a wall with a stile. There was a small queue of people waiting to cross over accompanied by a DS. I'd no idea if the DS was with a group, but he asked me what group I was with. When I told him he pushed me to the front of the queue saying if I was lucky I might still make it. I ran as hard as I could, using every scrap of energy I had left. As I came down to the finish line, the DS asked for my course number and scribbled my time down in his clip board. As I boarded the transport, I had no idea if I'd passed. A rumour went around the back of the lorry that there was going to be an extension to the allowed time for the Fan Dance as the unusually hot day constituted adverse weather conditions. I tried desperately to not get my hopes up.

Back at Sennybridge Camp, after getting showered and changed I joined a couple of Marines that I knew in the galley. Word was passed around that the list of failures for the Fan was posted on the course notice board. I finished my meal and headed over to check. My name was on the list of people who'd failed. I was devastated. The false hope when the DS at the stile said I still had a chance was smashed against the rocks of reality. Hope is a wonderful thing and often keeps us going when all logic tells us to stop, but the consequences of false hope are often shattering, and I was inconsolably miserable.

I walked dejectedly over to the Chief Instructor's office and waited with a small queue to be formally removed from the course. There had been extra time added to the Fan Dance because of adverse weather, but even with that, I was still a fair way over the time.

On the Monday following the Fan Dance, I reported to the SBS Training Wing. I waited outside the Sergeant Major's office, along with a couple of others who'd also failed.

'Right come on then, let's get this over with,' The sergeant major said as the first of us failures followed him into his office. I remembered him from the Briefing course, he had a wiry build but was very ordinary looking and you wouldn't be surprised if he sold you insurance. He was quite jovial and this added to his ordinary demeanour. Very soon it was my turn.

'Well come on then, what happed?' he asked as cheerfully as he could.

'I didn't cut it,' I replied.

He frowned, leaning slightly forward. 'What do you mean you didn't cut it?'

'I just wasn't good enough. You know those Bootnecks who never train and then go out and run six-minute miles, well I'm on the opposite side of the spectrum. I've always had to work hard to maintain normal fighting company fitness. I was always going to find it hard.'

He nodded and said 'OK.' And with that, he signalled that was the end of the interview.

Without any forethought, I said, 'It's a shame though, because I know I can pass'.

'How'd you mean?' He asked.

'Well I can plod for ever, if I could only get over the Fan I know I could get through, I never get threaders. You know that idiot still making jokes in the pissing rain on exercise when everyone else is in their chinstraps, well that's me.' I said.

'Wait there,' he said getting out of his chair.

I hadn't planned on saying anything other than not making any excuses and my little outburst had genuinely come from the heart, I had no ulterior motive in saying any of it. It certainly wasn't thought through, so I was a little bit shocked when he left the room, and I stood there uncomfortably waiting for him to return.

After a couple of minutes he came back into his office and said 'Follow me.' He led me round the corner to another office within the T wing building. He opened the door and sat on the other side of a desk was a very young officer with a massive bouffant of blond hair.

'Talk to him,' The Sergeant Major said and then left.

I sat down opposite the blond-haired young officer more than slightly bemused.

'Right, we're gonna try and get you back on selection for a third attempt,' he said.

This shocked me as I knew that there were only two permitted attempts at selection.

'We've got a good relationship with Hereford.' He said meaning the SAS and continued, 'Crack on training as if you're on the next selection. I can't promise anything, but as I say, we've got a good relationship with them.'

Shocked and a bit confused I thanked him and left.

Instead of returning to 40 Commando I was temporarily drafted to Air Defence Troop who were in the midst of converting to a new missile system and the conversion course was being run near Tenby in Wales, perfect for getting to the Brecon Beacons. Every spare moment through the course I spent yomping over the Beacons or running along the beautiful Pembrokeshire coastline. I reran the Fan Dance a couple of times the last time with weight and against the clock, purely for my own confidence. I was well within the times and what was more important, I felt strong and that I had more in the tank at each of the check points.

When the list for the next selection came out my name wasn't on it. I called the OC T Wing and asked if he knew anything. He took my name and promised to get back to me. I tried to carry on that day as normal and was in the supermarket when I finally received the call.

'Cpl Spencer? It's OC T Wing. I'm afraid it's not good news.' My heart sank. 'It's basically come down to a combination of two factors, your age and that you came off both times quite early on in the hills.'

'Great', I thought *'I'm basically old and shit.'*

'Either one and we may have been able to do something,' he continued.

I probably mumbled some thanks, but I was devastated. I felt numb.

'Spencer,' he said before I hung up. 'I want you to know that I tried everything I could.'

With that phone call, after years of training, two back-to-back selections and the half promise of a third, my goal of passing UKSF Selection and joining the SBS was finally over.

Would I have passed if I had a third attempt? Maybe. If I'd pushed for a medical withdrawal on the first selection with my heel injury, something that would've been nothing more than a trip to the small sick bay, then I'd almost certainly have got a third attempt. But you may as well ask, if the sun hadn't come out on the second attempt, then would I have passed? The point is that I didn't go to the sick bay and the sun did come out and I failed.

I've heard many people saying you need to be lucky to pass and maybe I was unlucky. But that's not what they are selecting for. UKSF Selection is not looking for lucky people, it's selecting for people who can get on with it and pass, despite being a bit unlucky. Being able to cope when things go wrong and have extra in the tank to complete the task is at the heart of being an SF soldier. UKSF selection served its purpose and correctly deselected me. The reality is that I failed selection at the first hurdle, before the Fan Dance, before the hills, even before the briefing course. I failed selection by not having the confidence to apply when I was younger and had a much better chance of passing. I'd dreamed of being a Royal Marine then for years I'd spent my time in the Corps, believing that I didn't deserve to be there. I then dreamed of being an average Bootneck then been promoted before I thought ready. Whilst I'd dreamed of being a competent corporal, passing selection seemed a step too far. I believed that I'd fail and the thought of failure stopped me applying. Fear of failure is the worst fear of all. Fear is a natural response to a situation that can be dangerous and often enables a person to make the correct decisions with proper caution. Fear can heighten the senses when needed and fear can stop you doing something stupid. But fear of failure is utterly pointless and will only ever prevent you trying.

After failing selection, I promised myself I'd never let fear of failure stop me from trying anything again. I didn't have a chance to contemplate this at the time as I was immediately called back to Charlie Company, 40 Commando. Whilst on selection the drums of war had been banging and 40 Commando would be in the thick of it.

Day 33

I ate breakfast and completed my morning routine. After phoning Izzy, Claire and filling out the logbook, I laid down to rest for 40 minutes before I started rowing again. My shoulders ached and I felt exhausted from two days of exceptionally hard rowing. My calloused hands and fingertips made it hard to function anything with a touch screen. As the minutes slowly ticked away, the cabin became a heat box as the intensifying sun beat down. I knew it was going to be another hard slog and reminded myself there was a few outstanding jobs on the boat.

It was another day of rowing through treacle as the currents slowed *Hope*. Without a hint of a breeze there was little relief from the relentless sun, yet the sea around me was still a mess of small waves and ripples. On my previous row, the sea was like glass on similarly windless days. Shafts of sunlight pierced through the clear water, producing mesmerising colours I'd never seen before. It shimmered between pitch black to vivid ultramarine and a million shades turquoise in-between. This time I was in a mess of conflicting currents disturbing the surface and pulling on *Hope*'s hull to slow her down.

I wondered if my slow pace may be due to leaks in any of the storage hatches meaning I was rowing a boat full of water. I spent my precious afternoon rest time unpacking each one and found a bit of water in each. I pumped them dry before repacking, but *Hope* continued her slow trudge.

I'd also scheduled today to check the water maker for leaks. The water maker was housed with the batteries in a small hold at the bottom of *Hope*'s hull, keeping all the weight as low as possible. Any leak could short the electronics. I switched on the water maker and then quickly dived back into the cabin with a head torch to check for leaks as it was running. It looked fine and the sponges placed to collect any unwanted water were thankfully dry.

The sea flattened through the night in the humid, windless conditions and a near half-moon kept me company through most of my midnight to two in the morning rowing shift, eventually setting into a flat sea. In the morning, any bitter disappointment I had about rowing a meagre 47.5 nautical miles, was overshadowed by passing the halfway mark. I was now on the downward slope to Cayenne.

Day 33 Logbook Entry

Position at 0800hrs (L) (0900hrs UTC) on 11th Feb 2019
17°57' 197N 028°08: 858W

Distance travelled 47.5nm at 238°t
Total distance 1633.5nm

1616nm to go Cayenne (Halfway Yay!)

Hot humid day with zero wind v strong current running at 1.5-2kts @238°(ish) turning more southerly through the night (210°)

Trying to not get carried away but I'm on course to take a month off the able-bodied record. A lot of ocean between here and there but so far so good. Conditions due to improve. Checked water maker for leaks (all OK). Holds have been taking in some water.

IRAQ

I returned to 40 Commando before Christmas and headed straight to Ben, my Sergeant Major.

A few of the personalities in Charlie Company had changed and Ben told me I'd be going to 6 Troop. The Troop Sergeant was a huge bear of a Mountain Leader called Craig. He'd been the ML who'd ran my Ski Novice and Arctic Warfare courses in Norway and had awarded me the Top Novice prize. The two other troop corporals were Topsy, a blonde-haired slightly chubby lad who could run like the wind, and Chal who always looked as if he'd just got out of bed.

We sailed for Iraq on 2 January on board RFA *Sir Galahad*. I was a section commander in charge of six young Marines, who were all very different characters, and my second in command (2I/C), a Lance Corporal (L/Cpl) called Titch. Titch was a shrewd northern lad who'd re-joined the Corps after a spell roofing in London. He had everything – intelligence, maturity, physical strength. He'd go on to have a successful career in the SBS.

We sailed through the Mediterranean, stopping at Cyprus for some section level training to form the section into the formidable fighting unit I hoped it would be.

There is a serviceman's mantra that every soldier is less robust and has had it easier than the generation before. It's a lie. It's also lazy thinking and assumes as fact that humans have become somehow fundamentally weaker in under a generation. War has changed beyond recognition and military training has adapted and changed in line with that. But the Commando tests and values are set in stone. I knew that every member of our young section had passed those tests and possessed those values.

We reembarked on *Sir Galahad* and set off through the Suez Canal. As we sailed closer to the Gulf, American and British politicians were desperately trying to justify going to war, with Blair's now infamous 'Dodgy Dossier'. Anti-war protests were rife, not only in the UK, but across the Europe. Being cocooned on the ship, we were sheltered from the news coverage. However, the closer we got to the Gulf, the more real it became and the tension on ship grew. With tension there was also an excitement. There was a feeling of standing on the edge of history. Most of the Corps had not done any fighting at a unit level since the Falklands War in 1982. All soldiers spend most of their careers training for something that seldom, if ever happens and all wonder how they will react if it does.

Being a Royal Marine isn't like any other job. It defines you, it's an integral part of who you are and how you view yourself. No sane person wants to be in a position where they are forced to kill another human-being and no one wants to be shot at. But every soldier wants to know, *'When it happens, will I cut it? Will I be able to do the job I've trained for?'*

For me there was a deeper significance. I knew this would be a reckoning with all those thoughts I'd carried since a toddler, petrified and unable to do anything when my Mum was crying for me to help her. That's why, the closer we sailed to the Middle East the more I felt like a boxer on the eve of a World Championship fight. For as long as I can remember I'd dreamed of being a Royal Marine, but what I'd really dreamed of being was brave, not the coward I believed I was. Finally becoming a Royal Marine hadn't made me feel brave as I thought it would. I fundamentally believed that I was a coward and that had been at odds with being a Royal Marine. I felt like a fraud since the first day I joined K Company from training.

When we got to the Northern Gulf, we were accommodated in the Kuwaiti desert under ponchos next to the massive impromptu camp that the Americans had named, with some genius, 'Camp Commando'. Once there we were taken out to the desert to an area of metal pickets driven into the ground joined together by orange mine tape.

Craig called the three section commanders and our 2i/cs into a huddle with the Boss, a young 2nd Lieutenant called Rich from South Africa. Craig laid out a large satellite photograph of some buildings in the desert. None of us had seen satellite imagery and we were awed by the seriousness of the situation. Craig explained the image was our troop's objective and talked us through the pickets and mine tape that were a life-size model that corresponded to the buildings on the image.

Nearly 500 metres from the town of Al Faw, south of Basra is the Manifold and Metering Station, (MMS) where nearly half of Iraq's oil passes through to reach jetties in the Gulf.

Craig explained how strategically important it was before adding, 'Once we secure the MMS, the rest of the invasion gets the green light. No one moves across their start lines until we secure the MMS.'

'So we'll be the absolute point troop of the whole invasion?' asked Topsy.

'Yes.'

Within the MMS, buildings housed the main workings for the station and the on/off switch. Prior to our landing, US Navy SEALs would be helo'd in to switch off the oil before it could be blown. We rehearsed with them repeatedly in the life-sized model of pickets and tape.

Chal's section would take the first building, my section the second. After all buildings were secure, my section would link up with a small team of SEALs in the south part of the complex to take over covering the western edge of the Company area.

When not rehearsing our attack, Chal, Toppsy and I would pore over the satellite imagery trying to glean every possible piece of information. There appeared to be trenches surrounding some buildings and we wondered how well defended they'd be. In between rehearsing the plan for the MMS, we practiced clearing buildings in some old derelict concrete compound out in the desert.

Day 34

The sun rose behind a bank of yellow-tinged clouds on the horizon and by the time I started my daytime rowing shifts, it beat relentlessly down through a hazy sky. The occasional thicker cloud gave little relief from the oppressive heat and humidity as I rowed through a breathless flat ocean.

The sea was calmer than I'd seen so considered going for a swim. I needed to scrape the hull to remove blossoming barnacles that would slow *Hope* down as they grew. It was something that needed doing every ten days, but conditions needed to be calm enough for me to safely enter the water. It was something I was looking forward to, especially on a day as hot and humid as this one. But despite the apparent calm of the sea, a very strong current was pushing *Hope* south and would quickly pull me away from her as soon as I entered the water. Becoming detached from *Hope* with a current running faster than I could swim would be an almost certain death sentence. I'd have to wait for the right conditions.

As the morning progressed more clouds bubbled and I could hear thunder rumbling. At about 3pm, a breeze suddenly blew from the north-west. It was a blessed relief from the stifling and muggy heat and made rowing a bit easier. I'd been slogging away in the airless conditions, barely getting above two knots all day, but *Hope*'s speed increased slightly in the light breeze and gentle waves. After I finished my evening meal at 8pm, I was about to get ready for my first nighttime rowing shift when the radio suddenly crackled into life.

'Hello *Hope*. I can see you, but I can't smell you', said a voice in an American accent.

I looked at the chart monitor, but nothing showed on the AIS. I quickly dived out of the cabin and, grabbing the handrail above the hatch, stood on my one leg to look around. I couldn't see anything. The clearness of the transmission suggested that whoever it was, they were extremely close and if it was a yacht, then I'd have expected to see a small light on top of its mast. I stuck my head into the cabin and rechecked the AIS. Still nothing showed. I quickly considered what to do. The most logical explanation was that it was a young lad on a yacht crossing the Atlantic who was alone on watch and bored. Not wanting to give them the satisfaction that I had heard the transmission, I didn't reply. I briefly considered turning everything off, but as creepy as the radio transmission had been, I knew it wasn't anything more sinister than some young lad stupidly mucking about.

I spent the next two hours rowing with my neck constantly craning around looking for any sign of another boat, but saw nothing. To add to the drama, lightning flashed all around me with the deep rumble of thunder rolling over the small waves. I didn't sleep on my first rest period from 10pm to midnight, I was unnerved by the voice, but exhaustion overtook fear as I slept through the rest of my off periods. I heard and saw nothing more through the night other than almost constant thunder and lightning.

Day 34 Logbook Entry

Position at 0800hrs (L) (0900hrs UTC)
on 12th Feb 2019
17°21'717N 028°57'901W

Distance travelled 59nm rowed
at 233°t
Total distance 1692.5nm

1558nm to Cayenne

No wind beyond a v gentle breeze all day until 1500hrs L when a brisk NW kicked in. A very strong current running at 1.5kts -1.8kts @ approx 210° T pushing the boat south. Overcast most of the day with thunder rumbling in the distance all day and lightning through the night. Hot sticky and humid. @ approx 1950hrs L a voice on the radio (English poss America accent) called for Hope then said 'I can see you but I can't smell you' very creepy and disconcerting. Radio signal suggests that whoever it was, was close, nothing showing on AIS.

After a week in the Kuwaiti desert rehearsing the plan repeatedly, we reboarded the ship and waited. One night a couple of us had a few beers and a game of poker that had gone on until about midnight when Scotty Mills came up.

'Frank, all the corporals are needed in the seniors' mess deck.'

I folded my cards and followed Scotty to the seniors' mess deck. Inside was all the sergeants and corporals, some of whom had clearly been woken up and were bleary eyed.

Ben said, 'Right lads, we've been meaning to invite all the corporals into the mess for a piss up for some time now.' He paused to pick up a bottle of rum. 'Well it's got to be tonight as the signal has just come in. We're going to war in the morning.' He then took a large swig from the bottle then passed it on.

We all looked at each other in disbelief. A few small cheers erupted. Scotty passed around cans of beer and I went over to Craig, Chal and Topsy. I opened my can and Craig raised his in toast.

'Here we go then,' he said and we all touched cans.

Ben soon produced a guitar and we drank through to the morning, stumbling back to our mess decks then packed our kit to go to war. The most important bergen I'd ever packed in my career and I, along with all the other corporals, was blind drunk.

We didn't go straight to war. We landed in the Kuwaiti desert again, where 40 Commando was lined out living under ponchos in company groups. We dug shell-scrapes, a kind of mini trench, and waited. We were given radios from somewhere that could only pick up one station that played Western music. It constantly played the same depressing songs, Dr Hook's 'Silvia's Mother' and 'Seasons in the Sun' by Terry Jacks, ad nauseum and we quickly nick-named it 'Suicide FM'. We listened to the BBC World Service for updates on the diplomatic farce as the UK and the Americans desperately tried to justify what was about to happen.

The Commanding Officer of 40 Commando, Lt Col Messenger, called the unit together near a derelict piece of scaffolding that he climbed and gave the whole of 40 Commando his 'going to war' speech. I can't remember it verbatim, but it went along the lines of, 'look we all know this is about oil, but we're here and we've got a job to do and we are going to do it with the upmost professionalism'. If Colonel Messenger had given his speech in Swahili we'd have still followed him. He was well liked and hugely respected in the unit. It didn't go down in history like Colonel Tim Collins' 'Magnanimous in Victory' speech that was printed in its entirety in the papers, but Colonel Messenger knew his men and knew that sentimental and meaningless lies wouldn't wash with us. Besides, I would've had to look up what 'magnanimous' meant.

Sat in the desert waiting for a war to start, we constantly pawed over all the satellite imagery of the MMS, talked it through with each other and rehearsed the plan again and again.

On the third morning in the desert, we woke to the news that the war had started. The Americans had seen a chance to kill Saddam and his sons whilst they attended a restaurant in Baghdad and so launched missiles. Either the intelligence was wrong, or they'd just missed them, but now it felt like the gloves were off and a line had been crossed. We all knew that the sham diplomacy was over and that we'd be going in.

Later that day, the sun shimmered a strange dull yellow as it dropped towards the horizon, a quiet descended on the desert camp, then almost immediately, a sandstorm blew in. War was placed on hold. We built shelters out of scraps of corrugated metal dumped in the desert, to shelter us from the wind and sand that turned the air a strange orangey yellow. It was a surreal time of laying in our shelter, jerboas, the cute but annoying rodent, bouncing all over our faces and then a flurry of activity as we scampered into shell-scrapes during the occasional Scud missile attack.

On the third night, the battering wind suddenly stopped as quickly as it had appeared and, in the morning, we all knew that we'd be going into Iraq that night.

We packed everything into webbing and day sacs that we'd need for the initial 24 hours of fighting. With all the ammunition, spare radio batteries, night vision goggles, 24-hours' rations and water, there wasn't much room for anything else. We divided the section ammunition of machine gun belts for the Minimis and spare underslung grenade launcher bombs amongst the whole section. Everything else, sleeping bags, spare socks, warm clothing, rations etc, went into our bergens. We'd go in Full Fighting Order with day sacs and our bergens would follow on later.

We were then ordered to sanitise ourselves and our kit, in case of capture. We removed every personal effect that we had – photos, wedding rings and letters and gave them in to Brum, the company TQ, for safe keeping. It would deny an enemy interrogator anything they could use against us. It was something I'd never done on exercise and brought the sharp reality of what was about to happen clearly into focus.

As dusk approached, I started to feel anxious about how I'd perform. The doubts I had about being a corporal and my deep-rooted belief that I was a coward, flooded my mind. I didn't know what to expect when we landed. I started to think about my young section, how my wrong decisions in the coming hours could cost lives. I knew that the next 24 hours would be the defining moment in my life. The dusk deepened and we sat on our kit waiting to go when the mail came around. I received a letter from Claire which I quickly read before burning it as we'd already sanitised our kit of personal effects.

We spent the last few moments in the desert, deep in our own thoughts, stood around small fires as our last letters from home burned. All our kit packed, checked, re-checked and checked again, weapons prepared, oiled and loaded, with little fires flickering in the desert gloom.

Day 35

I'd eaten porridge most mornings throughout the row and after completing my stats, I fancied a change so had macaroni cheese for breakfast. It was surprisingly good.

Halfway through my first daytime rowing shift, the gentle breeze that had offered a slight relief from the unrelenting sun, disappeared. I'd rowed through the strong currents of the previous day and the flat calm sea around me looked inviting. I stowed the oars, got the hull scrubber, my goggles and readied myself to slip overboard. During the day and only if the sea conditions weren't too challenging, I wore a rigger's belt with a strop that I attached to the deck instead of a life jacket. I detached the strop from the deck lines and attached it to the starboard jackstays. The jackstays were the two side lines that ran down each side of *Hope* and served to stop me from falling overboard. Happy that I was tightly secured to the boat, I then slid myself under the lower jackstay and into the water. I could feel the current pulling *Hope* away from me and held tightly to her side with one hand. Looking straight down, the perfectly clear water turned turquoise then deep blue as it disappeared into nothingness. The sense of floating above almost three miles of ocean was overwhelming. I scrubbed at the hull as best I could with only one hand. The current was a lot stronger than I first thought and made it difficult to properly get under the hull. I scrubbed at the tiny barnacles down one side then struggled back onto the deck. I moved the strop to the port side jackstay and repeated the process, but this time the current was pulling *Hope* over me instead of away. It made scrubbing under the hull difficult, and I soon gave up and tried to get back onboard, but every time I tried, my leg and body would slip under the hull as the current pulled the boat over me. It made getting back in almost impossible and I started to worry. I was trying to pull myself up and over the side of the boat, but my weight was too far under the hull to effectively pull myself out sufficiently. After quite a few failed attempts, I stopped and thought about how in training on the bottom field, I had to complete a regain by pulling myself back onto the rope. I laid back next to the hull and hooked the heel of my foot onto the deck and grabbing the higher jackstay, pulled myself sideways out of the water back onto the deck. I laid panting from the exertion of getting back in the boat, relieved to be out of the water.

As I finished my 1pm to 3pm rowing shift, the two flags that were hanging limp at the stern suddenly flapped into life as a strong breeze blew in from the north-east.

I had a closer look at the two so-called reconditioned autohelms that lasted three days and ten minutes respectively. I sat on deck in the relatively cool breeze and stripped both down. One looked like the motor had burned out and the other one's gears had seized. I swapped the broken parts with working ones before screwing this new bastardised contraption back together. I then opened the rear hatch, attached the newly created autohelm and plugged it in, crossing my fingers as I did. It instantly sprang into life, its piston pumping the rudder. I kept the old autohelm out, ready to instantly replace the bastardised one should it fail.

As the afternoon progressed the breeze stiffened and started to turn from north to west. A huge thunder cloud had been developing all day and drifted south towards me. Just after sunset, the moon disappeared ominously behind its huge bulk. Then, just as I started the first of the nighttime rowing shifts, the storm hit. Huge winds started to batter *Hope* from the west, driving short choppy waves against her starboard side and at an obtuse angle to the small swell from the north. It was impossible to row. I retired to the cabin and sat the squall out. For three hours the wind and waves battered *Hope* and she lurched from side to side. The blustery wind, stronger than any I'd had throughout the row, pushed *Hope* south. Then as quickly as it appeared, the storm rumbled overhead and disappeared. The sea remained choppy that made rowing very difficult. Another, but less strong squall passed by around midnight lasting just over an hour and by the morning, I had been blown 15 nautical miles off-course.

Day 35 Logbook Entry

Position at 0800hrs (L) (0900hrs UTC)
on 13th Feb 2019
16°33' 583N 029°45: 286W

Distance travelled 59.5nm rowed
at 230°t
Total distance 1752nm

1501nm to Cayenne

Very hot day wind died to nothing @ approx 1100hrs until 1500hrs L when a nice brisk breeze started. Strong current @ 220°T @ 1.5-2kts running. @ approx 20.00hrs L ran into a squall that lasted approx 3 hrs. Winds v strong @ 200°t. Boat was getting battered from starboard and running at 3-4kts. Another less strong squall @ approx 23.30 for 1 hr

Scraped some of the hull and bastardised a autohelm from the 2 'so called' reconditioned ones that's still going strong now. Fine red dust covering the boat for the last week or so.

The order to move came. The whole of 40 Commando stood in company group lines parallel to each other.

'OK lads, let's go.' I said simply. I put on my day sac and picked up my weapon.

As we walked to the waiting transport, all the men of 40 Commando formed a tunnel. Some clapped, some slapped us on the shoulders and arms saying, 'Good luck lads,' as we moved through. It was slightly unnerving and a stark reminder that we were going into the unknown. Every bit of training we'd ever conducted was for this moment. Several 4-tonne lorries waited for us at the end of the impromptu unit tunnel. We climbed inside for the short drive to the helicopters.

As dusk turned to night, we sat in our troops behind our respective Chinooks waiting. Our Chinook was called Vader One. I played the plan repeatedly in my head as we sat behind the Chinooks for what seemed an age. Whilst I was sat there in the desert contemplating what was to come, I picked up a heart-shaped stone and thought *'I'll keep that for Claire.'* I tried to push thoughts of Claire, the kids and home to the back of my mind, but try as I might, they were never that far away. Tension filled the air and a quietness as everyone sat deep in their own thoughts. Everything that needed to be said, had been.

Suddenly we were jolted back to reality as the Chinook engines whirred into life. The whole helicopter juddered as its rotors slowly turned before hitting full speed. The rotors kicked up desert dust as the loady looked towards us and gave a thumbs up. We walked as a troop towards the ramp of the Chinook. I looked across at the other two troops doing the same. As I got close to the ramp, I had to wait whilst those in front, turned to face the rear of the helicopter and squash as far back as possible. I was blasted by the hot air from the engines, before I walked up the ramp and turned to face the back of the helicopter. We'd loaded in the reverse order of how we planned to exit and were packed like sardines. I was stood at the very back looking straight out of the back of the helicopter. The rear ramp lifted slightly but remained nearly fully open with the loady sat behind the GPMG mounted on the ramp. The Chinook juddered violently and slowly lifted off the desert floor and climbed into the black sky where a full moon illuminated the ground below us.

We circled Babiyan Island on the southern tip of Kuwait for about 30 minutes and my body was aching with the weight of body armour, day sac and Full Fighting Order. The day sac was painfully pressing against the small 4-inch square ceramic bulletproof plate on my back, slightly offset to the left of my spine to cover my heart. I wished I'd brought my issue webbing instead of the cot vest I was wearing as it would have distributed some of the weight from my shoulders to my hips. As the Chinook turned, climbed and banked, the G force was pushing me into the floor, multiplying the weight of the kit. I could see the other Chinooks silhouetted against the moonlit desert night sky. The faint green glow of the night lights in the cockpit of the Chinook behind us, Vadar 2, just visible. Without warning, the Chinook dived out of the sky towards the ground before darting at low level across water, clearly reflecting the moon. It banked sharply to the left, then right, just metres above the ground that I now assumed was Iraq. I could still see the Chinooks behind, twisting and turning just metres above the ground. Lines of green tracer shot into the air as the Iraqi army started firing at us. With my heart pounding and my legs straining to keep me upright, I got a sharp tap on the shoulder.

Dave shouted, 'Two minutes.' Whilst holding two fingers in the air. It was the signal that we were just two minutes from landing. I passed the message on and waited, heart thumping in my chest.

Day 36

The storms from the previous night had cleared the air, but strong winds were now driving breaking waves with white horses on top that formed a mist around the horizon. The sun briefly shimmered as a yellowy-orange disc through the haze as it climbed out of the ocean and then shone brightly, lighting the haze on the horizon in brilliant yellow light. The wind steadily increased through the morning and the waves started to get bigger. They were coming from a more northerly direction than I'd have liked as I tried to claw back the 15 nautical miles I'd been pushed off course to the south. I was running *Hope* at a sharp oblique angle to the waves that were coming slightly from behind and to the starboard side, but as they got bigger and steeper later in the afternoon, I had to turn *Hope* in a more southerly direction.

The waves were steep and becoming angrier, making it near impossible to keep a more westerly heading. I was worried that as *Hope* was running down the front of a wave at too oblique an angle, the crashing white foam of a breaking wave would turn her fully sideways. She would then capsize, spinning uncontrollably down the front of a huge angry wave with me attached to her by a strop. The waves were also becoming less uniform. Sometimes whilst rowing in calmer seas, with a steady swell and uniform regular waves all coming from the same direction, a rogue wave travelling at a right angle to all the other waves would hit *Hope* on the side. These waves often drenched the boat, soaking me from head to foot as they smashed against the hull. There seemed to be lots of rogue waves, all doing their own thing and coming from lots of different directions. I assumed that it was caused by the storms and squalls from the previous night and a strong current. One big rogue wave hit the starboard side of *Hope* late in the afternoon and what seemed like a huge wall of water crashed over the deck absolutely soaking me.

I knew I'd pass the 030 Easting timeline and, at some point during the night, be two hours behind UTC Time or Greenwich Mean Time. It would mean another hour added to the night as my clock moved back an hour. I decided to split the extra hour between rowing and resting. The waxing gibbous moon shone white over the breaking crests of the large chaotic waves and after my first nighttime rowing shift, I laid in the cabin listening to the waves crashing against *Hope*'s sides. The deep rumble of the large breaking waves and the disconcerting sideways lurch whenever a wave crashed into *Hope* from the side, made sleeping difficult. I must have drifted off at some point, because just before my midnight alarm was due to wake me for the next rowing shift, the navigation alarm started beeping. I woke and immediately felt *Hope* roll dangerously on her side. I looked at the navigation screen and saw that the *Hope* was facing due west and therefore in irons. *Hope* was now side on to the waves and in immediate danger of capsizing. I donned my life jacket as quickly as possible and opened the cabin door. The thundering noise of big breaking waves rumbled around me as I attached the strop to the deck. This was the most dangerous point in exiting the cabin. As quickly as one leg would allow, I exited the cabin as *Hope* lurched from side to side and closed the cabin door. I grabbed the hand steering lines and pulled the rudder hard to starboard, grasped the oars and pulled as hard as I could. Slowly the forward momentum turned *Hope* out of irons back onto her correct course. As she settled, I fixed the hand lines and went to see what had happened to the autohelm that should've been steering. I was still using the bastardised autohelm and at first thought that it had burned out, but on investigation it had popped off the rudder. I assumed that a rogue, sidewards wave had smashed into the side of *Hope* violently enough to knock the autohelm off its mounting. I reattached it and it flashed back into life. I laid back down in the cabin just as my alarm alerted me that it was time to row. This time for two and a half hours.

I climbed out of the cabin and started rowing again. The moon was close to the horizon and illuminated the tops of the breaking waves. About halfway through my rowing shift, it set. Only the stars gave a sense of where I was and the uneven, irregular waves broke with crashing violence around me. In the pitch black it was impossible to gauge the size of the waves. Earlier in the day, they'd been as big as I'd ever rowed in, perhaps 20–25 feet. But now only the deep rumble of the largest breaking waves gave an indication of just how big they were. I could hear the guttural roar that reverberated in the pit of my stomach as they crashed in the blackness from behind *Hope*'s stern as if we were being stalked by giant monsters. A deep primordial fear coursed uncontrollably through my whole being and I decided to sit the rest of this rowing shift out inside the cabin. Fear made it impossible to sleep. The noise of huge waves rumbled in the cabin as *Hope* lurched in the angry ocean. I tried listening to some comedy podcasts to take my mind away from the violent conditions outside and eventually started drifting in and out of an uneasy sleep.

The wind picked up again at around 6am and just before sunrise, the autohelm popped off again. I rushed quickly out of the cabin as the greying horizon of the coming dawn gave enough light to see that the waves had got even bigger. I rowed *Hope* out of irons and reattached the autohelm. It had been a long night.

Day 36 Logbook Entry

Position at 0800hrs (L) (1000hrs UTC) on 14th Feb 2019
16°02′ 109N 030°40: 621W

Distance travelled 68nm rowed at 232°t
Total distance 1820nm total

1435nm to Cayenne

Strong NNE wind (210 t- 215°t) @ 15-20kts pushing 25kts from approx 06.00hrs L.

Autohelm has popped off twice in the last 24hrs at 23.20 hours L and again at 07.00hrs L. Passed 030° northing so L time now UTC – 2 hrs

The Chinook banked and span 180° in the air as it dropped out of the sky and landed with a jolt. Topsy who was just to my left, clattered into the floor of the Chinook with the impact. The rear door instantly plunged fully opened.

'Out!' shouted the loady.

It was too late. We were already moving. Craig charged out in front of me and Trouty tried to follow. *'You're not going in front of me,'* I thought and flung my right arm across and in front of him. I stepped in front of Trouty as Leighton, one of the GPMG gunners stepped over Topsy and we charged out into Iraq. Craig was first, then Leighton then me.

My first steps in war sunk into mud, something that was so unexpected after the constant rehearsals in the desert sand, I had to force myself from stopping. Other Chinooks landed behind us as we fanned out as a troop, all our weapons poised, facing towards our objective buildings, just as we'd rehearsed. After a moment on the ground, our Chinook thundered back into the air.

Craig, walking along the line just to our rear, called me, Topsy and Chal to him. As the other troops Chinooks took off, I knelt next to Chal in the mud facing Craig.

'Right, you happy?' We nodded in reply and Craig said, 'OK, let's move off.'

The first airstrikes lit up the night sky destroying the Iraqi army positions outside of the MMS as the Chinooks cleared the area. As we moved towards our target buildings it all felt very familiar, like a constant life size déjà vu and I had to keep reminding myself that I hadn't been there before. A huge metal pylon towered over and in front of us and I recognised it from our relentless studying of the air photo. I could hear the constant drone of the A-10 Warthog ground attack aircraft and a C-130 Spectre gunship circling above us. The gut-wrenching brrrrrrrrr of the 30mm Gatling gun mounted in the nose of the A-10 Warthog vibrated deep in my stomach and huge explosions thundered nearby, shaking the ground around us.

Chal's section readied themselves next to a four-foot bank of mud and dirt and I moved forward to get a first look at my section's building on its other side. His first men sprinted across to their building and then the rest of the section followed. They quickly cleared through and I heard 'Building clear.' Over the radio shortly after. My section was lined up along the bank, with Craig next to me.

'OK Frank, move now,' came his hoarse whisper.

I crouched next to Shnaggle and Bucky, my entry men. It would be their job to gain a foothold into the building. I pointing to the side of the building that I wanted them to go to, then slapped Shnaggle's shoulder and ordered, 'Move.'

Shnaggle and Bucky sprinted 20 metres to the dull concrete wall on the side of the squat, square building, then it was mine and Dave's turn. We ran over joining Shnaggle and Bucky. As we lined up against the outside wall, we could hear someone talking inside. Whoever it was, they were clearly agitated and shouting in Arabic in a one-way conversation down a phone. The front of the building was bathed in white light, so I kept Shnaggle and Bucky in the shadows and grabbed Dave to see if there was another entrance we could use. There was a couple of windows that were about 6 foot high at the back of the building, that looked like they would be a struggle to use as an entry point. I couldn't see a way in except from the front and that meant we would have to go around into the light and expose the section. Craig started to get impatient and I could hear him asking for updates over the radio. Panic started to build in the pit of my stomach as I struggled to see a way into the building. I could also feel Craig's presence on the other side of the mud bank willing me on and the whole of Charlie Company waiting for me to get on and clear this tiny building so they could move on with the rest of their objectives. At that moment, the entire invasion of Iraq was waiting for me and I could feel 160,000 soldiers from 36 different countries on my shoulders. Titch came up on the radio asking me something, but I couldn't hear what he was saying. This was my time, this was my chance and I could feel my control of the situation slipping through my fingers like dry sand. Craig then jumped over the bank and came to move the situation on. He stood there in the shadows, making his own mind up what to do. In the middle of all this I had a very clear thought that I needed to act and quickly. This was my moment and I would regret forever if I let it go. And the depths of panic, there came clarity. Out of nowhere I remembered a piece of advice from my corporal's course. Take a Condor moment. Stop, do nothing a just calm yourself down. I did this, then knew what I needed to do and exactly how to do it.

'Craig I've got this.' I said, then quickly explained my plan and without giving him the opportunity to question, I acted.

'Titch.' I called in a loud whisper. He jumped over the mud bank and joined me. 'Mate, move your fire team over there.' I said pointing to the far end of the rear of the building 'And act as cut offs.' A 'cut off' would stop anyone inside escaping and would also be additional fire to the east if we needed it. 'I'm gonna get Chal's section to cover us moving round the front.'

'OK Frank.' said Titch, then moved off to get his team in place.

I radioed Chal to cover my team as we moved round the front of the building. He took a couple of seconds before his section moved into fire positions and then started putting down covering fire.

Shnaggle was crouched, on the corner of the building with Bucky poised behind him. Dave and I joined them.

'Right, we're gonna move round the corner and into the building, it looks like there's an entrance there.' I said. 'Ready?' I asked, then 'Move.' I ordered.

'I can't, they're shooting at me.' Shnaggle shouted.

'Well fucking shoot them back, dickhead!'

We had no choice but to take this building and the only way was to go around this corner. I couldn't order anyone into oncoming enemy fire. I knew I'd have to lead my section from the front. This was my job. Without hesitating, without saying any prayers and without overthinking it. I was here and, in that moment, I knew what I had to do. Amongst the deafening racket of a full-blown invasion going on around us, I pulled Shnaggle back from the corner and shouted, 'Right, we're peeling round, me, then Dave. Shnaggle you and Bucky follow and get in the building. Move.' I shouted and then followed my own command.

Day 37

I forced myself to row for an hour in the early morning as the coming dawn began to lighten the chaotic sea. The small flags at the stern clacked loudly in the strong wind. The waves had got bigger with frequent side waves smashing against the small hull and as the biggest waves rolled towards me, it often felt that I was in a deep, watery trench.

After breakfast I rang Leven.

'Hello Captain.' He greeted me over the crackling line.

'I can't hold more than two thirty degrees true,' I said.

'That's fine, you can only do what you can do.'

Leven's calming voice soothed me instantly. Leven had given me a waypoint that I was heading towards and the wind and waves were making it impossible to hold course. I was now over 20 nautical miles south of where I should've been.

'At this stage Captain, it's speed over course,' he continued. 'Go with the weather, there'll be plenty opportunity to claw back some west.'

Leven also said I could expect a few more days of big winds and big seas. During my off periods I found resting difficult. I couldn't relax as *Hope* was violently tossed about by the sea. As each rowing shift approached, I could feel the tension build inside and I had to force myself out of the cabin to row. As the day progressed, a dread of the coming night began to form in the pit of my stomach. Late in the afternoon, a huge shark suddenly appeared behind the boat. Its dorsal fin protruded ominously out of the rough sea a few metres behind the stern. It looked about three metres long and a lot fatter than I imagined a shark would be. As quickly as it appeared, its tail fin flicked at the surface and it disappeared down into the deep.

After my evening meal, I tried rowing in the moonlight but lasted only 30 minutes. The crashing waves forced me back in the cabin. I desperately tried to ignore the furious sea outside and relax but the thundering noises and the violent rocking of the boat made resting impossible. Suddenly, a huge wave crashed against the starboard side. It boomed loudly then rumbled as *Hope* lurched violently over to port, then tipped. I could feel her being pushed violently sidewards through the water. I pushed against the inside walls of the cabin, bracing myself for the inevitable capsize. *Hope*, listing on her side at what felt like beyond the point of no return, thundered sideways. I could hear the huge breaking wave consume her. The wave rumbled on, like it had travelled under the boat and away. *Hope* returned upright. I couldn't believe that she hadn't capsized, it felt that she had tipped right over. I gathered my thoughts, my heart thumping in my chest. I knew I'd have to check the deck to make sure nothing had been washed away by the wave. I donned my life jacket and opened the cabin door, holding the handle ready to quickly pull it shut again. With my head torch on, I leaned out and checked the deck, but everything seemed to be in place. I spent the rest of the night with my life jacket on just in case, trying and failing to get any sleep. I was on edge, anxiety coursing through every part of my being. I was desperately tired and tried to go within myself, searching for a sanctuary from the dread, but every thought and every emotion was tinged with fear. Just before dawn, the navigation alarms brought me back from an uneasy doze and I instantly crashed out of the cabin as quickly as I could, rowed *Hope* out of irons then reattached the autohelm. I'd gone 48 hours without any proper sleep and the near-constant dread was wearing me down. I felt exhausted.

Day 37 Logbook Entry

Position at 0800hrs (L) (1000hrs UTC) on 15th Feb 2019	*Distance travelled 82nm rowed at 225°t*
15°03' 852n 031°40: 786w	*Total distance 1902nm total*

1358nm to Cayenne

V strong winds all day and night @25kts-30kts at 220°t. Big breaking angry waves, very choppy with lots of side waves. Closest I've come to rolling last night at approx 12.30hrs L. Big side wave hit the boat, I was in the cabin and braced myself as she began to tip, luckily she came back.

Saw a large shark (2.5-3m), briefly on the surface then shot off before I could get a photo.

Water maker has a lot of water underneath it, approx 200ml, dried it out and will check on the 17th.

In hindsight I'm not certain that we were under fire but whoever was talking inside the room had got out. Perhaps they had fired back at us as they ran into the night or perhaps the Iraqi soldiers stationed outside the perimeter of the MMS were firing back at us. But as I moved around that corner, I genuinely believed I was going to get shot. I took a half dozen steps and dropped to one knee. Instinctively bringing my weapon up on aim, trying to blend my body into the wall. 'Move.' I shouted again and Dave ran around past and in-front of me. I raised my weapon as he did and snapped it back into the aim position as soon as he cleared me. Dave dropped to his knee a couple of metres further along the front of the building then Shnaggle and Bucky ran round and entered the building, Shnaggle had the good sense to smash the florescent light in the entrance as he ran in, killing the light. We were in. We swept through the building and soon I called 'Room clear.'

I could hear on the radio net that the other troops in Charlie Company had moved onto their objectives and were soon clearing their buildings. As planned and rehearsed in the Kuwaiti desert, my section moved west of the main MMS complex and linked up with the US Navy SEAL team who'd been guarding that area. We took our position facing east towards Al Faw town and started digging a fire trench. The C-130 Spectre gunship and A-10s flying above fired on targets outside the perimeter of the MMS and occasionally we'd hear huge explosions as JDAMs, artillery and pre-planned air strikes dropped on Iraqi targets close by. We used the fire trench as our sentry position covering the company's flank and built up the entrance to a huge concrete pipe next to our trench with sandbags. We settled into a watch routine and rested in the safety of the concrete pipe.

I didn't have any time to properly comprehend what had happened. Titch's fire team joined us in the building and we systematically cleared through it as a section, room by room as we had trained. But I'd faced my biggest fear and overcome it. Not fear of getting hurt, not even fear of death. My biggest fear was that I was a coward and when tested, I'd be found wanting. That night I crossed a bridge, even though I had teetered on the edge of disaster, I had regained control of myself first, then the situation and I'd never doubt my own bravery again. From that point onwards, whenever that voice in my head accused me of not really belonging in the Marines because I was a coward, I could ask, *'I stared down death on that corner, where's your evidence?'* I know absolutely that I thought I was most likely going to get shot and I still went round that corner because it was my job. I didn't know it at the time, but from that moment on, I could say to that small, scared boy, paralysed with fear and unable to help his Mum when she cried for help, 'It's OK to be frightened. This isn't your fault.'

Day 38

Today was Morale Saturday. It felt anything but. I was extremely tired having not had any proper sleep in over two days and the constant anxiety that tinged every thought and emotion was wearing me down. I knew I was well over halfway, but I also recognised that this was unsustainable. I knew that I'd have to find a solution, a coping strategy to deal with the fear that pervaded every part of my consciousness. Before I set off, I'd asked people to suggest audio books I could listen to whilst rowing. Amongst the worst suggestions was *Bratavia* by Peter FitzSimons. I got as far as the very first line, 'Bolinda presents this unabridged recording of *Bratavia*. A tale of shipwreck'.

A friend's son called Tom suggested the *The Chimp Paradox* by Professor Steve Peters. I had listened to it a few weeks before on the boat and thought the way it likened our primitive emotions to a chimpanzee rampaging around our subconscious easily understandable. I also thought about how one of the methods of controlling the chimpanzee it described, distraction, may be applicable to the situation I was in. Fear is one of our most primeval emotions, keeping us aware of dangers, but fear was now taking over everything I was doing. Before the strong winds and massive waves, I'd been looking forward to Morale Saturday and had saved as many treats as I could. I'd now use these to distract the chimpanzee. I'd save every morsal of morale I had on the boat, my favourite snacks, my favourite meals, the best music and favourite podcasts for those moments when the fear was unbearable, hoping it would at least take the edge off.

Although the big waves and strong winds continued, the sea had become more uniform, less choppy with fewer rogue waves and I was making good progress. As the larger waves crashed around me, I was careful not to pull on the oars and initiate a surf down the front of them. They were too big. Just as I settled onto the rowing seat to start my second daytime rowing shift, a small orange turtle about the size of a large dinner plate bobbed past *Hope* on the starboard side. I was still being pushed too far south and my Cross Track Error was increasing all the time.

I rowed the first nighttime shift in the light of a nearly full moon and I could feel the fear and anxiety build. I counted down the minutes until I could get back into the cabin. Once inside, the noise from the vicious breaking waves kept me awake. At about 9pm, the alarms sounded so I instantly sprang into the, by now, well-drilled action. After rowing *Hope* out of irons and reattaching the autohelm, I returned to the cabin. Adrenaline coursed through me, and the sound of *Hope* being battered by the enormous angry waves filled me with dread. Exhausted, tired and thick with fear, I decided to try and distract the chimp. I listened to one of my favourite books that I'd read almost 30 years before, *The Hitchhiker's Guide to the Galaxy*. The still familiar words were strangely comforting and at some point, I drifted into a deep sleep. I woke after about three hours feeling amazing. It appeared that distracting the Chimpanzee had worked, but soon the cacophony of bangs from the waves smashing against *Hope*'s small hull brought the fear into sharp focus again.

The wind and waves had shifted around from the north to more easterly so I got out and changed *Hope*'s course, clawing back some valuable west. I rowed for about an hour before retreating into the cabin. I settled down and restarted the *Hitchhiker's Guide* at the last point I could remember, then drifted off into a deep sleep again. I rowed the last hour of the night as the coming dawn began to lighten the sky and when I checked how far I'd rowed in 24 hours, I was happy with 84 nautical miles. What I looked forward to most on Morale Saturday was the whiskey, but I was so afraid of something happening, a small emergency like the autohelm popping off and me not being 100 per cent focussed when dealing with it, that I didn't touch a drop. I was scared that in the heat of the moment I would make a mistake that could prove catastrophic or worse, fatal.

Day 38 Logbook Entry

Position at 0800hrs (L) (1000hrs UTC) on 16th Feb 2019
14°13' 529n 032°50: 368w

Distance travelled 84nm rowed at 233°t
Total distance 1986nm total

1276nm to Cayenne

Big waves and strong winds continue, wind turned more E to approx 240°t in early hours.

Saw a v small turtle about the size of a dinner plate around 1300hrsL.

Autohelm came off again at 2100hrs Local. Still using the bastardised one.

The rest of 40 Commando took Al Faw town and the next day, against all our expectations, our bergens made it forward to us. We started patrolling the newly liberated town of Al Faw and guarding the MMS. Al Faw seemed like a ghost town with Saddam Hussein's picture everywhere. But it didn't take long for the local Shia population to tear down and vandalise the mini-shrines to his reign.

After a few weeks Charlie Company handed over responsibility for the MMS to another company and we started patrolling. The whole company would move from large building to large building that we'd occupy and utilise as a patrol base. From these patrol bases we'd conduct patrols of the local area for about 24 hours then move on. We ended up in a large industrial area where we cleared the old factories and warehouses one at a time. We sometimes patrolled as a section and on the second night there, I was leading my section on a patrol when we were called back early to the troop's patrol base. The rest of the troop were waiting for us ready to go out on the ground. Craig called me over and said that he had to go to the Company HQ location for an 'O' Group. The fact that Craig was needed at the 'O' Group meant that it was likely to be a Coy level operation. He led the whole troop out on a patrol to the Company HQ location where we went into a defensive formation. It was the middle of the night when we got there, and Craig went into an old building that HQ had occupied. We tried to get as much rest as we could. I was right outside the window of the building and could hear the mumbled voice of the Company Commander Major Dewer. After a couple of hours, Craig came out and called the section commanders together. Craig then gave us Quick Battle Orders, a stripped-down version of a full 'O' Group. He told us that we were going to follow one of the other troops out to a point about 2 miles away where we would occupy a 'Start Line', ready to be the 'Point Troop' on a 'Company Advance to Contact'. An 'Advance to Contact' is where troops line up and advance towards the enemy positions line abreast until they come under contact, (get shot at by the enemy), and then clear all enemy positions by attacking them. The 'Start Line' is the start point of the operation where troops get up and start walking on a bearing towards the enemy and the time is called 'H Hour'. My section along with Chal's were the point two sections of the whole Company and 'H Hour' was first light.

We had no time to really sit and comprehend what was about to happen. I passed on all the information to the section, by which time the lead troop were ready to move to the start line. We patrolled the two miles where we pushed through the lead troop to fan out and occupy the start line, on the other side of a tarmacked road.

As 'H Hour' approached, the ground we'd be advancing over began to reveal itself in the grey light. It was relatively flat and open for about 500 metres then it started to close in with buildings and scrub. I was full of apprehension as I strained to identify potential enemy positions, choke points and danger points, looking as far as I dared over the bun-line we were behind. Then as the days first light spread across the sky and exactly on H Hour, I pressed the pressel switch on my radio and said as clearly as I could 'prepare to move.'

Everyone in the section, me included, crawled back into cover and shuffled on our bellies a couple of metres to the left or right.

After a few seconds pause I pressed the pressel again. 'Move.'

Shnaggle, got up, sprinted in a zigzag about ten metres to his front then settled down into patrolling walk, then it was my turn with Dave the other side of Shnaggle. The whole section repeated the process until we were all moving forward in a spearhead formation, a large upside-down 'V'. Chal's section had done exactly the same on my left and so with our two sections in spearhead formation, we led the whole of Charlie Company across the first 500 metres of open ground. As we moved forward, I was giving the whole section orders on what we'd do in the event of any enemy fire and in this way, we moved across the ground, everyone knowing exactly what to do the moment we were fired upon. As we started to move through the more built-up ground with its buildings, roads, tracks and ditches, command and control became extremely difficult. Coordinating the movement between mine and Chal's sections was crucial, but we were by now used to working together and it all flowed well.

My section hadn't slept for over 24 hours, and it was by far the hottest day since landing in Iraq but we continued to patrol tactically across the ground. Near last light, we finally took up a position at a large crossroads. It was one of the hardest days' work I'd ever done. Unbeknown to us, earlier in the day the Iraqi army in the south had taken off their uniforms and gone home.

Day 39

Distracting the chimp seemed to be working. I remained scared most of the time, but it was manageable. The sun rose into a cloudless sky and the wind continued strongly from the north, north-east. I'd arranged to call Leven and hoping for some good news on the weather front.

'Hello Captain.'

'Hey Leven. The waves are still horrific,' I said. 'I can't get anywhere 250 degrees in these waves.'

'Don't worry Captain. It's speed over course at this stage. Just run with it and get what west you can. There's plenty of time and sea to correct your course.'

Leven's soft Scottish Borders accent instantly soothed my anxiety and I was glad yet again for having the world's most knowledgeable ocean rower in my corner.

'The wind's due to drop tomorrow at some point. You're making excellent progress, Captain. Keep at it.'

Throughout the day the wind continued blowing 25–30 knots, driving huge, steep waves. I'd listened to podcasts on science, history and culture hoping to improve my knowledge of the world whilst at sea. But listening with any attention whilst trying to run *Hope* at as oblique angle to the massive, angry waves as possible, striving to push west, was hopeless. Instead, I listened to music and as my anxiety levels increased, so did the quality of the tunes. Whenever a particularly big or nasty wave hit and the fear got too much, I'd allow myself to listen to my favourite tunes. I kept coming back to 'Get Lucky' by Daft Punk. The rhythm of the song fitted perfectly with my cadence rowing which then became almost a dance, allowing me brief respite from the menacing, crashing waves.

Through the night, the sea continued to rumble as the biggest waves broke and rowing was, at times, terrifying. Around midnight, the wind drifted to a northerly, but I was still able to maintain my heading, which wasn't as westerly as I'd have liked, but more westerly than I'd managed in the previous few days. Thankfully the full moon accompanied me throughout the night and when I wasn't rowing, I distracted the chimp with the *Hitchhiker's Guide*.

Day 39 Logbook Entry

Position at 0800hrs (L) (1000hrs UTC) on 17th Feb 2019
13°33′ 899n 034°02: 144w

Distance travelled 79.5nm rowed at 240°t
Total distance 2065nm

1197nm to Cayenne

Checked water maker no leaks found and no water underneath, will continue to monitor.

Big winds with big waves continued through the night, wind shifted to a more northerly from approx 0000hrs to 0400hrs. Managed to hold 240° but really need to start consistently getting around to 250°t. Wind due to drop in next 24hrs.

After lots of false rumours about relieving troops, mostly started by me, and just in time for Glastonbury, I finally got home in late June, having been away for nearly seven months. I surprised Billy and Harriet, who didn't know I was coming home. My friend took them out to the shops then brought them to the local pub for lunch where I was waiting. Their faces lit up as they cried, 'Dad' in unison as they ran and grabbed me.

Iraq had been the first conflict to have media embedded with forward units and the oft-hidden realities of war were splashed across the news. Claire had tried to shield most of it from the kids but it had come crashing down amongst their lives on the first night that we had gone in. Two helicopters had crashed and one of the fatalities had lived across the road. I was oblivious to this and hadn't considered just how deeply me being at war had affected Claire and the kids. But I saw it in the pure relief and joy in their faces and it shocked me.

I had a lot of time off work through the rest of the summer with owed leave and spent it with Claire and the kids trying to make up for the last seven months. I felt guilty for putting them through the mill. Living in Poole, Dorset, meant and we had lots of afternoons at the beach in Sandbanks. I'd pick Billy and Harriet up from school with their swimming costumes and drive straight to the beach.

As summer turned to autumn, I returned to Air Def' and immediately applied for the Military Ski Teacher (MST) course, the next level of ski instructor who'd teach MSI's who, in turn, would teach novices. The MST course ran alongside the MSI's in Rjukan, Norway.

Whilst I'd been away in Iraq, Claire had been working full time in Bournemouth and my Dad had been helping with childcare. He'd come to stay to see the kids and had made himself as useful as possible. Claire said that he'd been brilliant and be dry for weeks.

In late September, after I was drafted back to Air Defence Troop in Plymouth, my Dad continued to come and help Claire with childcare. Throughout our marriage, my Mum and Dad regularly visited from Essex, but never together. Whenever they did, those visits followed a regular pattern. It would start about 48 hours before they arrived with a slow burning dread at what was to come. With my Dad, the dread proceeded the inevitable drunken state that he'd turn up in. The proceeding argument would end with him retiring to whichever of the kids' rooms was given over to him claiming he had chicken flu. He'd stay in there for a 24-hour period of drying out. We'd hear moaning and whimpers throughout the day and night, after which he'd re-emerge as if nothing unusual had happened. He'd stay sober for a couple of weeks before announcing that he was just going to nip to the pub for 'a couple of beers'. That was the cue for him to leave.

Within days of just having 'a couple of beers', he'd be in the park with a bottle of spirits in a brown paper bag.

In my Mum's case the dread preceded the near-constant arguments. She would always be just one sentence from a full-blown argument with me over the most inconsequential of perceived transgressions. I'd even dread phone calls with her as they'd mostly end in an argument.

Out of the blue our relationship changed. My Mum was prescribed anti-depressants and she transformed overnight. The arguments stopped and she seemed a lot happier. I always felt that her unhappiness was directed at me, that she resented my existence and even that she hated me. But after she started taking medication, I felt like she finally became like the mother I wished I'd always had. The difference was stark and I noticed it straight away, but by then, the damage to our relationship had been done.

Since I was very young, I couldn't bear any form of intimacy from my Mum, even physical contact of any sort would make me flinch. When my Mum changed and became more normal, the lack of intimacy between us was more noticeable and upsetting to her. I tried my hardest to control the flinching, but it was so deeply ingrained within, I'd unconsciously flinch before I could consciously override the action. In contrast, where my relationship with my Mum dramatically improved, the periods of sobriety between my Dad arriving and leaving after only having 'a couple of beers', gradually became shorter.

In 2003 he could go a couple of weeks sober and had been invaluable in helping Claire with childcare whilst she was working, and I was away in Iraq. Both my kids adored him and they'd laugh hysterically listening to hear his funny voices as he created fantastical stories such as the time he escaped from witches who had him in a big pot. He farted and the witches thought he was boiling because of the bubbles, or the time he nicked a parachute during the war and his mate jumped off the White Cliffs of Dover. Seeing how my Dad was with my kids made me feel sad at what could have been.

Throughout our marriage, we'd alternate between having my Mum and my Dad stay for Christmas. After my Mum started taking antidepressants, my relationship with her normalised enough to the point that I invited both of them to Christmas. Unsurprisingly, it ended in a massive row. The argument started over swimming lessons. Although it was Christmas Day and he'd been drinking, my Dad seemed OK. He claimed that he'd taught me to swim, something he'd never done. My Grandad Horder had taken me with my Mum to swimming lessons and at six years of age, I swam a length of Dagenham swimming pool. As I swam, I could hear all the other parents in the gallery cheering us along. The swimming instructor swam with her arm stretched out in front of me. And she kept saying, 'Just keep swimming to my arm.'

And I did. At the halfway point, a boy who was swimming next to me gave up and climbed out of the pool, I looked over at him briefly and thought, *'I didn't even know halfway was an option.'* About ten metres from the end of the pool, my instructor pulled her arm away and told me to swim for the finish. As I approached the end the noise from the crowed grew as nearly everyone there was now cheering me and I looked up and saw my Mum and Grandad standing and clapping. For years, my swimming certificate and my 'O' level in Art were my only achievements. Both were framed.

My Dad was adamant that he'd taken me and I kept replying, 'No Dad, you didn't.'

I was standing at the end of the kitchen next to the cooker and he was at the other end of the room by the door. I saw him lose control as if it was in slow motion. He pulled his clenched fists up and sprang towards me. I reacted instinctively and without thinking, dropping my right shoulder. I instantly saw what was going to happen and I knew exactly what I was going to do. As a child, I'd imagined going back in time, like *Back to the Future* and finding my Dad in a pub with all his friends and knocking him out for what he did to my Mum. I'd imagined myself stronger and harder than him, but ultimately knowing that it was fantasy and that I could never be 'the hard man' like him. But now I was a Royal Marines Commando, I was immensely fit and strong, I had just led men in war and even if it was only in my mind, I'd faced down death on a corner of an Iraqi building. I was no longer that small frightened little boy that stood petrified at the door as his Mum cried for him to help her. I saw that realisation in my Dad's eyes and then spread across his face as he lurched towards me. His angry sneer morphed into shock as he pulled himself up. He'd only taken one or two steps towards me and he now steadied himself, with a hand on the back of a dining room chair. That was the end to the swimming lessons argument and the whole incident had only taken a second. My Dad took himself off to bed and it was never spoken of again. It's possible that he suddenly realised he was running towards his son and had regained his composure. But that isn't what I saw. I saw the anger in his eyes change to fear. I saw him for what he was, a weak man. Whatever caused him to drink, whatever demons that he carried, it was more than he could handle. I don't understand addictions, I don't have the reference to make sense of not being able to control your own actions, to not be able to make the conscious decision to not drink. I can empathise with someone who is addicted, but I don't understand the mechanism of addiction. My Dad's sister, my aunt Linda once said to me, 'Lee you may as well get angry at someone who sneezes who's got a cold. Your Dad has an illness.'

And that, to a certain degree, is correct. But my Dad wasn't just an alcoholic, he was a violent alcoholic. His alcoholism drove him to drink, but nothing excuses him from beating my Mum and me. I loved my Dad, and I still do. I'd wanted to be a hard man like him. To have a reputation, to be feared and respected. But in that moment, I saw him for the weak coward that he was. More importantly, I saw myself for who I was, I was so much more than my Dad.

Day 40

The day started with a perfect orange sun rising out of the sea and illuminating a few wispy clouds that hung along the eastern horizon. Infinite waves reflected the deep orange tinged with reds and purples on the eastern horizon changing to the grey smudge of the retreating night that clung on in the west. It was stunning. Big clouds hung around the northern sky and just as the sun rose clear of the horizon and turned from orange to brilliant yellow, the wind suddenly dropped to a gentle breeze.

The waves were still big, but almost immediately calmed down. They were less steep and fewer were crested with angry breaking white froth crashing down their front. I turned *Hope* more west and felt the miles slip away as she surged through the water.

On my first hour off, I noticed some sores in the very earliest stages of development and realised that I'd neglected to properly wipe salt off my body. I'd battled fear and fatigue for nearly four days in huge angry seas and my body had paid the price. I was determined to religiously wipe myself down after every rowing shift from now on.

The waves gradually became smaller throughout the day and by evening I started to feel good about rowing. The past few days of huge angry waves and near constant fear was over and I began to relax. I rowed my first nighttime rowing shift to the light of a near full moon that occasionally hid behind small clouds, then just before midnight, I was awoken by the sounds of crashing waves. The deep rumble of huge breaking waves filled the cabin and my heart sank. I thought the big waves had passed me by, but as I looked out of the cabin, it was clear that they were back. The wind hadn't picked up and was still a gentle breeze, but the waves were big, steep and were angrily breaking around *Hope*. They'd suddenly appeared from nowhere, there was no discernible change in the wind and no logical explanation for the size and ferocity of the waves. It was as if the sea was reminding me of who ruled out here. I stayed in the cabin as *Hope* was battered and then a couple of hours before dawn, they disappeared as suddenly as the appeared.

Day 40 Logbook Entry

Position at 0800hrs (L) (1000hrs UTC) on 18th Feb 2019	*Distance travelled 70nm rowed at 247°t*
13°06' 797n 035°07: 370w	*Total distance 2135nm*

1127nm to Cayenne

Good day rowing. Occasionally overcast with light to stiff breeze (10-15kts) saw a very small turtle about 3 inches in diameter.

Salt taking its toll on my skin. Having to religiously wipe down after every rowing session.

Brilliant sunrise this morning.

On track 1000nm on Wednesday

In January 2004, I deployed to Norway as a skiing instructor, something that I loved. From day one in the Royal Marines, I'd been surrounded by incredibly fit and strong individuals. I'd always fought hard to maintain basic fighting company levels of fitness and knew it didn't come naturally. But the cold and immensely harsh conditions of soldiering in the Arctic were a great leveller. For once I excelled. Often the fastest runners in a troop tended to have very little body fat and therefore struggled with the cold. I never had that problem. Also, the hard slog nature of operating in the Norwegian mountains better suited my good endurance fitness rather than purely cardiovascular fitness. I was also a good cross-country skier. Good skiing technique will always trump blind fitness. But mostly, I loved instructing. I relished trying different ways to get across the information that I wanted to impart. Different people learn in different ways and one exercise or method won't work for everyone. I found a real affinity with helping the weaker members of a ski group and took pride in watching them improve.

Halfway through the deployment I was called in to see the RSM, who told me that I had been drafted to the Royal Marines Commando Display Team and would be flying back to the UK early. I didn't want to leave Norway and another Corporal in Air Def', Lewie, wanted to go on the Display Team, something that is called a swap draft. I went to see the RSM and explained the situation.

A couple of minutes later Lewie and I were waiting outside the RSM's office. He called Lewie in and then immediately sent him back out the room.

'He wants to see you.' Lewie said.

I walked in and the RSM said, 'It's got to be you.'

'Why?'

'Whoever it is, has got to be made up to Local Sergeant and Lewie looks too young.' Local Sergeant is a temporary rank without the pay of a full sergeant.

'So I'm getting spammed because I look old?' I said affronted.

'Pack your kit, you're going.'

'But Sir, I'm a soldier. Poncing off round the country with a bouncy castle isn't me.'

He smirked, something I'd not see him do often and said, 'Get out. You're going back.'

And that was the end of the conversation. A couple of days later I was back at Royal Marines Poole, the base of the Commando Display Team. Fortunately, my old mate Scotty was the PTI in charge of the team. After he'd explained what was involved, I realised that I'd almost missed out on what was going to be the best draft I'd have in my career.

I had to play catch-up as the team had been together for a month before I arrived, but I soon got to grips with it. As a team we rehearsed an unarmed combat display and for shows that were near a large body of water, a hostage rescue where we'd abseil from helicopters into speedboats then assault the target boat, rescuing the hostage. The unarmed combat display was extremely physical. No punch or kick was pulled. I partnered with a Marine from Essex called Jay. We rehearsed again and again, making sure our nods and winks to each other before a boot to the stomach or a punch to the side, were slick and indiscernible to anyone else. In one part of the display, Jay would attack me with a metal softball bat and I'd duck under the first swing, dodge the second to my midriff, then duck under the third, grab Jay and throw him over my shoulder.

As we got close to the start of the display season, and after a particularly gruelling practice run, I said to Jay, 'Mate, I reckon I'm gonna save a load of money once we're on tour. There's no way we can do this after being out on the piss.'

'Yeh mate. Imagine getting banged out in front of a big crowd.'

We never did it sober. What followed was a continuous round of parties and for the single lads, a fair amount of debauchery, with the odd helicopter abseil and a bit of unarmed combat in front of thousands in-between. It was a fantastic three months on the road and as close to living like a rock star that I'll ever experience.

At the end of the display season, I was called in to see the Boss who told me that I'd been picked up for a Senior Command Course, the course needed for promotion to sergeant. I'd stay under the umbrella of the Royal Marines recruitment but move to a Visibility Team waiting for my seniors in the new year. The Vis' Teams travelled around schools and colleges promoting a career in the Royal Marines. But my promotion to sergeant was put back a year after I had an argument with an old banister in a decrepit hotel in Kettering. It gave way and I fell several floors, breaking my pelvis. I had been incredibly lucky. Internal bleeding with a broken pelvis is very common and I'd laid unconscious for several hours at the bottom of the stairs. If I'd ruptured one of the many arteries that pass through the pelvis when I fell, I'd have undoubtedly died at the bottom of a rickety staircase in a rundown, decaying hotel in Kettering. Not the end I'd hoped for.

After a two-week stay in hospital, I was back home in Poole ready to spend Christmas in a wheelchair. In the new year I started my rehab. My seniors had been put back from January to August which gave my rehab a clear focus. I worked as hard as I could, running in water up and down the pool and weight training without putting pressure through my pelvis. I was unable to walk and in the wheelchair for three months. Progressing to walking with crutches felt like real, tangible progress. Rehab is extremely hard work, but the rewards are almost immediate and often there to see daily, encouraging me to work harder. As spring turned into early summer, I felt like I was in a race to get fit enough for the rigours and physical demands of the seniors.

During summer leave we moved home from Poole in Dorset back to the same village we'd lived in on Dartmoor. I joined the Senior Command Course at the end of summer leave in August 2005. The course starts with a test of physicality on the bottom field with the same bottom field tests that I did in training, 13 years before. It wasn't a mandatory pass or fail test, more a first look at you from the course DS and is affectionately known as 'Corporals in Destress'. Having been in a wheelchair just four months before, I knew that it would be a real hurdle, but my hard work through rehab paid off. The crux of the seniors is the two command appointments whilst on exercise. One as a troop sergeant and one as a troop commander and both need to be passed. Whereas I had started my junior command course doubting my credibility as a Royal Marine, let alone a corporal, I started my seniors confident in my own abilities. I actually enjoyed it. After a couple of months, I finished the course with a good pass, coming a very credible 4th out of 29. There's lots of Royal Marines who'd look at that and shrug, saying '*Yeh, that's not too bad*'. But for me, looking back at that little boy in the school hall being told by the recruiting sergeant from the Marines that 'I wasn't what they were looking for', I was immensely proud of a 'not too bad' pass.

Day 41

Good rowing conditions continued and the angry waves disappeared as mysteriously as they'd arrived. A brilliant sunrise heralded a new day.

After I'd entered my daily stats and filled out the logbook I rang Leven and told him about the big waves and how they'd just appeared from nowhere.

'You often get that after a big weather system as a kind of lag,' he said.

'What's the wind look like?' I asked.

'Nothing like you've had over the last few days. It's all looking fairly consistent. 10–20 knots in places but nothing untoward. Saturday is looking like a slow wind day, though. We need to talk currents, Captain. There's a strong current that runs north along the South American coast called Southern Equatorial Current. In places it runs at a couple of knots. We know it's there and we'll have to get some south in. Drop maybe 100 to 150 miles south of our line and use it to come up into our finish line.'

I ended the call with Leven feeling confident for the rest of the row. Leven's voice, always filled me with composure and confidence. I felt that at least one of us knew what they were doing.

The wind shifted just after breakfast and started blowing from directly behind *Hope*. The flags at the stern of the boat flapped in the breeze. Just after lunch I noticed a fishing boat running backwards and forwards about a kilometre to the east of my position. She looked fairly big, maybe 30+ foot and I was worried in case she was trawling. I didn't want to snag her nets. I tried calling on the radio but got no reply. I kept track of her through the afternoon as she zig-zagged back and forth, always just on the horizon to the east and behind me.

A shark's fin appeared five metres behind *Hope*. I scrambled to get the GoPro and film it underwater as it followed, but it flicked its tail and disappeared under the waves. I sat on the rowing seat shielding the GoPro's screen from the sun to see if I captured any footage of it. I couldn't see any sharks but noticed the hull clustered with barnacles. Late that afternoon the fishing boat disappeared north as a full moon rose out of the ocean to keep me company.

Day 41 Logbook Entry

Position at 0800hrs (L) (1000hrs UTC) on 19th Feb 2019	*Distance travelled 65.5nm rowed at 242°t*
12°35' 954nm 036°06: 616w	*Total distance 2201nm*

1062nm to Cayenne

Wind 10-15nts from NE (flowing 245°t) straight forwards to Cayenne. V large fishing boat approx 4-6nm to NE running N and South, backwards and forwards for most of afternoon. Tried calling on radio to no avail, wanted to warn them in case they were trawling.

Saw the tail of a shark slap the surface of the water approx 5m to the rear of the boat but again wasn't quick enough with the camera. When reviewing the footage noticed how fouled the bottom of the boat is, may be an opportunity to get in and clean it on Saturday, not sure if it's worth it. By Saturday I should be 800nm away. Just under 2 weeks.

Having been promoted to Sergeant, I drove to Faslane in Scotland to take over as a Troop Sergeant within Fleet Protection Group Royal Marines (FPG). I conducted my handover in a motorway service station on the M6 as my predecessor was driving south back home. I was taking over from Phippsy in one of the squadrons that guard Britain's Nuclear deterrent known as Op' Fardrum and I should've taken his over-keenness to get away from FPG as quickly as possible as a sign that it wasn't the greatest job in the Corps.

I drove into HMNB Clyde and made my way to the Sergeants' Mess. Usually when joining a new unit, you are required to complete a joining routine. This involves going around each department and getting a stamp on a joining routine card. It can be completed in a morning if all the departments are in but usually takes a day and a skilled practitioner of the joining routine can make it last a week. I wasn't due to start my new job and its inevitable joining routine until 0800 the next morning. But half an hour after driving through the main gate I met my new sergeant major, Dave and within 20 minutes, I was 'behind the wire' in charge of a troop of Royal Marines guarding Britain's Nuclear deterrent.

When I Passed out of training, the thought of one day being a sergeant myself seemed so far away, it felt almost unobtainable. But I knew that should I ever make it to sergeant, I wanted to be like Sid McCarthey, my Troop Sergeant in training. He treated us recruits like he was our Dad. He laughed with us, joked with us and when we needed it, handed us over to the corporals to be thrashed. If it ever got to the level where Sid thrashed us, then we knew that our transgression was sufficiently bad enough to upset him. A sergeant who just constantly shouts and berates his men has nowhere to go should he need to escalate a bollocking. Sid's thrashings therefore had gravitas. When we upset Sid, we knew it, but more importantly, we felt that we had let him down. A sergeant's job in war, first and foremost is 'bullets and beans'. Making sure those that are under him have everything they need to complete their mission, then comes the welfare of his men, a very close second. Outside of conflict a sergeant's job becomes the welfare of his men first and foremost and that's where a sergeant like Sid excelled. My close friend Budge, who I had met years before when our wives were pregnant, had a mantra on leadership within the military. Budge was an incredibly fit sergeant major in the Army who'd done the Commando course as a young soldier and had spent the majority of his career within Commando Forces. I liked Budge and respected him enormously. His mantra was simply, 'Standards. And the men come first'. 'Standards' means that as a leader, you have to maintain every standard that you expected your men to adhere to, be that physical, appearance and bearing, professionalism or effort. And the men come first, simply means that in everything you do, you put those under your command first. I wanted to be like Sid whilst keeping Budge's mantra sacrosanct. That was the sergeant I attempted to be from day one.

Keeping a troop of Royal Marines fit, motivated and out of trouble in a completely mundane but important and high-profile job like guarding Britain's Nuclear Deterrent took every scrap of experience I had. I was aided by a brilliant Squadron Commander called Dave and the best Sergeant Major I have ever worked for, also called Dave. Dave the Sergeant Major was tall, extremely loud and overly northern. His favourite saying was, 'Stop being a Cunt,' and he'd shout it at the squadron at every opportunity. He cared deeply for his men and they loved him in return. And that made my job as a Troop Sergeant easy.

Because of the boring nature of Op Fardrum, the unit tried to get as many of the lads rotated through going 'behind the wire' and then on to more interesting jobs within FPG. That meant that my troop was constantly changing with lads rotating through and it made creating a troop spirit and building cohesion difficult. When we weren't 'behind the wire', we were training, either in America, cross training with the USMC, or on the south coast at Lydd and Hythe ranges. The training packages were good and the runs ashore even better.

After a year behind the wire, I change squadron which meant no more 'going behind the wire' which was excellent news and soon I was knocking on the door of my new sergeant major. I walked into his office to introduce myself and froze in shock. I was immediately transported back 12 years when I'd been going through training. I poured a half-drunk cup of coffee out of the window of our accommodation. Almost immediately I heard someone shouting from a couple of floors below and like an idiot I looked out of the window. Below me was Paul, then PTI corporal in his formerly immaculate white vest and white shorts that were now splattered with brown coffee. He pointed up at me, his face pinched in fury and screamed 'You can fucking stand by!'

Blood drained out of my face and had spent the following days in a state of dread awaiting his retribution. But as the days passed nothing happened so I gradually forgot about it. But as I now stood gawping at him, the memory flooded back and with it fear and dread. It must have been buried deep within my subconscious for all those years. Paul quizzically looked at me as I stood floundering in his doorway and realising that I probably look very odd, I explained what had happened. 'I can't remember that,' he said.

'Well I thought I'd forgotten all about it, but obviously not,' I laughed.

He gave me a brief rundown of the new troop and highlighted a young marine called Blinky, currently on Commanding Officer's warning for discharge.

'Don't worry about him,' said Paul. 'He'll be a civvy soon'.

My new troop had two senior corporals called Bondy and H. Bondy was a very intelligent, level-headed PTI and one of the hardest marines I'd met. H was a tough Geordie with a reputation for fighting whilst ashore. I liked them both instantly.

On my first exercise, Blinky, the marine on a warning, stood out for his hard work and professionalism. I'd come across many marines in my career who weren't 'camp soldiers'. They invariably looked like 12 kilos of crap in a 6-kilo bag whenever in uniform, cared little for the tedium of camp life but flourished in the field. Blinky was beyond that. I'd never come across someone so bad in normal military life, but so good on exercise in the field. The difference was stark. After the exercise I called Bondy and H into the office.

'What's going on with Blinky? He can't be that shit on camp and that good in the field. Something's not right.'

'I don't know,' replied Bondy. 'It's all single man grots in the accom. Once they finish work, we rarely see them. It's not like the grots in a unit,' referring to commando units where marines tended to live in four and two-man rooms with communal areas for socialising.

'OK. I want an OP on him,' I said, meaning I wanted him watched.

Day 42

A good night's rowing gave way to a stunning sunrise and then a morning of near-perfect rowing conditions. I clambered into the stiflingly hot cabin at noon with the bright, burning sun directly overhead. I closed the hatch door, set my alarm for 1pm and lay on the thin mat to rest. Almost instantly I was raised from my slumber by the navigation alarm beeping. I sat up and looked at the nav' system. It flashed the 'Loss of GPS Signal' message. I opened the hatch and before I clambered out to right *Hope*'s course, I glanced at the two navigation screens at the stern. To my horror, the speed and the course over ground screen was blank. My heart sank. I quickly rowed *Hope* back on course and set the hand steering lines, then clambered back into the cabin. I switched the Nav System off then on again and the 'Loss of GPS Signal' message flashed back up again. I clambered out of the cabin and checked the rear hatch to see if there was anything obviously wrong. There wasn't. I sat on the deck, the ocean stretching out to the horizon all around me and suddenly felt so helpless and alone. I thought how critical the nav' system would be in the final stages of the row and how tricky the run into South America was going to be.

Rowing into the Canaries to get repairs wasn't an option this time. Feelings of desolation and deep anguish overwhelmed me. I blubbed. A single blub. Then suddenly thought, *'Well that's not going to help'*. The absurdity of the situation that I was now in, sat in the middle of the Atlantic Ocean on a rowing boat and feeling sorry for myself was almost comical. I tried to think logically and decided I needed to immediately strip the navigation system panel down to check all the connections. After checking methodically that everything was connected and there wasn't anything obvious wrong, I replaced the panel and called Tim the engineer in Gibraltar. He answered immediately and started to talk me through finding what had gone wrong. He gave me instructions, that I'd then get on with, then call him back with the results. It was time consuming, but methodical. After a few hours of systematically ruling out all other options Tim suggested the issue was at the back of the boat. Everything in the cabin was working and all the components talked to each other. I gave Tim a rundown on all the spares on the boat, including leads, junction boxes and two new navigation screens.

'Try the junction box first as that's the easiest fix,' he said.

'OK, I'll call you back in ten,' I said then clambered out of the cabin and down the stern to the rear hatch. The junction box was screwed to the inside wall of the hatch in the most awkward position and ten minutes turned into nearly thirty before I was ready to plug the leads into the new junction box. I sprayed the ends of the leads with

WD40 to clear all the moisture out, then plugged them back into the new junction box. The rear navigation screen immediately sprang into life and I very nearly screamed with joy. The navigation system in the cabin was on and working. I called Tim back.

'OK', replied Tim. 'Somehow moisture has got into the junction box.'

'I've got the EFOY in the rear cabin,' I said.

'Yeh that won't help. They produce a lot of water vapour. If you don't need it, I wouldn't run it. If you can, try and waterproof the junction box in some plastic bag and tape it up.'

I again thanked Tim, then taped some plastic bag around the new junction box. I collapsed in the cabin exhausted and recorded a video diary on the cabins GoPro.

The time was just after 5pm and I was completely wiped out. I decided to give myself a well-earned rest and start rowing again at the start of my nighttime rowing shifts at 8pm.

The sun set over my right shoulder and as it did the wind dropped to nothing. I rowed through the night in the light of a full moon reflected in the small waves around me and the luminous green glowing clouds of bioluminescence that faded to inky blackness behind *Hope* as she surged through the calm sea. After my midnight–2am shift, I laid in the cabin drifting off to sleep when I started to hear the clicks, high-pitched squeals and buzzes of dolphin chatter. I heard them from the edge of sleep like they were calling me back into consciousness. The cabin amplified whatever they were saying to each other. I opened the hatch to see how close they were and hoisted myself up onto *Hope*'s deck. A dolphin breached the surface of the dark water right next to me, moonlight glinting off its smooth skin, before it dived effortlessly back into the deep. More dolphins came around the boat, chattering away and I felt like I was transported to the very edge of their world. I sat watching them as they swam like Sirens from the deep. The ethereal beauty of the moon glittered off their skin and was reflected in the ripples as they dived down into the deep black water. I was spellbound. They eventually drifted away so I returned to the cabin and slept deeply for a change.

Upon waking I realised that I was two-thirds of the way across the ocean. It had been an eventful 24 hours on the boat.

Day 42 Logbook Entry

Position at 0800hrs (L) (1000hrs UTC) on 20th Feb 2019
12°11'. 129nm 036°53: 974w

Distance travelled 52.5nm rowed at 244°t
Total distance 2053.5nm

1009nm to Cayenne

@ approx 12.15hrs AIS failed then complete nav sys. Rang Tim at Sheppards in Gib, after 5 hours fault finding problem was with junction block or leads at end of boat. Changed and water resisted as far as possible with plastic bag and tape. Problem possibly caused by moisture/condensation from Efoy. Whilst fixing problem USB ports on control panel broke, using cigarette lighter port.

Wind dropped to zero through the night. @0200hrs dolphins around the boat. The moonlight glinting on their bodies and fins as they broke the surface of the water was beautiful.

Bondy soon came to see me to report back on Blinky. Within the base there was over 20 illegal bars operating and Blinky had been frequenting them every night with a couple of friends from the Navy.

'Right. I'll have a word with him but I need you to keep an eye on him at night.' I said.

I went to see Paul the Sergeant Major and it was a hard sell getting him to give Blinky another chance, but in the end he agreed. I then spoke to Blinky and laid it all out for him. This was a pivotal moment for him so told him how impressed I was with his performance on the exercise and how I couldn't square that with the marine who was on CO's warning for discharge that was stood in front of me.

'Blinky, you can't go on the piss every night. The way you're going you'll be kicked out within a couple of months. I've had a word with Bondy and H and the troop are gonna help. But ultimately, it's down to you.'

Within six months, Blinky was off CO's warning and been accepted on a driver's course. He rang me from Lympstone when he passed to thank me.

In 2007 I was too old for Special Forces, even if I hadn't failed selection twice, but since my six-month tour of Northern Ireland in 1994 alongside the Joint Support Group, volunteering for special duties had lurked in the back of my mind.

Over the years JSG changed its name to the Defence HUMINT Unit and Tommo, my mate from Air Def' troop, had passed a DHU selection. Unlike UKSF selection, there wasn't an upper age limit. I volunteered for Special Duties and was loaded on the next selection and in June I drove to the home of the Intelligence Corps with little idea of what to expect.

The first morning, I paraded in front of an old redbrick building, along with 63 other hopefuls ready for a BFT, a mandatory military physical test. It's a basic standard of fitness for the army that consist of press-ups, sit-ups and a mile and a half run. At the end of the run, we were given a coloured bib with a number to be worn throughout the selection. Mine was Green Seven. The next two days was a continued round of roleplay, classroom-based navigation and memory exercises. Group discussions and interviews followed, and it was all very unmilitary. I had no idea of what they were selecting for and how I was doing. There was no feedback or results. I knew that at some point there would be a cut, where I could expect over three quarters of the selection to be sent back to wherever they'd come from. I was desperate to be on the right side of the cut when it came.

The third morning started with a thrashing in the woods just outside camp. It wasn't anything I hadn't done before, although it lasted a couple of hours. There seemed to be a lot of instructors scrutinising everything, making it impossible to hide in the group. There was lots of fireman carries, uphill crawls, stress positions and was, overall, pretty unpleasant. After running back to camp, and a quick change, I sat in the classroom awaiting the next detail.

An instructor entered. 'When I read out your colour and number, dress outside.'

He then read out a series of colours and numbers. I realised that this must be the cut and waited to see if I was part of a large group or a smaller one. If I was part of the larger group then I knew I'd failed. Green Seven was called out and I got up and walked out. More candidates followed and I counted sixteen of us. I had made the cut.

The afternoon consisted of fighting each other in the gym and a few other tests after which two others were sent home.

By the final morning there was only 14 of the 64 that started. We were officially told that we'd passed. I left selection on the Thursday afternoon and drove straight to one of the wettest Glastonbury Festivals on record. After the selection and the very wet Glastonbury, I returned to FPG with only a couple of months to push until my DHU course.

Day 43

The sun rose into a cloudless sky and for once I was grateful. I needed the solar power to charge the few luxuries I had. The large solar panel on top of the front cabin produced enough power to keep the boats navigation systems going and run the water maker every other day. The water maker was the biggest draw on the batteries and I could only switch it on at midday with good sunlight. I also needed to charge the satphone, which didn't take much power, but every other electrical item I had was a luxury.

I had a waterproof Bluetooth speaker that played music, podcasts and audio books that I streamed from my phone. Both needed regular charging, but I considered them as near essential as they kept me sane. My electric toothbrush was a real luxury, having fresh breath and clean teeth is always a little boost to morale. But the biggest draw on power was the small fan I had in the cabin which became an unbearable sweatbox during the day. When I switched the fan on, I could see the voltage in the batteries drop, but the blessed relief of a tiny breeze across my face a body was bliss. Without the EFOY, I would have to be more stringent with my power output management.

As I rowed through the day, the sea appeared near perfect for rowing, but I was only managing to maintain between two and two and a half knots. Occasionally my speed would drop to almost nothing and it would feel like I was pulling the boat through treacle, but the sea looked exactly the same with no discernible difference. The oars would suddenly stop mid stroke. I'd pull with all my strength to try and keep some forward momentum for a couple of strokes, then suddenly, *Hope* would be released from whatever it was that held her. I assumed that I was rowing through an area of sea with a lot of strong swirling currents.

When I wasn't rowing through strong currents, the boat still felt sluggish. I knew the hull was covered in barnacles and that I'd have to get under her to scrub them off. It was a prospect I wasn't looking forward to after seeing the shark two days before. I also needed to re-enter the hatches to again check for water ingress in case that was weighing *Hope* down.

A near full moon rose out of the sea behind *Hope* as I began my nighttime rowing shift.

In the morning I was disappointed with only 54 nautical miles travelled in the last 24 hours. The conditions seemed good enough for much more.

Day 43 Logbook Entry

Position at 0800hrs (L) (1000hrs UTC) on 21st Feb 2019
11°45'. 938nm 037°42: 808w

Distance travelled 54nm rowed at 242°t
Total distance 2107.5nm

955nm to Cayenne

Boat feels sluggish. Feel that the conditions over the last 24hrs warrants a 60-65nm in 24hrs not 54. As soon as the conditions allow I will have to scrub the bottom of the boat something I'm not relishing especially after seeing 2 sharks.

Need to make time to get into all the hatches to check for water. I know the rear starboard one has a couple of inches.

In August 2007 I drove to Chicksands with Tommo, both of us ready to start the new DHU course. Since my tour of South Armagh in 1994, JSG had not only changed its name to the DHU but was now deployed to wherever British soldiers were on the ground. In 2007 that was Afghanistan and Iraq.

The high tempo of operations in both theatres not only stretched the Armed Forces in general, the need for intelligence, in particular Human Intelligence (HUMINT) increased beyond its capability. The high level of training meant that the course had a very high failure rate. It was producing too few agent handlers for what was required for both the Iraq and Afghanistan conflicts. To address this, the DHU split the course in two and introduced two levels of HUMINT Operator, the Basic (BHO) and Advanced (AHO).

From the very start, the course wasn't like any other military course I'd attended. Tommo and I started with 20 others from a wide and varied background, from a Colonel, an Apache pilot to Able Seaman and Privates from the Army. There was no rank and we wore civilian clothing. All military terminology and slang was banned. We had lessons in a wide range of subjects that often drifted into the bizarre. From practical lessons in chatting to people in pubs, how to tell lies and lessons in RIPA 2000, the complex laws that govern agent handling. All of this would have been enjoyable if it wasn't for the relentless pace and as there was no syllabus we didn't know what was happening from one lesson to the next. We had no time to ourselves, and I soon settled into a routine of trying to learn something new, failing it, then moving onto the next stage. The constant failures were soul destroying and I felt that I was always behind the curve. After a couple of weeks, we drew our pistols from the armoury. Once out they were carried 24 hours a day and we spent every free moment practising the motion of firing, called 'dry firing', in preparation for the next stage of the course, security and survival training (SST).

The SST was placed in the middle of the basic course, between lessons on how to debrief an agent and lessons in how the agent and handler meet, called mechanics. We spent the two weeks shooting, running and fighting. The days were extremely long and arduous and if I thought that I was behind the curve on how to debrief an agent, it was about to get a lot worse. I was a terrible shot with the pistol.

The SST culminated with a fighting assessment and a shooting test that was a mandatory pass before moving onto the advanced course. Throughout the shooting test day, I was praying for a miracle that just didn't come. I'd failed before the end of the basic course. But before I could feel sorry for myself, there was still the fighting assessment. It began with a thrashing in the woods for a couple of hours to ensure that we were exhausted before the assessment started. From the woods we ran straight into a circuit in the gym to ensure that the levels of exhaustion were maintained as we waited our turn. We were led, one at a time into the squash courts and then jumped by two assailants wearing full body padded suits and boxing gloves. The actual fighting part of the assessment only lasted three minutes but felt like a lifetime.

Deflated at not passing the shoot and, by extension, the SST, I moved to the next part of the course. Only a couple of others had passed the shoot and by now the course was down to 19.

How an agent handler and their agent come together without arousing suspicion is often done in plain sight and is beautiful in its simplicity. However, behind the simplicity is an intricate dance of mind-boggling complexity. The basic course only covered the very basic mechanic. Again, I settled into the familiar pattern of learning something new, fucking it up, then moving onto the next phase.

By the time we started the final exercise, I was struggling, but so were others. Each one of us in the team took it in turns to oversee an operation, with the rest of the team in a support role. When it came to my turn in charge, I mistook the rules governing how to operate and wrongly aborted the whole operation. It could not have gone any worse. On the way back, the instructor who was marking me, tried to console me by saying, 'Don't worry Frank. I failed the course first time as well.'

As I drove back to base and despite being devastated at almost certainly failing the basic course, something strange happened. I suddenly understood what it was I was trying to do. I'd been focussing on each of the different parts of the operation in isolation. Stupidly, in my head I hadn't put them together. I had the sudden realisation of what we were trying to do and why. Up until that point I'd been badly muddling through each of the lessons from the course in turn, instead of the operation as a whole. My turn as the lead had come and gone and I'd missed my opportunity, but the final exercise was still going. My final few jobs in a support role went without hitch for a change, wholly due to finally understanding the whole point of the course.

The course is unique in that you can attain a higher score by making a mistake and rectifying it, than if you hadn't made the mistake in the first place. On the final job, after realising I'd missed a turning, I called it on the radio in a textbook fashion. But I also knew that the chances of me passing the basic course were infinitesimally small so I needed something special. By calling in my missed turn, I'd done the proper thing, but if I could correct the action myself and carry on with the operation, then that would be something special. Having no time to think about the consequences, I quickly came up on the radio and gave my intentions and turned right. I turned into a particularly complex set of suburban roads, many of which I knew to be one ways and dead ends. I gambled on a 50/50 chance that the road I was turning into wasn't a dead end or no entry. The gamble worked and I managed to get back onto my route and complete my part of the operation.

On getting back to base, 'End Ex' was called, bringing to a close the basic course. The whole course sat waiting to be called into the office by the chief instructor for our results. The first name called entered the office, then shortly exited looking visibly upset. After five other failures, it was my turn. The chief instructor sat opposite a small desk. He was a short, mousy haired Sergeant Major from the Parachute Regiment and throughout the course had been quite dry.

He smiled and said, 'Well Frank, I'll put you out of your misery. You've passed the Basic, but as you know you won't be going onto the Advanced.'

I couldn't believe I'd passed. It was obvious that they'd called us into the office in reverse order and that I must have just scraped it as the first pass on the course. I thought again about that 50/50 right turn I'd gambled on during final Ex and how if it was a dead end, I definitely would have failed the Basic. Sometimes our lives change direction through massive cataclysmic events and sometimes they change on the flip of a coin.

Day 44

The day started with the sun again rising into a cloudless blue sky.

I ached from the previous days' exertions pulling on a sluggish boat through currents that felt like they were clawing at the underside of *Hope*. I settled into my daytime rowing routine and to my disappointment, it was much of the same as the day before. One minute I'd be flying along with a small swell behind me at a decent three knots. The next, I'd row into an area of sea that looked as if it was boiling. The small uniform waves that were about a metre and a half high, would suddenly disappear and the surface of the ocean would start bouncing up and down like a pool with a wave machine on. *Hope* would stop in her tracks and the oars would feel like I was pulling them through setting concrete. The sea would toss *Hope* around like a cork in a washing machine and the constant toing and froing made rowing near impossible. One second the port oar was high out of the water and the next it had plunged back in and the starboard oar was out. After what seemed an age of frustration and back-breaking effort, the sea would suddenly go back to uniform swell coming from behind. There was no discernible difference in wind speed or direction or in anything I could see on the surface of the water. When it stopped, it just stopped. I couldn't see the patches of boiling-like water behind *Hope* as I rowed out of them. It was as if someone suddenly turned the wave machine off.

Desperate to not dip below 50 nautical miles rowed in 24 hours, I pulled on the oars with all my strength. It was hard graft in the blistering heat. Even in the patches of sea that were good rowing, *Hope* still felt sluggish.

In the afternoon, I checked the hatches. I imagined them full of water sloshing around in the bottom, slowing me down, but they were nearly all dry. I spoke to Leven on the satphone.

After I explained to him about the rowing conditions, he said. 'You're doing great there, Captain. You're coming into an area of strong currents, and it'll be a bit stop and go.'

The North Atlantic Equatorial current had been pushing me along nicely from Cape Verde, but I was starting into an area where the North Atlantic Equatorial current bumped along next to the Equatorial Counter current that pushed back towards Africa.

'It'll be bumpy here and there, I reckon.' Leven continued.

'I still don't think that accounts for how slow I'm rowing,' I said. 'I haven't been able to get under the boat and clean the hull. I've checked all the holds in case they were full of water.'

'There's another strong current coming up that runs north along the length of South America,' he said. 'We may have to drop south about a 100-150 miles and use it to come up into the finish. I'll look at the data and calculate how far. But keep your heading for the now.'

Early in the evening, two shooting stars lit up the sky to the north of me as the moon rose in the east. They streaked, about thirty seconds apart, from almost directly overhead, down the sky to just above the horizon. They both burnt brilliant white and broke up as they fizzed through the upper atmosphere like fireworks.

I rowed through the night, shadowed by a waxing gibbous moon that glistened in the small waves. When I hit water that was full of current, boiling away on the surface, I gave up rowing and waited to be pushed through it. What was difficult in daylight was impossible at night, even under a near full moon.

Day 44 Logbook Entry

Position at 0800hrs (L) (1000hrs UTC) on 22nd Feb 2019	*Distance travelled 53nm rowed at 243°t*
11°22'. 366n 038°51: 056w	*Total distance 2160.5nm*

903nm to Cayenne

Long hard slog of a day. Boat still v slow. Checked all the hatches, a little water in the rear (autohelm) cabin and rear starboard hatch. Sea is one minute light swell (1.5m) and uniform then the next boiling over with waves all over the place and from difference directions, one minute gliding @ 3kts then without any notice it's like rowing through tar. There's no different in wind, speed or direction.

2 amazing shooting stars last night @ approx 21.50hrs L.

Wet rations tomorrow.

AFGHANISTAN

After getting the results, the whole course was taken up to our new unit, the DHU. If I thought the course was strange, then the unit was a lot stranger. We were kind of met by the RSM. He was a tall Warrant Officer First Class from the Intelligence Corps, with a mop of mousy brown hair and the look of a man who'd never heard of Christmas. He stood to the side of the Chief Clerk, a bespectacled RAF staff sergeant who mumbled his way through the joining admin. The RSM then sneered at us, presumably for having the audacity to join his unit, then stalked off without saying a single word. One of us from the course was needed to deploy to Afghanistan early in the new year and I volunteered.

On previous deployments, I'd been part of a unit that was deploying together. I'd known what I was doing and what to expect. This time I was deploying on my own, to join a small team, none of whom I knew well and to do a job I'd never done before. It was very disconcerting. Home was also different. When I'd left to sail to Iraq, war was a distinct possibility, but still far from certain. This time, Afghanistan was constantly in the news. Leading up to every deployment, there was always a tension in the air at home, this time it was magnified tenfold.

Eventually the day came when I said a hard goodbye to my family, jumped into the car and drove back to work to collect my weapons and kit, ready to fly to Afghanistan. I'd volunteered for Special Duties because I wanted to be someone I could be proud of. I had scraped a pass on the basic course. But now I was travelling alone to Afghanistan and I stood out wearing civilian clothes and sporting a beard. If I thought that I looked special, or Gucci in military slang, then I was about to come crashing down to earth. I flew from RAF Brize Norton with a quick refuelling stop-off in Cyprus.

Whist waiting for the plane to refuel, I met my old RSM from FPG who was now the Corps RSM. He'd been awarded the Queen's Gallantry Medal for gallant and distinguished service in Northern

Ireland and had also served as an agent handler with the JSG, the forerunner to the DHU.

'What's with the civvies and beard?' He'd moved on from FPG before I volunteered for Special Duties.

'I volunteered for the DHU.'

'Oh aye,' he said. "Course it's all changed since my time. They've got these basic handlers now. I mean what's the point of a basic? You're either a handler or not.'

He spent the next five minutes berating the basic qualification. I was too embarrassed to tell him I was a basic handler.

I landed in Kandahar Airfield (KAF), a sprawling metropolis of temporary buildings, tents, hangers, runways and barbed wire in the Afghani desert south of Kandahar city. Soon after I was on board an American Blackhawk helicopter, flying over the vast empty desert of southern Afghanistan with dusty, grey mountains hazy in the distance. Southern Afghanistan is predominately empty arid desert. Most of the population live in the 'Green Zone', the lush, green, fertile farmland irrigated by a myriad of small, interconnected ditches and canals that are fed from the Helmand River.

Before the Taliban, the powerbroker at village level was the local Mirrab who was in charge of which fields are irrigated and when. After the rise of the Taliban, this power switched to the Mullahs, or religious teachers. However, the irrigation ditches remain the lifeblood of southern Afghanistan and the Green Zone is where all the fighting took place. Occasionally we'd fly over the odd Kuchis encampment of ragtag tents, goats and a few camels. The Kuchis are a nomadic Pashtun people clinging on to an ancient way of life in the face of natural disasters, loss of ancestral pastures and pressure to settle by the Taliban.

The flat featureless desert gave way to a few fields as we approached the Helmand River and the Green Zone. We plunged down to skim over villages of a couple of mud huts, ramshackle buildings and large compounds with people looking up as we passed overhead. Moments later we were swinging down out of the sky and landing in a large, oblong HLS, surrounded by a tall HESCO wall. HESCO consists of large, square, metal wire crates, with hessian material inside filled with rubble and placed one on top of the other like huge Lego bricks. Main Operating Base (MOB) Lashkar Gah would be my home for the next six months.

Lashkar Gah is the Provincial Capital for Helmand Province and the MOB was the home to Head Quarters, Task Force Helmand, the name given to the mainly British Area of Operations. Lashkar Gah sits on the Helmand river in a large area of fertile land irrigated by both the Helmand and Arghandab Rivers. After the noise, downdraft and dust settled from the departing Blackhawk helicopters, I took in my surroundings. I gathered my baggage, weapons and guitar and walked over to a waiting battered blue 4x4 Toyota pick-up and Andy, my new boss. He greeted me and then drove the short distance to the detachment compound. After dumping my kit, I was introduced to the rest of the Det'.

I was to be mentored by Jules, the only other basic handler in the Det'. She was a Royal Navy cartographer and had an impressive reputation for handling the more politically sensitive cases and writing intelligence reports.

For something that was only glossed over on the course, intelligence reports are the bread and butter of agent handling. It is the ultimate product of everything we did. Doing it right is critical, not only ensuring that the information from an agent is correctly reported, but also for their protection. Knowing what could be reported at what level and protecting the agent, took an intimate knowledge of the agent and their background. I spent every spare moment reading up on the cases that I was Co-Handler on. As well as report writing, every single interaction with an agent was followed up with a detailed written report and once every year the agent would need to be authorised, which took a couple of days solid writing.

I had dreamed of being an Advanced HUMINT Operator, of operating undercover behind enemy lines, but now it appeared that I was an office clerk. And not a very good one. I left school with O' Level Art and only got GCE English as a corporal, paperwork wasn't my strong point.

As a basic handler, who'd just scraped a pass on the course, I wasn't trusted with the more complex and therefore interesting cases. I had an overwhelming sense of being pointless and when not feeling pointless, I felt completely out of my depth with paperwork.

Within weeks of getting to Lashkar Gah, the harsh reality of what we were doing was brought home to me. I was sat in the office that was incomprehensibly called 'the binner', when George, one of the two Bootnecks in the Det' came and found me.

'Do you know Big Dee Mullvihill, the Air Defender?' George was a short, wiry WO2, with a thick black beard who exuded competence. I told him I did.

'Mate, I've got some bad news for you. He's been killed in an IED.'

Big Dee was a rugby-playing Plymovian with a massive frame and bigger smile. I'd known a few lads killed in Afghan and Iraq, but Big Dee rocked me. He was a big character in Air Defence Troop and universally liked and respected. He was very close to my mate Doch and I instantly thought about him. I knew Doch would take the news badly. Our job as agent handlers was first and foremost force protection. Finding and reporting where the IEDs were planted, getting real-time information on attacks and preventing them. I felt frustrated that I wasn't being effective, a spare part in the Det' and therefore a bit pointless. From that moment on, every report of an IED blast or an ambush that killed a British soldier, resonated as a failure and drove home the feeling of how useless I was being.

Day 45

I started Morale Saturday with my favourite breakfast, scrambled eggs with peppers and potatoes with added fried chorizo and lots of chilli sauce. After breakfast I treated myself to fresh pants and later that evening, I knew that I would be eating the first of my boil-in-the-bag rations. Today was also wet rations day. Wet rations day was not only a welcome change to my diet, it was also a massive milestone in my row and signalled that I was now on the 'row in'. I had looked forward to today, but now it was here, I felt flat. Even though I was wearing fresh pants and had eaten my favourite breakfast I felt exhausted and 853 nautical miles to Cayenne seemed a very long way.

It had been ten days since I'd last scrubbed the underside of the boat and I knew I'd need to scrub it again soon. Although there was little or no wind, there was still a small swell coming from behind. But even if it was flat calm, the currents were too strong to contemplate getting out of the boat. Not only would it be dangerous, but it would also be nigh on impossible to get properly under the boat with the currents tugging at me. I knew the wind was due to pick up again in the next few days and although that would help push me along, it also meant that there was no foreseeable weather window for getting out of the boat and cleaning the hull.

Since leaving the Canaries, I'd rowed my heart out chased by Ralph and I'd kept that pace after Ralph pulled out. I had hit a period of massive waves and angry seas that had mentally and emotionally drained me, now the boat was slowing down as I hit the strong Equatorial Current. I was becoming completely exhausted. The patches of unrowable sea with strong currents continued throughout the stiflingly hot day and into the night. It was likely I'd not get over my 50 nautical miles target and had rowed hard in the patches of sea that were rowable. I finished my last night rowing session at 8am and collapsed into the cabin. But as I completed my stats for the last 24 hours, I was disappointed to be half a mile short of fifty.

Day 45 Logbook Entry

Position at 0800hrs (L) (1000hrs UTC) on 23rd Feb 2019
11°26'. 260n 039°19: 045w

Distance travelled 49.5nm rowed at 252°t
Total distance 2210nm

853nm to Cayenne

Another hard 24hrs rowing for only 49.5nm, really feel there should be more miles for effort. Wind and speed due to pick up pm tomorrow or am Monday. 1st day of wet rations ☺

The Det was commanded by Andy and next to him was Liam, the Det' Sergeant Major. Liam was keen for all the handlers to get orientated around as much of the area as possible and understand the complexities of Afghan tribal affiliations. I began to realise that this underpinned a lot of what I thought was incomprehensible about Afghanistan. I was co-handler on a couple of cases run by Beau, a young but very capable and ambitious Guardsman.

Throughout Helmand for two weeks in early April, everything stops. Every man, child, and thousands of migrant workers flock to the poppy fields to start bringing in the opium poppy harvest. Harvesting opium is labour intensive. Taliban fighters put down their Kalashnikovs and pick up the small, curved knives used to slit the poppy seed pods and collect the sap and join everyone else in the poppy fields. The lucrative trade in raw opium had become the lifeblood of the Taliban's insurgency and took precedence over fighting.

Liam sent Beau to FOB Jackson in Sangin and a couple of days later, I joined him. FOB Jackson was named after Private Damien Jackson of the 3rd Battalion, Parachute Regiment who was killed fighting the Taliban there in 2006 and the FOB was built around two massive buildings. One served as the Headquarters and had the main Operations Room on one side and the Galley tent on the other. The other Building was a large, oblong, three storied shell without walls. The sides were sandbagged up and it served as the Sustained Fire (SF) building with a 50-calibre heavy machine gun post on the roof. Both buildings were on either side of the large and fast flowing Nahr-e-Saraj Canal that flowed south from the Helmand River and split FOB Jackson in half. The western side was much larger, with the HQ building, main accommodation, shower blocks and the LZ, and it bordered the Helmand River. The eastern side as well as the SF building, also comprised a small ornamental garden and the main entrance to the FOB. The whole FOB was surrounded by a huge HESCO wall just over half a mile in diameter.

Sangin district covered the Green Zone from Nahr-e-Saraj in the south and Kajaki in the north. Most of the agriculture in the Helmand and Musa Qalai valleys was given over to producing opium poppy. The town of Sangin sprawls either side of Route 611, the main road that runs the length of the Helmand River from near Gereshk to Kajaki. It is also where the Musa Qalai Wadi, the route from Musa Qalai town joins the Helmand. Sangin was strategically important because it was where all the smuggling routes in northern Helmand, from Bagran to the mountains north of Kajaki converged before heading south to the Pakistani border.

I skimmed low and fast over the green zone in a Blackhawk helicopter that followed the Helmand River to Sangin. In every direction fields were mauve or purple with poppy flowers. They gleamed iridescent and reminded me of the purple tonic trousers that mods wore when I was a kid. I wondered how something so beautiful could be the cause of so much pain.

I was met by Beau who helped carry my guitar to my new accommodation, a large oblong building made from HESCO. The local soldiers were from the Yorkshire Regiment and I wasted no time in getting out on patrol. The Green Zone immediately surrounding Sangin was beautiful, in places it seemed like a biblical paradise. Lush green trees lined irrigation ditches with small bridges and walkways leading off between compound walls. Further out from Sangin town, every field was full of people harvesting opium. There was almost relief as the truce of the poppy harvest paused the fighting. As the harvest came to an end, the uneasy calm continued. Everyone expected to start fighting at any moment and every patrol was tinged with nervous excitement, but nothing happened. Up until that point the Taliban had been fighting in much the same way that the Mujahideen had fought the Russians. They ambushed the Russians and fought conventionally with a superior knowledge of the ground against a largely conscripted and poorly led army. They'd tried the same tactics against professional soldiers, who were largely better led and equipped and been mostly beaten.

Most soldiers who served in Afghanistan would describe the Taliban as brave to the point of stupidity. But that had taken a huge toll. From that poppy harvest the Taliban started to change tactics and rely more on IEDs and stand-off ambushes to direct confrontation with ISAF forces. In 2009 IED attacks across Afghanistan were up 120 per cent over 2008.

I returned to the Det' in Lashkar Gah in May to several changes. Tommo had joined the Det and Jules my mentor had left. In charge of both KAF and Lash' Det's and our company commander was a tall female major from the Intelligence Corps called Nicky. She wrote my mid-tour report and to my surprise it was glowing. I'd scraped a pass on the Basic course and had felt completely out of my depth in the Det', but I'd worked hard to gain as much understanding as possible and felt that the hard graft had paid off.

In early May I rescued Hannah the puppy, not realising how that one small act would change my life and eventually lead to me rowing across the Atlantic.

Nicky was replaced by a major from the Parachute Regiment called Paul and Liam was replaced by Suzie, who had been my DS on the Final Ex of the Basic course. Suzie had a very different way of working compared to Liam and they were very different characters. I struggled to adapt to the way Suzie worked and felt like I'd regressed.

I went out on as many patrols around the local area as possible and spent four days with a team of SAS reservists mentoring the Afghan police. We patrolled in armoured Land Rover snatch vehicles to several police outposts north of Lashkar Gah town. They were ill-suited to Afghanistan and particularly susceptible to IED's. Soldiers saw them as death traps.

An Intelligence Corps Corporal called Sarah would often pop round to the Det' to see Hannah. Sarah was there to say goodbye to her when she started her long journey back to the UK. A week later, Suzie came into the binner and gave me the news that Sarah, along with three members of the reservist SAS unit, had been killed when their snatch vehicle detonated a huge IED. It happened to be in virtually the same area and on an almost identical patrol as the one I did with them a week before. I didn't know Sarah well, but her death rocked me.

A week later I returned to the UK for my RnR and walked directly into the Glastonbury festival. It was a million miles away from the madness of Afghanistan. I kept thinking about Sarah and Big Dee and how everybody here in the festival was utterly oblivious to what was happening in Afghanistan. I was stood just inside the Acoustic tent, a huge blue marquee near the entrance when Billy and Harriet ran in, both jumping into my arms. I'd gone from Helmand in Afghanistan to the Glastonbury festival in under twelve hours. I was in a daze and struggled to adjust to the change but was glad to see Claire and we tried to make the most of the short time I was home. Later that night we were sat in a tea and toast tent talking about anything other than Afghan when from nowhere, I suddenly felt a crushing sense of grief and sadness well up. It overwhelmed me and I instantly burst into tears, sobbing uncontrollably.

My RnR flew by and it felt that I had just blinked and I was back in a hire car driving to RAF Brize Norton. I only had a couple of months to push until my End of Tour and I was just looking forward to getting back to Afghan' and getting it cracked.

Day 46

Aching and tired from the previous day's rowing in the stiflingly hot, still air, I was relieved when the flags at *Hope*'s stern began to flap in a welcome breeze. It not only cooled me as the sun beat down from a cloudless sky, it began to drive a small swell behind. Every so often, small regular waves would disappear and suddenly be replaced by waves in every direction. *Hope* would bounce from side to side on the surface of a chaotic, boiling sea. My course over ground would suddenly change dramatically as *Hope* was pushed south as the strong currents swirled around me. Rowing was extremely difficult as I was bounced from side to side.

In the patches of ocean that weren't so affected by the currents, I tried to make as much headway as possible. I'd pull hard on the oars, but it felt like I was pulling a big anchor behind me. With every pull on the oars, I imagined the barnacles under *Hope* clawing at the water as *Hope* tried and failed to surge forward. Eight hundred miles seemed a long way and I knew that I wouldn't get a chance to get under the boat to scrape them off in the foreseeable future. I thought about using a piece of rope under the hull and by pulling it from side to side it would scrape them off. I told Leven of my idea later in the afternoon on our scheduled call.

'We had the very same problem on a crossing and tried that exact thing,' he said. 'But it made no difference at all. The little it did do wasn't worth the effort.'

I resigned myself to rowing the rest of the way with the boat feeling this sluggish, and it filled me with dread. I felt so tired. Just getting out of the cabin and rowing on my shifts was becoming difficult. Every inch of my body ached. I concentrated on only thinking about getting over 50 nautical miles in 24 hours and not how far I had left to row.

The currents again played havoc with my night rowing as *Hope* was tossed from side to side in the chaotic ocean. I completely gave up trying to row in the pitch black before the waning gibbous moon rose into a cloudless sky just before 11pm. I clambered back into the cabin defeated. It took a massive effort to get out and row for the remaining night shifts. I was relieved I'd rowed 58 nautical miles when I finished in the morning.

Day 46 Logbook Entry

Position at 0800hrs (L) (1000hrs UTC) on 24th Feb 2019
10°14'. 265n 04°11 309w

Distance travelled 58nm rowed at 243°t
Total distance 2268nm

796nm to Cayenne

Wind increased through the day but strong currents are now pushing me south of my line. One minute the sea is normal with a regular small swell (1-1.5m from NW), then it's boiling with no discernible direction or change in wind speed or direction. It's un-rowable in places, in fact I gave up after an hour last night, the boat just rocks from side to side.

At present and for the last couple of hours my heading is 260°m but cog 230° but in bits where it appears boiling COG fluctuates between 225° – 250°t in seconds.

After a quick stop-off in KAF to collect my weapons, I was soon in another helicopter, flying across the desert to Lashkar Gah. Nothing much had changed in my absence and I tried to get back on with the rest of my tour from where I left off. I'd struggled to adapt to the way Suzie worked and felt I was starting from scratch. The more I tried the worse it seemed to get and to make matters worse, she loved Tommo.

Suzie had been my DS on the basic course final exercise and it seemed obvious that she didn't think I should have passed the course and, in fairness, she may well have had a point. But that didn't change the situation.

In the final week of my tour, I was called into Paul's office to get my 'End of Tour' report. It was shocking. It read that I wasn't suitable for HUMINT operations, I wasn't recommended for another operational tour with the DHU and I wasn't recommended for the Advanced Course. I wasn't expecting anything like my mid tour report, but the finality of what was written was shocking. It was an absolute nail in the coffin of any further career within Special Duties.

'Well that's not very good.' I said to Paul.

'I know. I didn't think you'd like it.'

I pointed out that there were instances within the report that were used as examples to my shortcomings that were factually wrong. Paul explained as nicely as he could that the report was standing and that was that.

It reminded me of the bad report years before from Jez when in Air Def'. It was also factually incorrect.

Determined not to make the same mistake, I went to see Andy. I went through the report line by line explaining where it was wrong and asking for real examples of supposed shortcomings. I knew I was far from perfect as a first tour basic agent handler, but nothing Andy could say justified the report, and he knew that.

Finally, I said to him, 'The real problem here is that my mid tour report doesn't reflect the end of tour at all. So what you are saying is that I, all of a sudden, became absolutely shit or that Nicky was wrong. Neither of those stack up, mate. We both know that the only thing that has changed is a new OPSWO.'

'OK, so what do you want me to do?' Andy asked.

'You're gonna have to rewrite it mate,' I said.

The day before I flew out of Lashkar Gah, Paul called me into his office. He started by saying, 'I've never had or seen a personal report rewritten in my entire Army career.'

I'm not sure it was meant as a compliment, but I took it as one. He then read my new end of tour report. It was a major change from the original one.

I flew out of Lash' and spent the night getting drunk in the new KAF Det' bar. Everyone drank into the night talking nonsense, listening to Pink Floyd's 'Dark Side of the Moon' whilst watching an impressive lunar eclipse. At midnight I realised today was not only the day I flew home, it was my birthday. As a blood-red moon slowly vanished in the black sky above the jagged hills south of Kandahar, I felt that the universe had come together just for me.

Day 47

I had a breakfast of chicken and mushroom pasta, my second favourite boil-in-the-bag military ration. I'd opened a day's rations and immediately found my favourite sausages in beans, but decided to save it for Morale Saturday.

I continued to pull the heavy boat through strong currents interspersed with areas of near-perfect rowing conditions. Even with the waves and wind behind her, *Hope* felt like a dead weight. Every sinew, muscle and joint ached from the exertion of pulling on a heavy boat. I felt utterly exhausted. It was a deep-down tiredness beyond anything I'd experienced before.

As I rowed through the day, the areas of strong currents where the sea felt and looked like it was boiling gradually subsided and I hoped that I was coming through the worst of them. The day wore on into the afternoon and the hot sun beat down over my shoulder from a cloudless blue sky. From directly to my right I suddenly heard a very loud 'Pshhhhhhh'. I almost jumped out of my rowing seat and immediately looked down to where the noise came from. In the sea right next to the boat was a huge sperm whale and her calf. The 'Pshhhhhhh' noise came from the mother as she spewed a cloud of mist out of her blow hole, then sucked in a lung full of air. I could see the white scars on her bulbous forehead and body as the pair gracefully dived under *Hope*. I quickly thought 'camera', but then panicked as it looked like they'd tip the boat over. I breathed in a lung full of whale's breath, it stank of rotten shrimp and halitosis. It made me gag. They slowly disappeared under *Hope*, their tails gracefully arching out of the water then sliding back in, following their huge dark grey bodies. I grabbed my iPhone that was on deck and waited to see them on the other side of the boat, hoping to get a picture. And waited. Then after what seemed an age, they both breached again about 200 metres to the north out of camera range. It was amazing. I felt so lucky to have been in touching distance to one of the oceans iconic creatures. I was still smiling five minutes later when I heard the same 'Pshhhhhhh'. This time from 50 metres behind. Another mother and calf breached and then slid back under the waves on the same journey north as the first pair.

Day 47 Logbook Entry

Position at 0800hrs (L) (1000hrs UTC) on 25th Feb 2019
10°12′ 600n 41°01: 99w

Distance travelled 60nm rowed at 241°t
Total distance 2318nm

736nm to Cayenne

Continued day of strong currents and disturbance in sea state and rowing conditions. Improved through later afternoon/ evening.

Saw 2 sperm whales (I think) appeared right next to port side of the boat. They were travelling north. They were about 1m away and I thought they were going to tip the boat over. They swam under the boat and off north before I could get a photo. Approx 5 mins later another pair appeared at rear of boat approx 50m away going in the same direction. 1st pair were so close I could smell their breath from their blow holes, amazing.

I went back to work in September 2008 and in my absence the unit had changed a lot. Out had gone sauntering around in civvies for a couple of days a week and in had come uniform, an almost proper working week and a semblance of a command structure. This meant I now had a boss and a Sergeant Major.

My new boss was Nicky, my company commander at the start of my tour, and I nodded a 'Morning Boss,' as I passed her office on my way to meet my new Sergeant Major in the office next to hers.

'Come in Frank,' He said as I knocked at his door. 'I'm Wez.'

Wez stood to shake my hand before we both sat down. Wez was a very young-looking Intelligence Corps WO2 with mousey blond hair and an open and friendly demeanour. He asked about my tour. I explained as diplomatic as I could about my change in fortunes with the change in OPSWO.

Wez said, 'We can't send you straight down on the advanced course.' I noted the 'We' and took it to mean him and Nicky. 'It wouldn't be in your best interests anyway. And another basic tour wouldn't be good for you. I think you'd benefit most from going down on the course as a basic instructor for at least a few months then going onto the advanced course.'

I walked out of Wez's office and nodded a greeting as I passed Nicky's door. I had an overwhelming sense that I was being looked after. I'd never met Wez and hadn't really had much to do with Nicky my new boss, even when she was in Lash'. I was reminded of the PRC before I joined the Marines and the Sergeant Major who'd called me back into his office and told me I would be a good Marine. There was the same feeling that someone had seen something in me that maybe others hadn't and I was being given a chance.

I felt quite nervous and uncomfortable going back down to the course as an instructor. Many of the instructors from my course were still there and we all knew how utterly useless I was as a student. Vinny, the instructor who marked me on the final exercise became my mentor.

On one exercise when following a student Vinny said, 'You know what, Frank? No one gets mechanics on the course. Everyone muddles through as best they can. You only really understand mechanics when you start teaching them.'

Vinny did his best to make me feel less of a fraud as an instructor on a course that I barely scraped a pass on. I started fitting in as an instructor and just before I started working on my second basic course, I was told that I'd be going onto the advanced course. I couldn't join students I had just been instructing, so I sat out instructing the basic course.

Before the start of my advanced course, the chief instructor of the SST had changed and with him so had the course. The new instructor was an intense, wiry WO2 from the SAS called Gaz. Gaz had brought an old friend from the RAF Regiment called Tommy to help instruct pistol marksmanship. Tommy was 'Yoda with a pistol' and had got Tommo through his shooting test. Gaz very soon identified me as one of Tommy's' special children and I was taken off to the side. Tommy had a near-continuous smile and spoke with a cockney accent.

After some one-to-one coaching from Tommy, I stood in front of a target and fired using a counterintuitive technique that he'd shown me. After I unloaded, I looked at the target with five neat holes in the centre, all right next to each other and then at a smiling Tommy.

'How the fuck has that just happened?' I said with genuine bewilderment.

I've still no idea how the technique that Tommy showed me works, but I passed the shooting test. The SST culminated with a live firing exercise and two days of tests in Kent where all the skills learnt over the previous two weeks were put to the test. I passed and passed well.

The advanced phase of the course flew by in a flurry of extremely long days, lessons in advanced mechanics, test exercises, planning and recceing jobs culminating in a ten-day final exercise. The difference from the basic course was stark. I'd been blinkered by constantly failing every aspect of the basic course and never considered the actual reason behind everything taught until the very end of a disastrous final exercise. On the advanced course I was confident in knowing what I was doing and more importantly, the 'why'.

We were called in one at a time for our course results, the first three failing the course. If they were calling us in reverse order, then I came a very credible second. I had a couple of weeks leave that was owed that led straight into Christmas leave. I returned to the unit in January 2010, ready to deploy for a second time, this time as an Advanced HUMINT Operator.

It'd been a far from straightforward journey from selection, through the basic course then my first tour as a basic handler. But Tommo and I were two of only three from around 120 who started selection to have passed. That was something to be rightly proud of.

Day 48

Strong easterly winds began blowing through the night and built a decent swell behind *Hope*. By morning, the waves were quite large, steep and occasionally breaking around me.

Hope surged down the front of them in perfect rowing conditions. Any satisfaction of getting pushed closer to Cayenne was tempered by my previous experience when the waves were terrifyingly huge. The fear from those four days of huge 30–40-foot waves still lurked within, raw like a festering wound. I knew the strong winds were with me for the next couple of days and hoped that the waves wouldn't build to the same size as before.

I continued to row through patches of strong currents, and my COG would dramatically shift to the north. Over the previous week, the areas of strong currents were inconsistent in where they pushed *Hope*, sometimes south, sometimes north and other times she'd almost stop dead, as if being pushed back. But the last couple of days the currents were consistently pushing *Hope* north. In between areas of strong current I was managing a very respectable three and a half knots, then without warning, the sea would boil, my oars would stop dead as if in custard and *Hope* would slow to an almost stop as she was pushed north. I reasoned that I was leaving the Equatorial Counter Current behind and starting to hit the Southern Equatorial Current that pushed north along the South American coast. It was a sure sign of progress and that I was now on the run in to Cayenne.

Through the second half of the night, a half-moon occasionally broke through the clouds to illuminate the pitch-black sea. The strong winds continued, and rowing was hard in the infrequent combination of the moon poking through the clouds and a regular swell behind *Hope*. The rest of the time, in the pitch black or in areas of strong current, rowing was nigh on impossible. I struggled for motivation and getting out for every rowing shift, was an increasing challenge. I felt utterly exhausted. In the morning I was pleased with 73 nautical miles rowed and with 665 nautical miles to go, ten days to reach Cayenne was a distinct possibility.

Day 48 Logbook Entry

Position at 0800hrs (L) (1000hrs UTC) on 26th Feb 2019	*Distance travelled 73.5nm rowed at 237°t*
09°44'. 147n 042°10: 802w	*Total distance 2401.5nm*

665nm to Cayenne

Another day of strong currents pushing me N of the line and lots of periods of turbulence in the water.

Saw either a v large shark or medium to small whale that followed the boar for about 2 mins, again couldn't get a phot.

Overcast most of the day with a strong wind. Speed dropped significantly when I hit the strong current pushing me N.

Maybe 10 days to go ☺ (despite that I have zero motivation)

After completing Pre-Deployment Training, in spring 2010 I was ready to deploy back to Afghanistan. The 12 months between the summers of 2009–2010 would prove to be the costliest of the war in Afghanistan and the bloodiest and most violent fighting took place in and around Sangin, the small town on the Helmand River where I'd spent six weeks in 2008.

My upcoming tour coincided with 40 Commando Royal Marines' deployment to Sangin, so it was deemed a perfect fit for me to go straight out to Sangin as a Forward Deployed Operator (FDO) to provide HUMINT directly to them. In the lead-up to my deployment the news was full of casualties from Afghanistan, particularly Sangin. Royal Wootton Bassett became the focal point of a nation's mourning as the whole town lined the streets as funeral corteges of fallen soldiers passed through from nearby RAF Brize Norton. Throughout 2009 and the beginning of 2010 it was almost a daily occurrence. It was a very strained period for the family. Every service family who has had to wave goodbye to loved ones has felt the tension that builds throughout the household for weeks beforehand. In the early years of our marriage, Claire and I had argued a lot before long deployments. Later we recognised the tension for what it was and had learned to mitigate for it. But as my departure date to Afghanistan came closer, there was an extra intensity to the tension that ran through the house. It was difficult to hide the anxiety everyone felt, especially the kids.

My imminent departure was heralded the night before by the dropping of the hire car that I'd use the next day to drive to RAF Lyneham. After a particularly stressful night of all the family trying and failing to be as normal as possible and a day of checking I had everything I needed, the time came for me to say goodbye to Claire and the kids. Harriet was going to stay with her friend who lived in a nearby village, so the plan was for me to say goodbye to Claire and Billy then drop Harriet to her friends and then continue onto work.

'I'll be OK I promise,' I said to Claire on the doorstep, trying to reassure her as best I could. We hugged, there was a few tears as I said goodbye to Billy with a pat on his head. 'Be a good boy, alright mate?'

'Yes Dad.'

'Love you.' I said as I turned towards the car.

'Love you too.' Came their reply in unison.

The drive through the Devon lanes to Harriet's friend was awful, we both tried to talk about normal things but as we got closer to her friend's house the more upset Harriet became and when we arrived, she was in floods of tears. Her friend came and hugged her as she sobbed. I said goodbye as best I could then started to drive away. After a mile I had to pull over as I couldn't see through my tears. I was sobbing. Leaving Claire and the kids was extremely traumatic for me, but more so for them. In all my years in service and the countless goodbyes we as a family had endured, this was by far the worst, and an all too familiar occurrence for service families up and down the country at that time.

A day later, I landed in KAF, which by now was a huge, sprawling, desert metropolis and home to nearly 50,000 soldiers, medics, mechanics, chefs, cleaners and contractors from a hundred different nations.

Going to war in KAF was a very different experience to what soldiers in the Forward Operating Bases experienced. Many FOBs lacked basic sanitation, often there was no fresh water and of course, FOBs were where the actual fighting took place. The Det in KAF was used as a staging post for all the DHU Operators flying in and out of Afghanistan. I was expecting to only be there for a matter of days before flying forward to Sangin. The KAF Det was also the staging post for all the DHU alcohol that was smuggled from Kabul to the other Det's and the KAF Det always had a healthy bar fridge. Afghanistan was a dry military theatre with alcohol banned for all troops; however, I was looking forward to a few beers with the lads in the KAF Det before I flew out to Sangin. I was met by my good friend Mike and he helped carry my kit to my temporary room. As soon as I saw him, I could tell something was wrong. The office where all the Operators worked from was nicknamed the Binner and when I entered the Binner, the atmosphere was awful.

'What's wrong with them lot?' I said to Mike referring to the Operators in the Binner.

'This is a broken Det,' he replied.

Before I could ask anything I was summoned to see Paul, the OPSWO. The office he shared with Mark, the boss, was across a very small courtyard opposite the Binner. Rank within the DHU was extremely flexible, most soldiers would be promoted by their respective regiments in line with their own promotional requirements and would bear little or no reflection to an Operator's experience and often performance within the DHU. This meant rank had little relevance and it was experience as a Handler that counted making first names the norm with all but the most senior ranks.

On the door to their office was a big sign that read 'Knock & Wait'. This was a bit unusual as the Boss's office in all other Dets was almost always open. I knocked and waited. And waited a bit more, then knocked again thinking they hadn't heard my first knock.

'I heard you, just wait,' came the muffled reply from within.

After another wait a voice shouted, 'Come.'

I opened it and stepped inside. Hunched over their laptop computers was Paul and Mark Ian. Both ignored me so I just stood there in an awkward silence. After what seemed an age Paul, a short un-athletic, middle-aged man looked up at me with as much faux indifference as his weasel face could muster. 'Erm, you're not going to Sangin,' he said.

'OK.' I replied, a little shocked.

'This Det isn't functioning as it should,' he continued. 'The handlers are not up to much and we need your experience.'

This confused me as I'd just finished my Advanced course. I'd done well on it but would never describe myself as experienced. I walked back over to what I thought was my temporary room and began to unpack.

Day 49

The day started with a stunning sunrise into a clear blue sky. The strong wind continued from the east and the waves were big and steep. Despite these favourable rowing conditions, *Hope* seemed soul-destroyingly slow in the water. I pulled on the oars as hard as I could but only managed a meagre two-and-a-half knots between areas of strong currents where *Hope* would almost stop dead. It was backbreaking work, frustrating and exhausting in equal measures.

After dinner, I struggled to get out and row for my first nighttime rowing shift. I forced myself to climb out of the cabin to row in a pitch-black, boiling sea. Rowing was almost pointless as the big waves tossed *Hope* around. With no visual reference other than the stars, it felt like I was falling into an inky abyss. During my second shift at about 00.30am, a half-moon rose out of the sea directly behind *Hope*, its pale light scattered across infinite waves. After my second nighttime rowing shift, I drifted off to an uneasy sleep. I could feel a sense of anxiety as waves began to break around me. I knew the wind was due to increase before it died down again. As I slept I had a nightmare, where I was absolutely alone in the middle of the ocean in a rowing boat. As I drifted back to consciousness, there was a brief moment of elation where I realised I was only dreaming, but then as the real world imposed itself, I suddenly knew that my nightmare was reality.

I sat up in the small cabin, the noise of the sea smashing against *Hope*'s hull and laughed at the absurdity of waking from a nightmare into an actual nightmare. The wind increased just before dawn as Leven predicted and so did my fear. I decided to distract the monkey and treated myself to curry for breakfast.

Day 49 Logbook Entry

Position at 0800hrs (L) (1000hrs UTC) on 27th Feb 2019 09°10'. 721n 043°01: 997w	*Distance travelled 60.5nm rowed at 236°t Total distance 2461.5nm*

605nm to Cayenne

Pattern of periods of turbulence with strong currents continued through the day. Felt more frustrating than actual miles covered and COG wind picked up significantly with dawn @ 0715L. Have seen some big breaking waves this morning: ☹

I'd assumed that KAF Det was broken due to the unfriendly management style from Paul and Mark. It soon became apparent that it was the tip of the iceberg. The purpose of the Det was to wring as many intelligence reports out of the stable of agents as possible. It didn't matter how true they were as long as the report stats were up and the Det looked productive. It was obvious what was unverifiable to the agents and we were encouraging them to make stuff up. Whenever any of the handlers raised any concerns about the validity of any intelligence, we were told repeatedly 'Let us worry about that.'

I had a growing sense of pointlessness. I'd worked hard to qualify as an Advanced HUMINT Operator. I'd hoped that I'd have had a greater sense of achievement, but I felt a long way from special as a volunteer for 'Special Duties'. This was not what I expected or hoped I'd be doing. I was operating covertly in Afghanistan, but it felt hollow.

OP MINIMISE, the shutting down of all communication back home whilst a family was informed of a death or very serious injury of a loved one, was enforced regularly. Many of the reports that followed were from Sangin and I knew that it would most likely be a Royal Marine who'd been killed or badly injured. I felt that I'd be better off back with the Royal Marines, proper soldiering, actually doing something that mattered. This growing sense of pointlessness was accompanied by a sense of almost two years' bloody hard work for nothing.

One morning at prayers, the meeting that started every working day, we finished with everyone saying what they were doing and what their agents were doing. I said I was completing a renewal of an agents annual RIPA authorisation paperwork, a huge legal form that gave the legal framework and justification for running an agent. RIPA paperwork typically took a couple of days to go through and was dreaded by everyone.

'What's your agent doing?' asked Paul.

'Nothing today', I replied. 'He's off to Marjeh on a tasking tomorrow.'

'Ring him up and tell him to get some intelligence, we don't pay him to sit on his arse.'

'I can but he'll just make something up,' I replied.

'You don't know that.'

'Yes I do.' I said, 'It's why I'm a handler.'

'Just do it.'

'I'm telling you, if I ring him up and tell him to get some intelligence, he'll just ring back with some bollocks about an IED in Marjeh.'

'You don't know that,' said Paul, then repeated 'Just do it.' It ended the conversation.

I called my agent straight after prayers and berated him saying, that he wasn't paid to sit on his arse. Within 20 minutes he'd rung back in with a report of an IED at Loy Cherrai, which literally translates as Big Junction, in Marjeh. He may as well have said there's an IED in Afghanistan. Marjeh was full of big junctions. It was also a regular report from him when he couldn't be bothered to make anything else up. I went back into the office and told Paul what had happened.

He looked up from his laptop with a smug look on his face and said, 'See I told you.'

I was thrown by his reaction and took a couple of seconds to recover, 'No I told you. This is exactly what I said he would do, this is a load of crap.'

'It could be true,' he said.

I stood looking at Paul, my jaw hanging open in disbelief. He somehow managed to look as if he'd won an argument and I was stupid for doubting him.

'Write it up as a threat warning,' he said.

The threat warning went out and made the report stats from KAF DET look better and the war in Afghanistan rolled on. Except I was now done with Paul, Mark and the DHU.

Day 50

The strong winds that were driving big, breaking waves continued through the morning. I knew from my conversation with Leven the previous day, that the wind was going to drop at around lunchtime, but whilst it was blowing and the waves were crashing around me, I tried to get as much distance as I could.

With aching muscles and no motivation, I thought *'I want this to be over as soon as possible'* and used it as a mantra to drive myself to row as hard as I could. As the morning progressed, the strong wind continued from directly behind *Hope,* but the waves started to almost peter out and a strange side swell started to push waves from the south at almost 90 degrees to the wind. The occasional rogue wave doing its own thing was a normal occurrence, even in a steady swell, with uniform waves and a constant wind, a random wave coming from a completely different direction would saunter past. Sometimes at night they'd smash against the side of *Hope* without any warning, sending a spume of cold sea water over the deck and completely drenching me. But this was different, the waves from the south started to become more frequent as the morning wore on. The wind finally dropped around midday as the sea became more confused with what felt like waves from multiple directions.

Rowing was both physically draining and technically difficult as waves from different directions tossed *Hope* around. I was also rowing through areas of strong currents where an already confused sea turned into an un-rowable mess. These instances of strong currents became more frequent through the day and were pushing me south. I'd hoped that I'd cleared the Equatorial Counter current, but it was clear from the southerly direction that I hadn't.

I called Leven late in the afternoon. 'Leven, these currents are almost un-rowable and they're pushing my south,' I explained.

'Lee that's OK. We need to get some south in because of the currents coming into the finish line. They'll be fairly strong going south for a day or so. Go with them, put some south in. Try to get some speed,' he said before his own mantra, 'Speed over course, Captain.'

After talking to Leven, I called Claire. 'I'm really finding it hard now,' I said.

'You're doing really well,' she replied. 'I've been speaking to the French Navy and they're going to meet you at the finish.'

My good friend General Ed, the Governor of Gibraltar, had put me in touch with the defence attaché in Paris before I'd left, who, in turn, put me in touch with the French Navy, or Marine Nationale, in French Guiana. Claire had carried those conversations on whilst I was at sea.

'Really? That's amazing,' I said.

I still wasn't sure where I was going to land and that would be the first thing the back-up crew would need to sort when they got to Cayenne. I was heading for the Mahury River estuary, south of Cayenne. The finish line would be where I crossed from the Atlantic Ocean and into the Mahury River estuary and, by extension, continental South America. There was a Marine Nationale base and a tiny marina about six kilometres from the mouth of the river. Depending on tides when I arrived, I'd need towing from the finish line. It would be impossible to row against the strong tidal flow and river currents.

'We're looking at flying out on Tuesday to arrive on Wednesday,' said Claire.

The back-up crew would be Claire, Ivor, Billy who'd be helping Ivor and Izzy. After the call I felt better, not only from talking to Claire, but the conversation had been about finishing.

Day 50 Logbook Entry

Position at 0800hrs (L) (1000hrs UTC)	*Distance travelled 59nm rowed*
on 28th Feb 2019	*at 228°t*
08°31'. 114n 043°46: 481w	*Total distance 2520.5nm*

549nm to Cayenne

A very hard fought 59nm with a good head start of v strong winds in the morning from 0700hrs L to approx 1200hrs l pushing the boat at around 3-3.5kts.

Incidents of turbulence in the swell is now less associated with change in COG but it appears to be part of a strong side swell from the south.

Strong current pushing boat south of line from 0000hrs. Heading approx 245°T in line with wind direction but COG 215°T – 225°T. Further south the COG the more speed it appears generated.

I'd made up my mind that I wasn't going anywhere within HUMINT and I became quite open in my disdain for both Paul and Mark. I felt that the hard work I'd put in, doing a six-month tour as a Basic Handler, working as an instructor and finally passing the Advanced Course, was all for nothing. I'd hoped that by volunteering for Special Duties and working undercover in the most dangerous place on Earth, I would finally realise a childhood ambition of being someone I was proud to see staring back in the mirror.

I couldn't stand by, pumping out pointless reports whilst Royal Marines were fighting and dying. I now openly questioned every decision I thought was stupid and regularly raised my concerns over the cases I was running. My days in the KAF Det' were numbered as with every handler who openly questioned Paul and Mark.

I was called into Paul's office. 'There's been a fast ball, you're on a plane to Bastion then Sangin tonight to replace Harry who is End of Touring.' He almost looked smug as he told me. Mark stared intently at his computer screen.

'OK,' I replied. 'What time?'

Harry was a lean, fit-looking RAF Regiment Sergeant from Northern Ireland. He was popular and a good friend. His End of Tour date would've been set in stone for months beforehand. Going to Sangin wasn't a fast ball. I was going two weeks before my RnR to hand-over from Harry and then on my return, he'd fly out on the same helicopter that I'd fly back on. We'd high five on the helicopter Landing Zone in passing. I didn't know exactly that this was going to happen, but I wasn't surprised either and I wasn't disappointed. I quickly went to my room and with a strange sense of relief, shaved off my beard and packed my bags for the worst place on God's Earth, Sangin.

Paul's parting gift was the interpreter I'd be taking with me, Freido. Freido was an ethnic Pashtun from Pakistan, he'd joined the many Afghans in exile who'd found lucrative work interpreting for the various armed forces and intelligence agencies back in Afghanistan. Freido was a short, jovial, older gentleman like a kindly old grandad. He was also the worst interpreter in the Det. His poor grasp of English was exacerbated by my Dagenham accent and as a result, Freido barely understood a word I said. He was the oldest interpreter by far and was definitely not up to the rigors of living in a Forward Operating Base. He was also a Pakistani and spoke Pashtu with an obvious Pakistani accent. Most ethnic Pashtuns in southern Afghanistan hated Pakistanis. He was the stupidest choice for an FDO's interpreter, especially in Sangin. For all his faults, Paul wasn't stupid, this choice was calculated to make life as difficult as possible for me. My job as an FDO was to often provide critical, time sensitive life-saving information to soldiers fighting on the ground and Paul was prepared to hinder that.

After overnighting in a transit tent at camp Bastion, Freido and I arrived in FOB Jackson, Sangin by Merlin helicopter at first light. It was the second time I'd been to Sangin and it hadn't changed much in the two years since. Harry met me from the Landing Zone with Pete, the National Directorate of Security (NDS) Liaison Officer. The NDS were the Afghan Government's Intelligence service. Pete would be my boss for the NDS mentoring side of my job in Sangin. Pete was a very experienced handler from the old days in Northern Ireland and was someone who couldn't do enough to help anyone. Pete and Harry helped carry my kit, equipment, guitar and weapons whilst I carried Freido's bag, straight to what was going to be our new home for the next four months. It was a small mud-built Afghan outbuilding with half-a-metre thick mud walls and no windows giving it the impression of being a cave. In 2010 Sangin district was strategically important as a smuggling route for raw opium and heroin, also the flourishing Bazaar in Sangin town was held as a beacon of hope for Afghan government stability. British soldiers first fought in Sangin in 1878 during the second Anglo-Afghan war and it was a ghost town when British soldiers went back in June 2006. In the years leading up to 2010, a third of all British deaths in Afghanistan occurred in Sangin as British soldiers paid the ultimate price for bringing a touch of normality to this small corner of Afghanistan by keeping the bazaar open.

In April 2010 40 Commando took over from 3 Rifles in Sangin. Both the Rifles and 40 Commandos' tours would prove to be the deadliest year of the war in Afghanistan, as the Taliban continued to lace the countryside with IEDs. However, 40 Commando's tour would be remembered for the phrase that permeated every tactical decision made on the ground and became a byword for fighting with both hands tied behind your back, 'Courageous Restraint'. Courageous Restraint was a term first adopted by General Stanley McChrystal in 2009. It was intended to limit civilian casualties by reducing indirect fire from aircraft and artillery and instead placing the onus on soldiers on the ground in contact fighting the enemy with rifles and often bayonets. However, by 2010 'Outrageous Constraint', as it was called, was interpreted to mean reducing all lethal force and was hated by every Royal Marine. By the time I arrived in Sangin at the beginning of July, the Marines felt that whenever they went out of the gate on patrol, they were truly on their own. Any requests for support from heavy weapons, artillery, mortars or air strikes would fall on death ears, no matter how dire the situation. And more crucially, they felt that they would also have to answer for every shot fired. But to fully understand what Courageous Restraint was and why it was implemented so rigidly as a tactical approach to fighting in Sangin, you need to understand the complex and murky world of Afghan tribal politics. In Sangin they were more complicated and baffling than anywhere else.

Afghanistan is an ethnically diverse country; the Afghan National Anthem and the Afghan Constitution mention a total of fourteen different ethnic groups. Southern Afghanistan is predominantly populated by ethnic Pashtuns, who are again divided amongst a complex myriad of different tribes and tribal federations. Tribes had powerbases and their loyalty was governed by whoever was supplying them with weapons so they could protect and control their part in the lucrative opium trade. Often families had divided loyalties with family members fighting with different militias against each other, so the family had a stake in the winning side. Sangin district was the deadliest place in Afghanistan, but perversely had a tenuous and often strained relationship with the Taliban. Sangin sits between the Alikozai tribe territory north of Sangin bazaar and their tribal enemies, the Ishaqzai tribe to the south. It had been fought over since before the time of the Soviets and had changed hands many times. In 2010, Sangin District was under the control of the Alikozai tribe, because they were heavily represented within President Karzai's newly-installed government. The Afghan police, Afghan National Army and local district governors were nothing more than Alikozai tribal militias in American-supplied uniforms. After the fall of the Taliban in 2002, the Ishaqzai tribe lost a lot of their influence, especially in Helmand. Tribal politics mattered in Sangin because of the lucrative drugs trade and this was controlled by the Alikozai tribe in the north. The Taliban relied on the drugs trade to fund their religious insurgency so tolerated the Alikozai despite their alignment with the government. The fragile truce that existed between the Taliban and the Alikozai tribe in Sangin broke down in 2007 when they kicked the Taliban out of the Sangin area under the influential Alikozai tribal leader Dad Mohammad Khan. For some time before 40 Commando's tour, the British were quietly talking to the Alikozai in Sangin District. These talks were through intermediaries and were top secret. The secret talks with the Alikozai in Sangin had initially been thought to be productive and was the reason behind the enthusiastic enforcement of Courageous Restraint by Lt Col Paul James, the CO of 40 Commando. He didn't want the talks derailed by fighting. To put this into some context, if the talks with the Alikozai tribe succeeded, it had the potential to change the whole war in Afghanistan. In the spring of 2010, the Alikozai tribe again teetered on the edge of revolt against the Taliban. The Taliban's representative in the area was Mullah Mohammad Akunzada. Akhundzada was once the Governor of Helmand but was sacked on the insistence of the British, for dealing in opium. His power-base was Musa Qalai to the north of and west of Sangin and shortly after his expulsion from the government, he turned himself and his fighters over to the Taliban, but perversely still held a role within the Afghan government. Mullah Mohammad Akunzada was from the Alizai tribe, a rival tribe to the Alikozai in the upper Sangin Valley. Akunzada shot and wounded a senior figure in the Alikozai tribe called Mullah Bakari, over the control of opium. Mullah Bakari controlled opium production and the drug laboratories that turned it into pure heroin throughout northern Helmand and parts of eastern Farrah Province. The reverberations of this were felt throughout the whole of Afghanistan as the Alikozai tribe tried to consolidate their control of the drugs trade. It was into this tinderbox of tribal tensions, constant bloody fighting with the Taliban, the deadly threat of IEDs and deep resentment with the Commanding Officer, that I had landed.

Day 51

Along the horizon to the east, a noticeably warmer, hazy orange glow heralded the day. After completing my morning routine of stats, filling in the logbook and breakfast, I tried to rest. My back ached and I stretched out as best I could in the cramped cabin.

Hard rowing under an unrelenting hot sun continued through areas of strong currents. In these areas, *Hope* was pushed south and the oars would stop, often mid stroke, like they were set in concrete. Despite feeling like I was rowing through cold treacle, my speed would increase the further south I was being pushed.

Throughout the day I was struggling to keep to my heading, but I was over 500 nautical miles from land and still a lot of sea between me and the finish line to correct any south I was getting now.

That afternoon I spoke to Leven.

'The south you're getting is looking to continue until about lunchtime tomorrow, Captain, he said. 'I'd go with it for the now and you should be able to head towards the waypoint tomorrow. Speed over course at this stage and there's the North Atlantic Equatorial current that we'll be heading into soon, that'll give us some north.'

As I sat in the cabin eating my evening meal, the navigation alarm bleeped and with dread I looked at the screen on the control panel. To my utter horror, it went blank and was displaying the message 'Loss of GPS Signal'. Instantly my heart sank, but before I could do anything, the screen flashed back into life. I sat staring at it, willing it to stay as it was. Nervously I continued eating my dinner, but the Nav' system stayed on. Through the night the currents were pushing *Hope* almost due south even though I was pointing her near due west.

Day 51 Logbook Entry

Position at 0800hrs (L) (1000hrs UTC) on 1st March 2019 07°47'. 533n 044°18: 326w

Distance travelled 54nm rowed at 216°t Total distance 2574.5nm

504nm to Cayenne

Another hard days rowing in strong currents at points during the night my heading was 245°t-250°t COG 200°t – 205°t. Strong current pushing me south is expected to carry on for a few hours today after which I should be able to head towards the waypoint. Really finding it hard now: ☹

AIS and sat dropped momentarily last night, been OK since but to say I'm nervous is a massive understatement.

As an FDO I had two distinct jobs. Firstly, I'd help run and mentor the local NDS, ensuring that all the intelligence that they gathered through their own sources would be shared and fed into the main coalition forces intelligence streams. The second was to be the HUMINT representative to the local Battle Group, 40 Commando.

Harry and Pete gave me a brief overview of my job in Sangin and touched on the local NDS station.

'I'll show you the office then we'll go over to the NDS station before it gets too late. They wrap their tits in and get their heads down for a couple of hours after 11,' Harry said.

My office was a large metal container on the perimeter of the LZ. Inside was a small desk, a phone and a laptop. It was already heating up like an oven in the early morning sun.

'You have to shut the doors when any Helo's approach, it's really shit mate,' Harry laughed before explaining the complicated and overly convoluted way of sending my reports.

Outside the container the normal background hum of life in Sangin rattled on. I could hear a gun battle that sounded quite close, a couple of helicopters overhead, and the constant drone of the generators giving FOB Jackson its power. Suddenly we heard a huge bang.

Harry looked up at me frowning and said, 'That sounded,' then stopped as Pete shouted from outside, 'Fuck me.'

We ran outside into what sounded like the world erupting into gunfire. Pete was looking up in the air behind us, pointing. We ran forward and turned just in time to see a Blackhawk helicopter billowing black smoke spinning towards the SF tower.

'Fucking hell it's gonna hit the tower,' said Harry

Somehow it span out of control past the SF tower and disappeared behind closely followed by a second Blackhawk helicopter, the tracer from the 50 cal' and GPMGs clearly visible in the bright morning sun.

'Quick, let's go to the Ops Room.'

We ran as fast as possible but before we reached the Ops room door, we heard the sickening crunch of the helicopter hitting the ground above the deafening gunfire. We both entered and a Royal Marine Sergeant that I vaguely recognised looked over to us and shouted, 'Go over to the sick bay.'

We ran to the sick bay just behind our cave. The whole FOB had sprung into action like a well-drilled machine. Marines carrying fire-extinguishers and water jerry cans sped past us on quad bikes towards the crashed helicopter. The sickbay area became a hub of organised chaos as marines came as quickly as they could to help.

The Doc appeared. 'Harry, grab some plastic gowns and gloves and triage out here, Stu and I will be inside.' Harry followed the Doc, a chubby blond-haired Royal Naval surgeon, into the sick bay to grab the gowns and gloves. 'Don't give me anyone that isn't going to make it,' said the Doc.

I stood outside of the sickbay with my Royal Marine Commando flashes and Colour Sergeant rank slide clearly visible on my uniform and noticed the younger marines looking at me for some direction. *'Don't look at me,'* I wanted to shout, *'I don't know what the fuck I am doing'*.

Harry handed out the surgical gowns and gloves and said, 'Welcome to Sangin.'

After about ten minutes we were told that all the wounded had been taken to hospital by the second helicopter and we stood down. However, four crew members of call sign Pedro 66 were killed in the crash. The aftermath of the incident hung in the air as did the acrid taste from the smouldering mangled hulk of the helicopter and more tellingly, in the exhausted faces of the marines, many off whom I knew.

Later that afternoon we went to see the NDS. Their station was a large compound just outside of FOB Jackson's main gate. The NDS had a contingent of a dozen guards, two of whom were in a drab grey uniform at the compound's entrance. The rest were lounging in the large garden. We walked through the garden to a large plain room with a couple of old sofas and a large Afghan rug on the floor. Pete greeted the two NDS commanders with a hug and introduced me to them with Friedo interpreting. Captain Maboob was small, very dark-skinned Pashtun about 30 years old. He had a round kind face with tidy and thick jet-black hair. He looked every inch the efficient bureaucrat. He was second in command to Captain Saiid Nabi who

I greeted next. Pete had warned me about Captain Nabi's ethnicity. He claimed to be a Pashtun but had very distinct Tajik features and was very touchy about this. His long, deeply lined face was a portrait photographer's dream, with deep set, oriental eyes that twinkled with mirth and a long, thin wispy, white beard. He looked like a mystical oriental sage. He smiled and shook my hand with his long bony fingers. After the inevitable prolonged Afghan pleasantries, the conversation quickly turned to the crashed Blackhawk helicopter. The name Gulab came up again and again. Gulab was a notorious Taliban fighter who had gained his reputation in Sangin as a sniper in the preceding years but now commanded the area to the south of Sangin. He was directly responsible for every ambush, IED and firefight in the area and was no doubt responsible for the attack on the helicopter.

Captain Maboob motioned for me to follow him, and we walked outside into the bright sunshine. I followed him up a small ladder leading onto the roof and looked out across the wadi. Frowning, he pointed to the mangled hull of the smouldering helicopter 100 metres away. We stood motionless looking at the destruction and thinking about the families that would now be devastated by the loss of loved ones.

We climbed back down into the garden before saying our goodbyes. As we passed the guards they greeted us, shook hands and smiled.

'What the fuck is he doing here?' said Harry.

He immediately turned and walked back to confront Captain Maboob and Nabi. I looked at Pete who frowned and walked over to what was obviously a heated discussion between Harry and Nabi, with Freido doing his best to interpret.

We returned to the galley tent in the FOB and over a hot cup of tea, Harry explained what had just happened. Months before the previous NDS commander, Colonel Rahman, had been expelled from the area. Rahman was a Captain in the NDS but had given himself the rank of Colonel. He was also a high ranking and influential Alikozai tribal leader in the Upper Sangin Valley with close links to both the narcotics trade and Taliban. He was a local warlord who'd used his position as NDS commander to further his own interests in the area. Being the local NDS commander gave his tribe, the Alikozai, controlling stake over Sangin Bazaar. Whilst Rahman was in Sangin, his sidekick was one of the NDS guards who also happened to be the nephew of Mullah Abdul Khaliq, an influential Taliban fighting commander in the Upper Sangin Valley. The nephew was also expelled at the same time as Rahman but was now back in the NDS station. Harry had recognised the nephew amongst the guards. Nabi had told Harry that his appointment had been ordered directly from NDS headquarters in Lashkar Gah and there was nothing he could do about this.

I didn't know it then, but this tribal politicking within the NDS and Colonel Rahman would dominate my time in Sangin.

Day 52

Good rowing conditions lasted all day. A good-sized swell drove *Hope* along and the regular waves made the mechanical part of rowing easy. With every stroke the oars bit into the water, but it still felt like I was dragging a ton of flotsam behind me. *Hope* felt sluggish and I felt energy drain out of me through every two-hour rowing shift. The currents that were pushing me south seemed to be gone and I was pointing the boat almost exactly at my waypoint. My heading and COG were momentarily aligned.

Without the interference from the currents, I could see how much *Hope* had slowed down because of barnacles that infested the hull. I was struggling to row *Hope*, even in excellent rowing conditions, at anything over three knots. I reckoned I was losing about half a knot and conscious that I'd have to maintain a decent speed as I approached the South American coast otherwise the Southern Equatorial Current would push me too far north and I'd miss the finish line. Between rowing shifts I studied the French Guiana coast on the chart. I was aiming for the Mahury River and thought about the possibility of not hitting it. Just north of the Mahury River was the Cayenne River, but I had nowhere to land and would need to be towed back around Cayenne to the Mahury River, something that could be quite dangerous in coastal waters. North of the Cayenne River, I knew the coastline was virtually all mangrove swamp and impossible to land the boat. I had to keep rowing and keep my speed up.

At 6.15pm, the AIS and Nav' system went down again. The alarms bleeped and the screen again displayed 'Loss of GPS Signal'. It flashed again and instantly came back on.

Throughout the afternoon the hot sun had beat down unrelentingly on the rear cabin. I wondered if the heat was producing a lot of water vapour that was getting into the junction box of the Nav' system. It was more than a coincidence that the Nav' system had briefly gone down again at almost the same time as it did the day before. I decided that I wouldn't put the EFOY on again. I tried to get some sleep before my first nighttime rowing shift, but the Nav' system played on my mind. I was dreading it going down this close to the end and having to navigate with the chart and handheld GPS, my back-up Nav' system. It would mean even less time sleeping and I was exhausted. It took every scrap of determination to row through the pitch-black night, even under the billions of stars that hung majestically in the sky. I hated rowing without the moon and added to the utter exhaustion that I felt. It took everything I had mentally, to row. I knew I couldn't miss any rowing shifts as I closed into the South American coast and the finish line. I forced myself out of the cabin for my last nighttime rowing shift and a thin sliver of a crescent moon hung low in the eastern sky.

Day 52 Logbook Entry

Position at 0800hrs (L) (1000hrs UTC) on 2nd Mar 2019
07°08'. 057n 045°00: 380w

Distance travelled 57.5nm rowed at 226°t
Total distance 2632nm

452nm to Cayenne

Seem to be past the worst of the current that is pushing me south.

Sunny day with cloudy intervals. Worried about power as I don't want to turn EFOY on in case if effects the AIS/sat nav which briefly went down again last night at exactly the same time. The sun was directly on the rear cabin. I wonder if it's creating water vapour that is getting in the system. AIS went down only for a couple of seconds @18.15L

That night we ate with the NDS and their guards, Pete had given them enough money to buy a goat that they then killed and cooked. We all sat around a large tablecloth that was placed on the floor and all the food laid out on it in small metal plates. We ate the goat with rice, tomatoes, okra and warm naan bread. We finished the meal with sweet green tea and then headed back to the FOB. Pete was due to leave the following day and promised to get to the bottom of why Mullah Abdul Khaliq's nephew was back in the NDS station in Sangin.

The next morning Harry told me about the secret talks with the Alikozai tribe. My first case as an agent handler in Lashkar Gah, two years before, was a reconciled Taliban commander and it had given me a good working knowledge of the murky, complicated world of Afghan tribal politics. After breakfast, Harry took me round to meet everyone I needed to know. I knew a lot of the personalities in 40 Commando, but I'd never met the CO before.

Harry knocked on the CO's office door and walked in. 'Hi Sir, this is Colour Sergeant Spencer who will be taking over from me when I end of tour.'

'Colours,' the CO replied, looking up at me.

I just nodded in response. He then looked down at his work, heavily indicating that it was the end of the conversation. Next was the Political Advisor to the CO, a civilian diplomat from the Foreign and Commonwealth Office (FCO). Phil was tall and slim with short dark hair and a neatly trimmed black beard lightly flecked with grey. He smiled confidently and greeted us both with a friendly handshake. Both Harry and Pete had been instrumental in setting up the initial meetings with the Alikozai tribal leaders and therefore party to the ongoing secret talks.

'Any news from our friend from Yakchal?' Harry asked.

'No nothing,' said Phil frowning slightly.

'I'll drop it into Saiib to see if he's heard anything,' said Harry meaning Saiib Nabi, the NDS commander. 'I'll hide it amongst a few other TB commanders' names.'

Phil shook his head and said, 'No not yet, it's only been a couple of days.'

'Nice to meet you Frank,' Phil said as we turned to walk away.

'What was that all about?' I asked.

'Mullah Hikmatullah is our friend from Yakchal and is the one talking to us about the Alikozai reconciling. He's gone quiet. No one's heard from him in a few days.'

Over the next two weeks of the handover, I gleaned as much information from Harry as I could, but one thing became glaringly apparent. The steady stream of intelligence from the NDS informants and agents had dropped to zero. No local would go anywhere near the NDS station while Mullah Abdul Khaliq's nephew was there. To do so would have been an immediate death sentence from the Taliban.

Pete was also hitting his head against a brick wall with the Helmand NDS headquarters in Lashkar Gah. It seemed that the appointment of Khaliq's nephew as a security guard had been made at a high level and the NDS headquarters were reluctant to talk about it. This was highly unusual. In the hierarchy of Afghan security forces, the NDS guards were at the bottom and for someone in a position of authority in the NDS to get involved in where one of them was stationed reeked of corruption. Especially when the guard in question was the nephew of a mid-ranking Taliban commander involved in the day-to-day attacks on local British forces.

At the end of the two weeks, I packed a bag, said goodbye to Harry and Freido, flew out of the most dangerous place on the planet and headed to the Glastonbury Festival for the start of my RnR. The juxtaposition of being in Sangin almost hours before being surrounded by thousands of carefree revellers was hard to deal with. It was annoying that these people had no idea of what was happening to my friends, but it was also reassuring how easy it is for humans to just be just nice to each other. But mostly I was just glad not being in Sangin. But it didn't last long and soon Sangin came crashing down around me.

The day after arriving, Bondy, one of my corporals when I was a sergeant in Scotland, found me. 'Frank, I've got some bad news. Darbs has been killed.'

Darbs, or Sergeant Steven Darbyshire, was a fellow air defender. He was the most northern bloke I knew to the point of almost being a caricature. He 'smoked tabs' and 'drank beer' and had an infectious wit. He was always laughing and was universally loved and respected. I took the news in but didn't properly process it and got very drunk. That night I again sobbed my heart out in a Glastonbury Festival bar at the loss of a friend.

It felt like I'd blinked and was back in a helicopter flying from Camp Bastion to FOB Jackson. The arid desert dropped away to the River Helmand and the helicopter followed the contours down and then sped low across the cobalt blue water. It landed with a bump and after a few moments the RAF loady gave the thumbs up for us to disembark. I grabbed my bag and ran off the back ramp of the Merlin helicopter looking for Harry.

I ran over and shouted over the din of the aircraft, 'Have a safe trip, mate.'

Harry had that end of tour glow and was grinning like an idiot. 'Stay safe mate.'

We embraced, shook hands and then he was off running to get on the helicopter and out of this hell hole. Freido was waiting for me just outside of our cave. We embraced and I asked how he was.

'OK,' he said, but he looked anything but OK. He'd aged years. The rigors of living in a cave in a Forward Operating Base in Afghanistan were obviously taking their toll on him.

Nothing had changed in the two weeks I'd been away, but more importantly, there had been no intelligence gained from the NDS in over a month.

I grabbed my pistol, 'Come on Freido, let's go and see the NDS.'

The NDS guards greeted me as I walked in with broad smiles and lots of hand shaking. Captain Maboob greeted me with his usual reverence. I followed him into the small room and sat on the sofa. We talked with Freido interpreting which was a slow and painful process. Harry had a broad northern Irish accent that Freido had no problem understanding but he couldn't understand a word I said. I asked Maboob if there had been any change in the situation and if they'd seen any of their informants. As Freido translated I noticed how uncomfortable Maboob was. He shifted in his seat like an embarrassed child. He talked for a couple of minutes about how difficult the situation was in Afghanistan. Notably he didn't mention the elephant in the room – a Taliban commander's nephew guarding his NDS station.

A guard brought in some green tea that we sipped in silence for a few moments. I asked where Saiid Nabi was. Maboob answered that he'd gone into the bazaar to talk to some farmers in an attempt at gaining some intelligence. I finished my tea and said I'd be back later that afternoon. As I stood up ready to leave Nabi walked in wearing a spotless light blue dish dash. We exchanged pleasantries then I asked how his trip to the bazaar had been.

'I hoped to meet with a friend,' said Nabi, 'But he didn't come.'

'Have you met with anyone new?' I asked.

'No, it is difficult with people coming here.'

'OK, I'll come back this afternoon.' I said and shook both Maboob and Nabi's hand.

'Has he been going to the bazaar much?' I asked Freido as we walked back.

'I think so.'

'But still no intelligence.'

Nabi had been trying to meet with informants away from the NDS station but his distinctive Tajik features stood out. I doubted anyone would risk being seen talking to the well-known and recognisable NDS commander amongst the prying eyes of Sangin bazaar.

My job was to mentor the NDS in running agents to gain intelligence and to provide that intelligence to commanders on the ground. If the NDS couldn't get intelligence because their agents wouldn't go near them, then I'd have to get my own agents. I spent the next few weeks out on as many operations, patrols and chasing as many dead-end leads as possible, all with an increasing sense of frustration.

Firefights were an almost daily occurrence often right next to FOB Jackson. But it was the deaths of young marines that hit everyone the hardest. We'd hear the bang of an explosion and everyone would be thinking *'I hope that was one of our bombs'*. The immediate eruption of gunfire would tell you that it wasn't. Somewhere a soldier had stepped on an IED and waiting Taliban had ambushed the rest of the patrol. The OP MINIMISE sign would go up and a name would filter back through. Finally, word would come from the hospital in Bastion that whoever it was, a mate, often a husband and father, hadn't made it. It became a familiar cycle of near hopelessness to everyone, and I felt useless. I had no way of doing my job of finding and reporting on IEDs. The Taliban were winning and we were very much on the back foot, set against this backdrop of the despised mantra of Courageous Restraint.

As the weeks passed, I was no closer to finding an agent. Phil the Political Adviser became increasingly worried. His contact had disappeared and there hadn't been any communication with the Alikozai tribe. The negotiations hadn't just stalled, they had ceased to exist without any explanation.

Day 53

Another hot, hard days rowing followed in much the same conditions as the day before. I continued to row the increasingly slowing boat as hard as I could, but I could feel my energy sapping away.

In the afternoon I had a scheduled call with Leven. He read out coordinates for what I hoped would be my last waypoint. It was right on the edge of the Southern Equatorial Current and where I'd begin my run into the finish line.

Getting out to row each session was becoming harder as deep fatigue set in. I'd never experienced feeling like this before. It was beyond tired, beyond exhaustion. But what was becoming harder, was the mental gymnastics I was having to go through to force myself out to row. It seemed that it was also taking a toll mentally. I tried to hold my heading, but a strong current was pushing me north of my line. I worried that I wouldn't have the energy to fight the Southern Equatorial Current if I couldn't maintain my speed.

After my midnight to 2am rowing shift, I laid in the cabin exhausted and just as I was drifting off to sleep, I heard a bang on the cabin door. I opened the hatch and a storm petrel was lying motionless on the deck. I carefully picked it up in both hands, cupping its soft black feathers. As I held it, Hamish bird seemed a fitting name for such a solitary animal. I'd seen them flying around the boat from the very start and they offered a welcome if odd company as they swooped inches above the waves. This Hamish bird had flown straight into the cabin door and stunned itself, but as I held it, it fluffed itself right and twisted its head, so its ink black eye could stare straight at me. I opened my hand, and it paused momentarily before flying off in a flurry of wing beats.

Day 53 Logbook Entry

Position at 0800hrs (L) (1100hrs UTC)
on 3rd Mar 2019
06°39'. 539n 045°48: 170w

Distance travelled 55.5nm rowed
at 239°t
Total distance 2687.5nm

398nm to Cayenne

New waypoint on edge of Cayenne current approx 165nm away @ 233° t current heading 240°t, worried that I'm getting pushed (or going to be pushed) too far north to counter the Cayenne current. Storm petrel crashed into the boat last night @ approx 0200hrs L. Clocks went back one hour on Cayenne time UTC -3hrs, predicting a Sunday 10th finish or early Monday 11th.

I chased every tenuous lead, visited Patrol Bases and joined as many patrols as I could. As the weeks passed without any intelligence from the NDS, the reason behind the reinstatement of Mullah Abdul Khaliq's nephew as a guard at the NDS station began to take shape. A rift began to appear between Saiid Nabi and his deputy Captain Maboob. Nabi was clearly taking the blame for the ineffectiveness of his NDS station and there began calls from NDS headquarters in Lashkar Gah that he be sacked. Maboob could see the winds of change coming and had thrown his lot in against Nabi. Pete finished his tour and changed over with Dave who I knew from my course back in Chicksands. Dave was aware of the situation with the NDS in Sangin and had been digging around to see if he could find any answers. As the calls for Saiid Nabi to be sacked grew it soon became apparent that the chief candidate to take his place was Colonel Rahman. He'd been the instigator behind the appointment of Mullah Abdul Khaliq's nephew and was now poised to return to his powerbase as NDS chief in Sangin. This typically murky Afghan politics and intrigue made little difference to the men on the ground in the Sangin area. IEDs were still getting laid, patrols were still getting ambushed and marines were still dying.

After another fruitless patrol with Charlie Company through the Bazaar I took my body armour and webbing off and took Freido to get a drink in the galley. Jim, a corporal in the Intelligence cell, called to me from across the courtyard.

'Frank, have you got a sim card reader?' he asked.

'No I haven't, but the Det's in Lash and KAF have. Why?'

'Teahouse have asked for one. Apparently they've got a picture of Gulab.' Gulab was the Taliban commander responsible for the majority if not all the attacks south of Sangin town including shooting down the helicopter on my first day in Sangin.

'How have they got that?' I asked, my interest suddenly raised.

'No idea, mate.' Said Jim.

If someone had managed to get close enough to Gulab to get a photo of him then they might have good access to him on a regular basis.

And if they were prepared to give us that photo they might want to meet and give me information as well.

Observation Post TEAHOUSE was on the edge of the green zone next to route 611 and once an impressive concrete building before being destroyed by a large bomb and it was now an Afghan National Army (ANA) patrol base. About thirty ANA soldiers lived and operated from the bottom floor and it was an ANA soldier that opened the steel doors to me a couple of days later. Another ANA soldier led me to a damaged staircase that led to the first floor. The OP commander, a South African corporal called Greg, met me at the top of the shattered, rickety stairs. Greg was in his mid-twenties with broad shoulders and an assured confidence. FOB Jackson's Ops room hadn't informed Greg I was coming so he looked a little shocked to see me.

The upper floor comprised several rooms, some destroyed with collapsed concrete ceilings held in place by twisted steel struts and the floor in several places tilted at odd angles. Greg commanded six other marines who operated the observation balloon tethered to the shattered building. The green zone was covered by several observation balloons similar to the one in OP TEAHOUSE. The large helium-filled blimps carried powerful cameras that enabled observation into hard-to-reach areas. They provided constant target practice for the Taliban who were always trying to shoot them down. Their altitude made them hard to hit but it also meant that the slightest breeze would force them back down.

Greg led me into the small Ops room that contained a desk with a television with a live feed from the camera on the balloon and the radio. A young marine called Si sat at the desk monitoring the radio and balloon feed. I asked Greg about the photo of Gulab.

'The ANA Sergeant showed me a phone with a video of the fucker on it.'

'A video?' I asked. 'How'd he get it?'

'He's got a mate who he sees. I think it's his phone,' said Greg.

'His mate?' I asked.

'Yes mate. Si, go and give Mahmood a shout,' Greg said turning to the Marine who was on duty.

'It sounds like he's been running this bloke as his own personal agent,' I said to Greg.

'They always seem to know when an attack is gonna happen and a few weeks ago we were watching them patrol and he just suddenly stopped the lead men and uncovered an IED dug into the bank. Fuck knows how he knew it was there, there's no way he could see it.'

This all sounded positive and once again I tried and failed to manage my expectations.

'Who's your terp?' I asked.

'No one, Mahmood, their sergeant, speaks pretty good English.'

That was unusual in itself. Mahmood entered the small Ops room. I stood to shake hands with the tall, wiry ANA sergeant. He looked like no other ANA soldier I'd ever seen. His uniform fitted him well and gave his bearing a professionalism missing in every other Afghan soldier I'd met. His greeting also lacked the usual Afghan smiles and over-flowery pleasantries. Greetings and hospitality are serious business in Afghan culture. Instead, he held my gaze with his shrewd, black eyes and asked, 'You have card reader?'

'No, I'm trying to get one from Lashkar Gah. I've come to see if the photos or footage are any good. Do you have the camera with you?'

'No, it is my friends, I will ask him and bring it to you tomorrow,' he said in his educated voice. And with that he turned and purposely walked out of the Ops room.

I awoke the next morning when the first rays of sun touched the olive-green mosquito tent. Greg made me a cup of ration-pack tea with dried milk powder.

Mahmood the ANA Sergeant came striding up the broken stairs. 'I have my friend's phone but must give it back soon.'

'OK, let's go to the Ops room and take a look,' said Greg.

We grabbed our drinks and walked into the relative gloom of the Ops room. Mahmood showed us the phone. He had the video ready to go and pressed play. The footage was of a group of Afghan males swimming in the canal. Mahmood paused the video and pointed out a slender Afghan male sat on a wall watching. He was wearing a brown waist coat and a distinctive light brown Kandahari cap. A traditional Afghan circular cap with an upside down 'V' cut out of the front that is often worn under a turban. 'This is Gulab.' he said. His face was too grainy to be of any intelligence use.

'Can I have a look?' I asked and held my hand out. Mahmood reluctantly passed me the phone and I replayed the footage again trying to get a usable screen shot with no success.

'How did your friend get this?' I asked Mahmood.

'It is his friend's video. His friends are swimming.'

'We can't get a good enough picture to use with this video. That's a real shame,' I said with a sigh. 'Can I meet your friend?'

'It is very difficult for him to come here,' said Mahmood. I noted he tensed at the mere mention of me meeting his friend. 'If you tell me what you want to know then I will ask him and tell you the answer,' he said.

'Thanks, that's really good of you,' I said with a show of earnest sincerity. 'But I would like to meet him so I can ask other questions that might come up from what he tells you. It would be easier if I can meet him with you.'

'I will try.' Mahmood said before holding out his hand for the phone. 'I will have to go now,' he said, then turned and walked out of the Ops room.

After he left, Greg and I hatched a plan that would involve me coming back with an interpreter. Firstly though, I'd have to get back to FOB Jackson, something that wasn't straightforward. Greg radioed through to the Ops room at Jackson and I waited. My transport arrived two days later without any notice.

Day 54

The good rowing conditions continued throughout the day, but the combination of getting pushed slightly more north than ideal and *Hope* slowing down worried me. I thought that if these conditions continued, I was in danger of not being far enough south to counter the Southern Equatorial Current that would push me north when I hit it. I reckoned that if I could maintain 50 to 60 nautical miles a day, I may only have a week left rowing. But it was becoming clearer that the harder I was rowing, the distance I was able to cover in 24 hours was coming slowly down. As hard as I was pulling on the oars, I couldn't get much over two knots. I felt utterly physically exhausted and the mental strength it took to force myself to row each shift was wearing me down.

I called Claire who was in Paris with Billy, getting their connecting flights to Cayenne. They were meeting Ivor, who was going to help recover *Hope* when I finished. The back-up crew on their way out to Cayenne was a sure sign that I'd started the row into the finish line. From as far back as when I first made the decision to row again and all the way through the planning, training and even through the two postponements, I'd looked forward to this very moment. But now it was here I felt far from elated. The finish line seemed as far away from me now, as it had when the pod of dolphins kept me company on my first night rowing. My margins for navigational error were becoming smaller and smaller and every decision and every rowing session was becoming more critical. I knew this row was far from over and could end with the very next wave.

The alarm woke me at midnight for my second rowing shift and I felt so tired. After a ten-minute mental struggle, I got out and started rowing only to be woken minutes later as a random side wave drenched me. I'd fallen asleep rowing. My arms were going back and forth, but

I was fast asleep. I rowed through the night underneath a cloudless, black sky filled with a hundred billion stars. They gave me a slight spatial context as I rowed in an invisible ocean. I kept feeling that I'd rowed off the edge of the world and was falling through space, then a wave would hit the side of *Hope* without warning and bring me back.

The navigation alarm sounded just before I was due to get up for my last nighttime rowing shift at 6am. I donned my life jacket, attached the strop to the deck and scrambled out of the cabin to row *Hope* out of irons. As soon as she was out of irons, I locked off the steering lines and clambered down to the rudder at the stern on my bum. The brass pin that attached the autohelm to the boat had come away. I quickly changed it for a brand new spare autohelm and fixed the brass pin back into the old one. It was the autohelm that I had bastardised from the two broken ones and marvelled that it had kept going for nearly three weeks. The brass pin looked secure, so I decided to keep the new autohelm working and the bastardised one as spare. The thinnest slither of a crescent moon hung in the sky then disappeared as the coming day turned the eastern sky from pitch black, to blue then brilliant orange.

Day 54 Logbook Entry

Position at 0800hrs (L) (1100hrs UTC) on 4th Mar 2019
06°13'. 693n 46°36: 248w

Distance travelled 54.5nm rowed at 241°t
Total distance 2742nm

346nm to Cayenne

Finding everything a massive struggle as I go into what I hope is the final week. Conditions pretty much the same for the last few days. Still going more north than I'd like. Autohelm broke this morning @ approx 0600hrsL. The pin that holds the connecting rod (the metal rod that attaches to the boat) came away. Seemed OK otherwise, so fixed problem and changed autohelm. Autohelm being used at mo is the new one, the one I fixed is now spare and is the one I bastardised from broken parts.

Military interpreters were in short supply and back in FOB Jackson I went to see my old friend Sam who was Charlie Company second in command. He saw the worth in my plan and agreed to let me take one of his Company's precious interpreters. It also highlighted how utterly stupid the decision was to send Freido with me to Sangin. He couldn't deploy out of the FOB with me. Charlie Company's interpreter was a young marine called Stevie and before we left, I'd rehearsed what I wanted him to say with Freido. I also instructed him to at no point let anyone know that he spoke Pashtu. Two days later we were back in OP TEAHOUSE and I asked Mahmood the ANA Sergeant if he'd bring his friend to meet me. Mahmood made excuse after excuse, but on the third morning, he strode up the broken stairs and announced that his friend would come to the PB after dark.

That evening as the sun slowly disappeared over the desert beyond the Helmand river, I went through the plan again with Greg, the Ops room marine Si and Stevie the interpreter. At last light, we all moved into position. Si went up to the sentry position above the Ops Room, Stevie sat at the desk in the Ops' room monitoring the feed from the balloon camera, Greg and I sat cross-legged on the floor in the style of a typical Afghan Shura. We were talking in hushed voices when Mahmood suddenly appeared in the doorway. He strode into the room and ushered in a slight, hunched figure in a light grey shawl. We stood to greet them as the figure straightened and pulled back the shawl to reveal a slim, dark face with a thick black beard and large hooked nose. His face smiled with ease and his dark eyes followed suit. I liked him instantly. We earnestly clasped hands before sitting down opposite each other. Mahmood spoke to his friend and he pulled out his phone and started talking to me.

'He says he cannot get any more videos of Gulab but it was his friend who took it and gave it to him.'

I spoke directly to Mahmood's friend, keeping eye contact and smiling as I did, 'Who is your friend? Is he one of Gulab's fighters?' I then looked at Mahmood and said, 'What is your friend's name?'

Mahmood frowned at me and said, 'Hamid.'

I then repeated my questions using his name and Mahmood translated. I asked as many questions as I could, taking lots of notes and appearing as interested in Mahmood's translated answers as possible. After ten minutes whilst Mahmood was talking to Greg, I glanced at Stevie who was sitting just behind me at the desk and gave him the slightest nod. He then pressed the transmit switch on the radio twice, briefly transmitting over the radio net. Si, positioned above us, heard the familiar double click and hiss and fired two shots into the night. Below in the Ops room we jumped up. Greg ran as fast as he could up to the sentry position and returned shouting, 'Mahmood, quickly I need to show you something,' and beckoned him to follow.

As Mahmood disappeared Stevie came from behind his desk and like an actor on an opening night, faultlessly delivered his lines.

I grabbed Hamid's hand and said, 'I want to meet you at the main base in Sangin in three days' time at 9 o'clock,' then waited for Stevie to translate. Hamid looked shocked then recovered his composure.

'I will pay you 40,000 Pak Rupees,' I continued and again waited for the translation.

'If you walk straight up to the gate, don't look to your right at the NDS station, just keep walking and I will be ready to open the gate just as you get there.' Stevie translated again.

'Don't tell Mahmood, he will want to take half of the money I will give you,' I said and with this he gave me a knowing smile.

'Do you understand?' I finally asked. Hamid nodded. 'At 9 o'clock, exactly 9 o'clock, in three days' time. Walk straight at the gate and I will be waiting.'

After Stevie quickly translated, he rushed back behind the desk, just as Mahmood and Greg came back down into the room.

'What was that?' I made a show of asking.

'It looked like some TB moving into a position. They were preparing to do something but Si fired some warning shots,' said Greg.

I went to sit down, but Mahmood said, 'Hamid will have to go now.'

Mahmood was keen to get Hamid out of the base as quickly as possible and we said our rushed goodbyes. As they walked out Hamid smiled at me and that gave me a small piece of encouragement that the plan had worked. 'What were they saying to each other?' I asked Stevie as soon as they left.

'They were talking too quickly, I couldn't get any of it,' he said.

'Well done mate,' I said.

Stevie and I returned to FOB Jackson the next day, which gave me a day to prepare for Hamid. I thanked Stevie and made a note to ask for him again if I needed an interpreter.

The following day I woke before the sun got too hot and filled out the paperwork for the meeting. I rang and spoke to Dave in Lash and gave him a brief on my few days in PB TEAHOUSE. I'd been continuously briefing him with everything that I was doing in the hope that he'd see that I wasn't accepting the status quo and that I was being proactive.

The next morning, I woke with the sun rise and prepared the office for the meeting. I made sure we had refreshments in the fridge, all the mapping was ready and gave the place a good clean. Freido and I readied ourselves and then walked down to the main gate ready to meet Hamid. I was nervous and despite actively trying to prepare myself for the inevitable disappointment, I was excited and optimistic.

As we approached the gate, we became aware of an argument. One of the NDS guards in his distinctive grey uniform was berating a local

Afghan and trying to usher him out of the camp. The marines on duty on the gate looked on bemused as this appeared to be NDS business and they didn't want to get involved.

The duty corporal saw me. 'Ah Frank, we just sent someone round to find you, he was asking for Harry and we thought you might know who he is.' The Afghan looked up and obviously recognised Friedo and starting earnestly talking to him.

'What's going on, Freido?' I asked.

'I met him with Harry while you were away.'

'Tell him to go, Freido. Tell him I'll sort this now.' I said indicating to the guard who now looked sheepish. Whatever was going on, it was blatantly obvious that this NDS guard didn't want me to see this Afghan. Freido interpreted and the guard sloped off out through the gate.

'Right, now what's going on, Freido?' I asked.

'This is the friend of Mullah Bakari,' said Freido. 'He's come to find Harry.'

Mullah Bakari was the leading narcotics producer in the whole of Helmand and beyond and was the one who was shot and wounded by Mullah Mohammad Akunzada, the previous Taliban district governor. I'd been told by Harry that one of his friends was a source for the NDS and now here he was. I looked at him properly for the first time. He was fat with a very dark complexion, a large, hooked nose and a thin wispy beard lined with grey. He was wearing a tan coloured dish dash with a black turban. I looked at my watch, it was 8.55am. '*Afghan agents must be like buses, you wait all month then two come at once.*'

'I want you to go back out and go and see the NDS and tell them that you was looking to get some compensation from ISAF. Tell them that I said no and we had an argument.' Freido translated for me as I spoke. 'Tell them I'm a bastard, call me names and say you'll never come here again.'

I handed him some of the money I'd set aside for Hamid. 'Go to the bazaar and get a light blue dish-dash with a light-coloured turban. Then come back here in exactly 4 hours.' I said hoping that my meeting with Hamid, if it happened, would be over.

As Freido interpreted he looked at me and lifted his arms to show me his bare wrists.

'For fuck's sake,' I muttered to myself. 'OK, buy yourself a watch.' I said handing him the rest of the money I had. 'Four hours, not before, not after, exactly one o'clock. And don't look at the NDS, cover your face as you walk past them.'

I opened the gate and ushered him out. As he walked past, I glanced up the road at a figure approaching. He looked about the same size and build as Hamid and he covered his face with a shawl as he passed the NDS station, as instructed. I closed the gate and waited for him to get closer. As he reached the gate, I could see it was Hamid so opened the gate to greet him. I gestured for him to pull his shawl back over his head as there were plenty of local Afghans about the FOB and I didn't want anyone to recognise him.

Once in the office it became clear that Hamid would be able to report on Gulab and his small cell of fighters. They were all well known in the area and they at least kept the locals aware of new locations of IEDs. This would be invaluable information for the marines as they patrolled the ground. He was clearly intelligent, but nearly every Afghan I had met was useless at pointing out places on maps or aerial photography. I showed Hamid an aerial photo of the area surrounding OP TEAHOUSE, but he looked baffled by it.

'Have you ever seen a map?' I asked him.

'No, never,' he replied.

I then drew out a view of the office from above explaining as I did. 'Imagine being above and looking down on us,' I said. 'There's the bin,' I said pointing out the circle I had just drawn in the corner of the paper. 'This is you,' I again pointed out where I had drawn Hamid from above in relation to the bin. I continued like this, explaining as I drew and gauging Hamid's understanding. I then went back to the aerial phot and started pointing the biggest features, like the road and the Helmand River. He let out the universal sigh of 'Ah, I get it now'. I pointed out the building that contained PB TEAHOUSE and said, 'This is where I met you.'

Hamid stared at the aerial photo intently then pointed to distinctive buildings and features naming each one correctly including his own house. He looked intrigued as he recognised the structures in his own compound.

I pointed to what appeared to be a prominent track junction just to the west of PB TEAHOUSE and asked Hamid, 'Do you recognise this place where the two paths cross?'

Hamid nodded. 'In three days' time at exactly two hours before midday at ten o'clock, stand exactly there and count to thirty. Once you've done that move you're shawl from your left shoulder to your right then follow the path.' I then gave Hamid a route to follow as a test. I got him to repeat exactly what I had said and show me the route a couple of times to ensure that he had understood.

'Come back here after three more days at the same time so we can meet up again.'

I gave Hamid the 40,000 Pak Rupees as promised then escorted him back to the gate. I shook his hand and said goodbye, then rushed back to the office. I turned on the computer and quickly searched for any information Harry had on Mullah Bakari's relative before going back to the gate and welcome him in. As we walked to the gate, I suddenly realised I didn't know his name.

'Shit. What's his name, Freido?' I asked.

'Isatullah.' Freido thankfully replied.

Day 55

I finished rowing and tried to complete my stats for the last 24 hours and eat breakfast quickly so I could rest as long as possible. I'd just managed to keep above my target of 50 nautical miles in 24 hours, but still felt utterly demoralised. I'd rowed as hard as I could through the night, in back-breaking conditions for what felt like little or no distance. I thought about how little energy I seemed to have and decided to eat one of the high-energy, freeze-dried breakfast instead of the wet boil in the bag ration. I poured boiling water into the little orange pouch of porridge with blueberries and waited a couple of minutes for it to hydrate. But I struggled to eat it and managed only half a portion. It was as if I didn't even have the energy to digest the food and my body was rejecting the high calorific content of the hydrated meal.

After breakfast I laid down in the already hot cabin with my thoughts. Claire was travelling, so I couldn't call her, and I wasn't due to call Leven until later that evening. As I was thinking about how exhausted I was, my alarm went off for my next rowing shift. I couldn't believe it, I must have slept for over an hour, yet felt as if I hadn't slept at all. I couldn't recollect closing my eyes, let alone sleep. I checked and re-checked my watch, but it was time to row again. I struggled to sit-upright and pushed myself to get ready to row again.

The sea conditions were the same as the last few days and I again pulled on the oars as hard as I could in the hot, sticky and humid air. A shark followed me for a few minutes, its large, distinctive dorsal fin glistened above the water a couple of metres behind. It then slipped away as its tail fin slapped the surface and disappeared into the deep. Later in the afternoon a huge dorado dived out of the sea right next to me. I'd often seen them swimming around the boat and on my first row, Cayle had almost caught one. But this dorado stunned me with colours I'd never seen before. Its flank dazzled iridescent turquoise in the sun, and it exuded raw power as it effortlessly flew through the air and dived back into the sea near the end of the boat. It was truly awesome and a welcome highlight in an otherwise demoralizingly hard days rowing. After my last daytime rowing shift, I called Leven.

'The wind is due to increase slightly in the afternoon tomorrow and should give you some momentum,' he said.

'I hope so, Leven.' I replied. 'It's really hard rowing for little or no distance.'

'The currents are fairly strong there or thereabouts and will play havoc with your course over ground. We need to keep as much south as we can for the now. It'll pay dividends as we come into the equatorial current in a couple of days.'

I rowed again in pitch black and then almost on the stroke of midnight, *Hope* just stopped. A current started to push me north and as I altered my heading south, the boat felt like it had just frozen. I pulled on the oars but could only manage a meagre one-and-a-half knots. I rowed my heart out through the night for little or no speed and when awoke and got ready for my last nighttime rowing shift, I couldn't move. I wanted to get out of the cabin and row, but I just sat there instead. I told myself that if I rested, I'd be stronger and be able to row faster, but I knew that was a lie. I knew it was my mind playing tricks and once this rowing session had gone, it was gone forever. I'd never get it back again. But still I couldn't move. I felt like I was welded to the floor of the cabin. I counted to ten, urging myself to get out and row on ten, but as it approached, I knew I wouldn't be able to move. Utterly exhausted, both mentally and physically, I tried again, but as I reached the number ten, I was still unable to move. I felt powerless and wanted to cry. I knew that I couldn't give in, I was too close to the finish and without rowing I would drift too far north. I tried counting to ten again but still I couldn't move. After 40 minutes, trying and failing to get out and row, I finally managed to get out of the cabin and rowed for an hour and 20 minutes. Afterwards I collapsed exhausted in the cabin, disheartened with a miserable 46 nautical miles covered in 24 hours.

Day 55 Logbook Entry

Position at 0800hrs (L) (1100hrs UTC) on 5th Mar 2019
05°55'. 213n 47°14: 747w

Distance travelled 46nm rowed at 246°t
Total distance 2788nm

300nm to Cayenne

Conditions v similar to last few days until 0000hrsL when boat started going north and slowed down considerably. Now COG 255°t – 260°t and heading 225°t – 230°t. Speed 1.5 -1.7kts where for the wind it should be 2-2.5kts. Saw another shark at the end of the boat @1530L and large fish (dorado) dived out of the water v impressive 3-5m jump v powerful and the colours of the fish were stunning, shimmering deep emerald green and turquoise.

I peered through the spy hole again and saw Isatullah walking towards the gate. The NDS guards were their usual lackadaisical selves and didn't give him a second glance as he walked past. I opened the gate, let Isatullah in and closed it quickly.

'Salaam Alaykum, I'm glad to meet you properly.' I said. 'Harry told me about you, where have you been?' I continued as we walked through the garden on our way to the office. The small garden was a mini oasis within the FOB and I often saw one of the many wild mongooses hunting amongst the small shrubs, nooks and crannies along its edge.

'The guard is Abdul Khaliq's brother and is passing information back to him.' he said.

'So why did you come?' I asked.

'I wanted to see Harry' He offered as explanation. I noted the slight embarrassment to his tone and demeanour. We reached the office, but it was too hot to sit inside so we sat on chairs under the shade of a poncho.

'Why did you want to meet with Harry?' I asked as he settled down.

'I just hadn't seen him for a long time,' came his evasive answer. I again noted his uncomfortableness in talking about his reason for coming.

The big news in the Upper Sangin Valley that week was an American air strike on a very senior Taliban figure. He'd been travelling in a convoy in an area between Lashkar Gah and Gereshk when the convoy was attacked. The aircraft had reported seeing figures escaping from the destroyed car and the Americans wanted confirmation on whether they'd killed their intended target. I asked Isatullah if he knew anything about it. He told me that he'd been at the bedside of this senior Talib a couple of days before along with a comprehensive list of who's who of the most senior Taliban leaders in northern Helmand. The senior Talib had been hit in the chest by shrapnel and was too weak to travel to Quetta in Pakistan to receive proper medical treatment. Instead, a doctor had been dispatched to treat him in situ but didn't think that he would survive. Hence the reason for the Taliban delegation visiting him the day before. They were there to pay their respects to a dying comrade. I went through all the information logically and it felt good to finally be doing what I was supposed to do. I noticed with interest that Mullah Hikmatullah, who was supposedly talking to us, was absent from everything Isatullah was saying. I would have to find a way of bringing him up in conversation without alerting Isatullah to my interest in him. But I wouldn't be able to do it now. It would be too obvious. I arranged to meet him again in a week's time to allow me to get to PB TEAHOUSE and back. I finished with Isatullah, saw him out of the gate and watched him pass the NDS guards without incident. From having no work for a month, I now had a mountain. I'd have to get all my paperwork done before I left for TEAHOUSE the next day.

A couple of days later I was sat in the tiny Ops room in TEAHOUSE staring at the TV screen waiting for Hamid to appear. Greg sat next to me and we chatted as I moved the camera around the local area scanning for him, checking the most likely approaches to the crossroads. As the allotted time approached my nervousness grew. I spotted what I thought might be Hamid. He was walking up from direction of the Helmand River heading directly for the track junction and looking at my watch, it seemed that he had timed it perfectly.

'Well this looks promising,' I said to Greg.

'That definitely him?'

'Looks like him.' I replied. 'We'll find out in a second.'

The small figure shimmering in the already hot morning sun approached the junction and then stopped. It had to be Hamid. I counted to thirty with a nervous excitement. *'Go on then, don't forget your shawl'*, I thought as I willed him to change it from draping over his left shoulder to his right. The small figure on the TV screen then looked directly at the camera high up in the sky then turned away and started walking along the path in the direction I'd instructed him, moving his shawl as he did.

'Go on,' I said out loud with increasing relief and excitement.

'Is this good?' asked Greg, sensing my obvious excitement.

'Yes mate, this is not usual,' I replied, smiling as I did. Hamid then reached a bigger track next to a compound where I'd told him to turn right. He paused, then turned left and continued along the path in the opposite direction. 'Fuck.' I shouted at the TV.

'I take it he wasn't supposed to go that way,' said Greg.

'No mate.' I felt like my horse had fallen at the last fence after leading from the start. He'd at least started well, and this was something I could build on.

Three days later I was sat with Hamid in the office with an aerial phot between us on the floor. 'OK Hamid, show me exactly what you did and where you went.'

Hamid pointed to the track junction and said, 'This is where I started as you said. Could you see me from the balloon?' He asked.

'Yes I could.'

He smiled and looked back down at the air phot. His brow furrowed as he concentrated. 'I followed where you said,' his finger tracing the route along the path I'd seen him walk three days earlier. 'And then I came to here,' pointing at the junction where he should've turned right. 'And Gulab was there planting an IED.'

I heard 'Gulab' and 'Minuna', what Afghans called any explosive buried in the ground, before Freido had chance to interpret. 'He told me to go away, so I couldn't go the way you told me.'

'Where exactly was he burying it?'

Minutes later I ran into the Ops room with a ten-figure grid reference of the newly emplaced IED. A ten-figure grid reference gives you an area of only one metre square and as near as dam it, an exact location.

I ran back into the office and asked Hamid, 'Do you know any more places where there are "Minunas"?'

A couple of hours later I'd reported the exact locations for most of the IEDs in the area around PB TEAHOUSE. I said goodbye to Hamid after arranging our next meeting and immediately started the worst part, but the majority of a HUMINT Operators job, the paperwork. For once though, I relished it.

40 Commando and the British were preparing to leave Sangin for good and hand over control of the area to the Americans. An increasing number of US Marine Corps soldiers had become common in FOB Jackson and the other patrol bases as they began to build numbers ready to take control as 40 Commando ended their tour in October. New faces in USMC uniforms had become the norm, so I wasn't overly surprised to see a few Yanks at the daily Int' briefing later that day. For once I had a lot to say and outlined the locations of all the IED's that Hamid had given me. After the meeting a tall, muscular yank Marine introduced himself.

'Hi I'm Corey. I'm the battalion HUMINT guy,' Corey was handsome in his immaculate uniform, his thick black hair pulled back smartly and shaved 'high and tight' Marine Corps style. His quick, sincere smile made him instantly likable.

I'd taken to wearing shorts, T-shirt and flip flops about the place and my hair was far too long and dishevelled for how much I had left. We couldn't have looked any more different.

'I'm Frank. Shall we go and get a wet in the galley?' I said then quickly added, 'A coffee in the chow hall.' When he looked confused.

As we talked it became clear that the NDS would also come under Corey's remit and I explained the problems at the NDS station. Corey looked understandably shocked as I told him that one of the guards was a well-known nephew of an influential Taliban fighting commander. I also explained the background to the previous NDS chief, Colonel Rahman, who'd been expelled but was probably pulling strings in the background, hoping to get reinstated in Sangin. We agreed that Corey would accompany me on my daily meeting with the NDS starting the next day, but first I had to meet my other agent, Isatullah.

Day 56

Once I was sat on the deck, I could row for two hours but every rowing shift through the day started with a torturous struggle to simply get out of the cabin and start rowing. On my hour off, I'd lay in the cabin, trying to rest as best I could, dreading the inevitable internal fight to get out and row. The mental effort was as draining as the physical effort of pulling on the oars.

The previous night's currents continued and rowing through treacle for a meagre one and a half knots was soul destroying. As the hot day wore on into the afternoon, I could feel what little energy I had, slowly ebbing away and the struggle I had to start each rowing shift, became increasingly harder. Again, I thought about resting, reasoning with myself that I'd be stronger afterwards. But again, I knew that was a lie. I remembered back to my time in Royal Marines training and how I believed that I'd be one of the first to fail from the troop and kicked out. I remember being astonished every time someone left who I thought of as stronger than me. I particularly remembered one of the first to give up. He was physically fitter than me and after he went to see the training team to tell them he wanted to leave; I asked him why. I was desperate just to still be with 635 Troop at the end of each week and couldn't understand why someone would voluntarily give up.

'It's just not for me,' he'd said, but I knew it was a lie. You can't simply join the Marines, you must put in a lot of effort just to get into training, so it must have been for him at some point. And training isn't the Marines, it's the hurdle you must jump over to become a Royal Marine, so how could he know that it wasn't for him? I knew he was lying to himself and he was leaving was because he'd simply just had enough. I remember being astonished at how he could believe his own lie. It was as if that memory shone a light on my own lies to myself, that by resting and not rowing, I'd somehow be faster. It kept the lies at bay.

I called Claire after dinner and spoke to both Billy and Ivor who'd joined her in Cayenne. They were all excited to be in a new country and had that 'first day of a holiday' vibe that was completely at odds with my feelings. I didn't say anything to Claire other than I was struggling.

'Don't worry, you're nearly there,' she said.

After the call I sat in the cabin and thought about why I was putting myself through this. I'd rowed my heart out all day and I knew that barring a miracle, I wasn't getting anywhere near my 50-mile target for 24-hours rowing. I was utterly exhausted, physically and mentally and thought *'no one cares what I'm doing'*. I couldn't see the point and felt stupid about the apparent absurdity of being in a tiny boat out in the ocean and rowing myself into complete exhaustion.

I called Scotty. 'Oi oi brother,' he answered, recognising the satphone number.

'Hey Scotty.' I said. 'Mate, I'm . . .'

'I'm so proud of you, brother. You've gone and put your head above the parapet and you're doing the extraordinary. You are inspiring so many people and we're all rooting for you.'

We chatted more before I put the phone down. I burst into tears and sobbed my heart out. It was as if Scotty knew exactly what to say in that moment.

Shortly after the call it was time to clamber out of the cabin for the first of my nighttime rowing shifts. At the end of the boat was a large black sea bird. It had a long black beak and a light grey patch on its head. It cocked its head to one side and stared at me with its beady eye as I settled myself onto the deck.

'Hello,' I said, then slowly shuffled down to the end of the boat, trying not to startle it. It stayed where it was, appearing totally unconcerned. I took a photo of it then sat at the end of the boat for a few moments chatting to it. When it didn't answer, I went back to my rowing seat and started rowing. It was a little bit of company through the night and when I got up for my last shift before morning, it had gone but had shat all over the solar panel.

'That's really ungrateful,' I said to myself and smiled for the first time in days.

Day 56 Logbook Entry.

Position at 0800hrs (L) (1100hrs UTC) on 6th Mar 2019	*Distance travelled 41.5nm rowed at 247°t*
05°39'. 330n 47°57: 095w	*Total distance 2829.5nm*

260nm to Cayenne

V frustrating and worrying 48hrs of a current pushing me N. Boat progress across the ground is pitiful 1-5kts – 2kts when rowing; Back-breaking and demoralising. Picked up a hitchhiker last night, bird happily sat on the end of the boat bumming a lift. Then the bastard shat of my solar panels before flying off, very ungrateful.

I ensured that my next meeting with Isatullah was properly prepared. Our first meeting was rushed because I hadn't known he was coming. I planned on asking who he knew in the higher echelons of the Taliban hierarchy and therefore who he'd be able to report on. This I thought would be a good opportunity to throw Mullah Hikmatullah in amongst a host of names without arousing suspicion that he was the intermediary in the reconciliation talks between the Alikozai tribe and the British.

I got up with the first rays of the morning sun, prepared the office then walked down with Freido to the main gate. Isatullah walked straight past the NDS compound and came through the gate without incident. Once sat in the office, I started by going through the Taliban command structure as we understood it. Afghan tribal politics was as complicated as a bucket of live eels and often made as much sense and the list and organisation of Taliban commanders was no different. There was no command structure as we'd understand it, it was more a complex and ever-changing group of allegiances based on tribal loyalties and shifting influence. Any up-to date information on this was valuable intelligence. I went through the list of names with Isatullah telling me as much about them as he could.

'Mullah Hikmatullah?' I asked.

'He's been sent to Baghran,' he said.

'Baghran north of Masu Qalai or Bagram near Kabul?'

'Masu Qalai,' he confirmed. 'Mullah Bakari has many drugs labs there.'

Baghran north of Musa Qalai is a long deep valley in the mountainous far north of Helmand province and totally inaccessible to conventional ISAF troops. It was also the reason there had been no contact with him. I thought for a moment that this would be a comfort to Phil the political advisor and to the CO.

'Is that why he's been sent there?' I asked.

'No,' replied Isatullah before dropping the bombshell. 'Abdul Zakir sent him to stop him talking to ISAF.'

Abdul Zakir was the Taliban senior commander in Sangin. I steadied myself before asking the next question, concentrating on not giving away the significance of what Isatullah was saying. 'What do you mean "talking to ISAF"?' ISAF was the collective name Afghans used for any foreign soldiers.

'Mullah Hikmatullah was talking to ISAF for the Alikozai and Abdul Zakir wanted to stop that, so he sent him to Baghran,' Isatullah said matter-of-factly.

If the Taliban shadow district governor of Sangin knew about the secret talks, then the Taliban senior leadership in Quetta, Pakistan would also know. The secret talks with the Alikozai tribe brokering a peace in the whole upper Sangin Valley, the talks that had been the focal point of 40 Commando's tour and had underpinned nearly every tactical decision had not only stalled, they were dead in the water. I asked as many questions as I dared without alerting Isatullah to the significance of what he was telling me before moving on to the rest of the who's who of Taliban commanders in the upper Sangin Valley.

After saying goodbye to Isatullah I rushed back to the office to call Dave, my boss in Lashkar Gah. I told him about Abdul Zakir sending Mullah Hikmatullah to Baghran and more importantly about his knowledge of the talks. If Isatullah knew about the secret talks between the UK and the Alikozai tribe, then it must be common knowledge. This information was a massive bombshell and I needed Dave's experience in how I was going to report it. I felt the implications of 'Courageous Restraint' every time I went out on the ground on patrol. I knew how every soldier hated it and felt let down by the chain of command. But I also knew the implications of what was trying to be achieved. If the Alikozai had reconciled, it had potential to change the whole course of the war. I could totally understand the marines hating 'Outrageous Constraint' and I sympathised with them, but what I knew and couldn't tell them was that what it was trying to achieve was worth it. But now I had to go and tell the Commanding Officer that the focus of his whole campaign had just gone up in smoke and to be honest, I really didn't fancy doing it.

I anxiously walked through the Int' cell and into the corridor leading to the Ops room. The CO's office was halfway down the corridor on the right and as I approached, I could see him in his office sat at his desk.

I knocked at his door and said, 'You got a minute please, Sir?'

He looked up from behind his desk and said, 'Come in Colours.'

'I've got some news about our friend from Yakchal,' I noticed his attention focus. 'What I'm about to tell you I'll be reporting tonight, and I can't say with certainty whether it will be released as an intelligence report tomorrow but it's very likely that it will.'

'Go on,' he said, sensing my apprehension.

'If it does go out, it'll have the lowest grading, that's because it's from a source that is still being assessed so can only be released that way. Despite that grading I assess this information as being highly credible for several reasons,' I took a deep breath and continued, 'Our friend from Yakchal was sent to Baghran north of Musa Qalai some weeks ago by Abdul Zakir. The reason for sending him was because he was aware that we were talking to the Alikozai about reconciling. Also, it's no secret in the Upper Sangin Valley about the talks.'

The CO stared at me for a few moments like a statue, frozen. I couldn't read what he was thinking or if he believed me. He sat staring at me and I started to wonder how I was going to end this conversation and extract myself from his office.

Still staring at me he said, 'Thank you Colours.'

I walked out of his office and went to find Phil the political Advisor to repeat the process.

The next day Colonel Rahman came back to Sangin. As Corey and I approached the NDS compound I could tell that something had changed. The guards, usually happy but lackadaisical were now quiet and subdued. Freido greeted one of them as we entered the compound and after their brief exchange, he turned to me and said, 'Saiid Nabi has gone.'

Before I could respond, Rahman strode from the building. He was a huge bear of a man with a large black beard, massive hands and a sneer that told us exactly what he thought of us and that he didn't care that we knew. I shook his hand and introduced myself with Freido interpreting, then Corey did the same with his interpreter. Rhaman then went into a small speech about how bad Nabi was, how he'd shared too much information with us and that things would change now. As he spoke, I followed Freido's translation but I was engrossed by Rahman's small bloodshot eyes. They were the eyes of a murderer, bereft of all humanity. I've never seen eyes like them before or since.

In the small meeting room we sat on the sofa while Rahman sat on the other, his large bulk taking up most of the seat. He continued his sermon on how things were going to change and I asked how he was going to get intelligence. The question shocked him as if he hadn't considered the priority for the NDS station. It was clear that everything I'd heard about Rahman was true. He was only interested in furthering his family's influence in the Upper Sangin Valley and that I'd have to be doubly careful when meeting Hamid and Isatullah.

As we left, I passed Captain Maboob sat at his desk. He looked up at me with an almost terrified expression on his face. It was clearly going to be a challenge working with Rahman, but at least not as challenging as working under him.

I continued meeting Hamid and started to build a comprehensive picture of how the Taliban were operating south of Sangin town. Gulab's little cell of fighters continued their attacks and laying IEDs but as they were digging them in, I was reporting their location.

Gulab was operating from a compound so I began to build a detailed picture of not only the day-to-day goings on in and around the compound but also a thorough layout of the inside of the building. Isatullah was giving me excellent information on everything that was going on in the higher echelons of the Taliban hierarchy in the Upper Sangin Valley and importantly how there was no change with Mullah Hikmatullah, our friend from Yakchal. As my reporting began to fill out our understanding of the Taliban leadership in Northern Helmand, in most cases it tied in with what we knew from other sources giving Isatullah's reporting more and more credibility. As the weeks stretched into months since the last contact with Mullah Hikmatullah, all hope of a reconciliation faded.

After a particularly fruitful meeting with Hamid, I put out a threat warning for an IED he'd seen being dug in by two of Gulab's fighters near a PB next to a bridge over the Nahr-e-Saraj Canal called PB Almas. The following day started as so many of them had before with a sign saying 'OP MINIMISE now in force'.

Later that day, Jim the Int' Corporal approached me. 'Frank, we've had a request from PB Almas that any threat warnings you get from that particular source who reported the IED yesterday, can you let them know that it's from that one.'

'Why's that?' I asked.

'The casualty this morning stepped on the IED from yesterday's threat warning and it seems that this source is bang on.'

'Mate they should treat all threat warnings as serious,' I replied.

'Yeh, I know but that one is bang on mate'.

Utterly deflated I walked away. All the hard work I'd done to get that IED location was for nothing. The whole point of what I was doing, the real buzz in being an agent handler was knowing that you were saving lives. My feelings turned to anger, not at the soldiers for not listening to the threat warning, not to the patrol commanders for not using them in planning their patrols. I was angry with Paul, the Det sergeant major in KAF. He was only interested in producing piles of intelligence reports and higher and higher threat warning statistics that he could then brief to the chain of command taking the credit for his Det's hard work. My report of a location of an IED had been lost in the chaff of vague reports, often made up and reported as threat warnings and a Royal Marine had been seriously injured as a direct consequence.

Day 57

The day started the same as the past few, with back-breaking rowing through strong currents that slowed my progress west to a pitiful one and a half knots.

Whilst resting, I'd lay dreading the mental struggle to row again. But row I must. The hard truth beyond all my dread of the coming day and its inevitable hardships, was that I knew I had no choice. I was at sea, I couldn't stay where I was, the currents would send me away from the finish. My only option was to row. I began to notice a current that started to push me south. As the first two hours' rowing wore on, it got stronger and by the time my two hours were up, *Hope* was moving through the water at almost a right angle to the way she was facing. This current was totally at odds with what I was expecting. I rowed hard, fighting against the southerly current, inwardly dreading another day battling an ocean that was doing what it wanted with me and my small boat. As I laid in the cabin after another two hours hard rowing, I could see how quickly I was moving south without any forward momentum and I started to worry. If I was pushed too far south, getting into the Mahury River estuary and the finish line could become difficult. I continued to fight the southerly current through the day and my speed was pathetic. I struggled to get close to one and a half knots when rowing and when not, *Hope* was being pushed worryingly south. It was gruelling hard graft. In the middle of the afternoon, I saw a container ship to the north-west on the horizon. I realized that it was the first human thing that I'd seen for weeks beyond my tiny universe that was *Hope*. I had an overwhelming sense of being on the other side of the vast emptiness of the Atlantic Ocean. I knew how far I'd come and how far I had to go. I pencilled it into the logbook every morning when I completed my morning stats. It was part of my daily routine but seeing that ship on the horizon brought the numbers to life. For the first time throughout the whole row, I had a real sense of closing in on the finish line. I was careful not to allow myself to get too carried away, there was still a lot of ocean between me and Cayenne.

After my last daytime rowing shift, I opened a hatch and laying sideways, reached in right up to my shoulder and dug around the bottom to get an evening meal. I touched a couple of breakfast ration packs then felt my hands close round a circular metal object. I guessed what it might be but tried to not get my hopes up. I pulled it out and with a huge smile saw it was a tin of fruit salad. Twenty minutes later, I was sat in the cabin eating a tin of fruit salad thinking all my Christmases had come at once. It tasted amazing. My first nighttime rowing shift seemed easier, it looked like I had cleared the strange southerly current and my speed increased slightly. The black bird was back and hitched another lift with me through the night.

Day 57 Logbook Entry

Position at 0800hrs (L) (1100hrs UTC) on 7th Mar 2019
05°07'. 506n 48°28: 534w

Distance travelled 44.5nm rowed at 224°t
Total distance 2874nm

225nm to Cayenne

Surprise strong southerly current from 1000hrs L until approx 1800hrs L gave a good bit south! The boat is still very slow which is demoralising. Hopefully as I go into the Cayenne current its westerly but will give some momentum.

Found some tin fruit last night, essence ☺

The balloon in FOB Jackson was in constant use tracking patrols on the ground and on the odd days when no patrols were out, it would be used for a myriad of different tasks or be grounded getting repairs. When this happened shots would ring out with the Taliban taking the opportunity to shoot at it whilst it was briefly in range.

A couple of days after the incident with the reported IED, Jim found me in the office, 'We had the camera trained on the compound your source has been reporting on and they all came out carrying a couple of vallons, it looks like they are testing their IEDs to see if we can detect them.'

A vallon was the front line in detecting IEDs for all British troops in Afghanistan and was a slightly more sophisticated metal detector carried by the point man of every patrol. I followed Jim to the Ops room. On the way Jim told me that they had a rare free slot on the camera and had decided to check out Hamid's reporting on Gulab's base because of the correct reporting of the IED. This free slot had coincided with Gulab checking the IED's that he and his fighters had buried to see if we could detect them with a couple of captured vallons. I walked into the Ops room and a large compound filled the huge screen.

'That's the compound,' Jim said.

Gulab and his fighters had just unwittingly shown us the locations of at least some of the IEDs they'd emplaced. The balloon had corroborated Hamid's reporting. I borrowed a phone and called Dave my boss in Lashkar Gah to tell him. This was significant because the reports on the building were no longer single source. Dave told me that getting as much information on the building would now be a priority for my future meetings with Hamid.

As my End of Tour date approached, I began to pack the office up. I continued to meet with Hamid who furnished me with excellent intelligence on Gulab's base. He also continued to report the locations of new IEDs. The British were also preparing to pack up and leave Sangin and as they did, the numbers of USMC steadily increased. Finally, I counted up all the money, closed down everything that could be closed down and padlocked shut the container before it was shipped back to Camp Bastion in a huge military convoy.

I arranged my next meeting with Hamid as an introduction to Corey. The fact that the British were handing over control of Sangin to the Americans was common knowledge throughout Afghanistan and was no surprise to Hamid. The handover went well as I explained that Hamid would now be meeting Corey who'd be feeding intelligence directly to 40 Commando whose last men would continue to patrol for another few weeks through the staggered handover.

My work in Sangin was over and feeling pleased with myself I walked round to see the CO. I knocked at his door. 'Hi Sir, I'm just letting you know that I've just had the handover with the USMC HUMINT guy and he'll be running my source from now on. I'm flying out the day after tomorrow.'

'Can you stay on for a couple of weeks?' he asked.

The question took me by surprise. I'd assumed that the CO wasn't my biggest fan as I was always bringing him bad news about Mullah Hikmatullah and the reconciliation of the Alikozai tribe. Practically, everything that I needed to run agents had been packed up and shipped back to Camp Bastion.

'No Sir,' I smiled. 'I'm getting the flight back.' The CO thanked me for my work.

I walked back to the cave feeling pretty happy with myself.

My first day in Sangin started with a Blackhawk helicopter being shot down above me. My last day started with a rocket-propelled grenade whistling a couple of metres over my head as I walked to the shower block. It came from the same firing point as the one that hit the Blackhawk, narrowly missed a CH-53 helicopter that was landing, and then exploded over the wadi on the other side of the HESCO wall. As it did, the whole of the FOB exploded into action with the familiar drum of heavy machine guns, 50-calibre and small arms fire. I continued walking nonchalantly towards the shower clutching my towel around my waist and my wash bag in my hand. This was just another day in Sangin.

After lunch I went over to the Ops Room to check my flight and walked straight into massive argument. On the screen from the balloon camera were six Afghans sat in a semi-circle in front of two Afghans digging a hole. The diggers were partially obscured by an overhanging branch, but you could clearly see the shovel come out from behind the branch with the digging action and the spoil fly off the shovel.

The Special Forces Liaison Officer, a tall wiry colour sergeant from the SAS called Billy, was pointing at the screen and shouting, 'How can you not see what this is?'

'We don't know that's what they're doing,' replied a major from the Royal Artillery.

It didn't take long for me to get the gist of what was happening. Earlier, the camera on the balloon followed the Taliban fighters from Gulab's compound with a captured vallon to where they were now digging-in an IED in what could only be a 'How to dig in an IED so the vallon can't detect it' lesson. The artillery major's argument was that the hole they were clearly digging was obscured by some branches. The fact they'd come from a known and reported Taliban compound with a captured vallon and were undeniably digging a hole, despite the obscuring branch, was obviously lost on him. The CO came into the Ops room, I guessed to see what the commotion was all about.

Billy said to the CO, 'Look, this is a blatant IED laying lesson with a vallon.'

'We can't know that for certain,' interrupted the major which made Billy even angrier.

Jim came into the Ops room. 'We've just had a single direction radio transmission cut on Gulab and it goes straight through that group.' He said indicating the screen. I looked closer at the Taliban on the screen and the more I looked the more one of them stood out. I had seen the footage of Gulab sat on a wall on Hamid's phone and now here he was on the screen in front of me, the same slender build wearing the same distinctive brown waist coat and light brown Kandahari cap. I walked up to the screen and pointed at and said, 'That's Gulab.'

'How do you know?' asked the major.

'I've seen him on a phone and my source described the same clothing, that's him.'

'We can't just kill people because you don't like their clothing, Colours,' he sneered.

Billy said to the poor young Marine writing the logbook. 'Right I want all this logged.' He then reeled off a list of what we were watching, the fact they'd come from a known Taliban compound with the Valon, they were digging in something and the single direction radio transmission of Gulab.

Finally, the CO very reluctantly said. 'Right. I now want to prosecute this target.'

'But Sir,' the major started but the CO cut him off.

'I've made my decision.'

'OK then.' said the major from the Artillery. 'I'll order an Exactor strike.'

'What?' cried Billy in exasperation. The Exactor is an optical guided missile known by soldiers on the ground as the 'exaggerator' because of its inaccuracy. An argument then began between Billy and the major about his choice of weapon system that was cut short by the CO who said, 'We'll go with Exactor.'

'I want it logged that in my opinion this is the wrong choice of weapon system for this target.' said Billy to the Marine now overwhelmed by writing the log.

The major called in the Exactor and we waited. We heard the dull thud of the Exactor hitting the ground. On the screen the Taliban fighters all looked up as one at the same sound we'd just heard. The Exactor had missed by so much, they hadn't realised they were the intended target. They shrugged and carried on. The OC fires looked mortified.

'Right, call-in fast air,' Said the CO.

The duty signaller then started talking to an American F-15 pilot and gave over the fire mission of a 500lb bomb. The pilot's voice relayed via a speaker for all to hear.

'I've got visual on the target,' came the crackled voice over the speaker. 'Ninety seconds till weapons release.'

'This can't be happening', I thought to myself. *'This is too much of a fairy tale.'* My reporting had led to this moment and we were going to finally get the most effective fighting Taliban commander in the Upper-Sangin Valley. On my last day in theatre.

'Sixty seconds,' came the voice again and as it did, the Taliban fighters on the screen started to get up and shake each other's hands.

'No. No' and 'Fuck', came the cries from the Ops room as they started to get on motorcycles, bikes and walk away in different directions.

'Abort,' ordered the CO.

The Det in Kandahar had completely changed in the three months I'd been in Sangin. Paul, the Det sergeant major, had been replaced and the Det was better for it. While I waited for my flight to the UK I thought about the missed opportunities and poor leadership, both from Paul in KAF and the CO of 40 Commando in Sangin. At least the latter was trying to achieve something, Paul was only interested in furthering his career. I thought about the limbs that would be lost and the lives that would be devastated by those poor decisions. The consequences of decisions made in Sangin would reverberate for years to come.

Those thoughts stayed with me for months whilst at home. I'd uncontrollably, and mostly without reason, burst into tears. As I sobbed, I thought about Darbs and the families that had been devastated. The tears gradually faded, but the consequences of my own decision to leave Sangin and not stay a couple of weeks came to haunt me years later. I met a big Cornish Bootneck called Big Al who stepped on an IED and lost his leg in Sangin. He'd been in the same FOB when Darbs was killed and Darbs had been his troop sergeant in PB Almas. We talked and reminisced about him. Darbs was a massive character and Big Al loved him. As did I.

I asked Al when he was injured and when he told me, I realised it was just after I left. If I'd stayed, I'm certain Hamid would have reported that IED. I burst into tears and sobbed how sorry I was. Big Al is a huge bear of a man, with a mop of black hair and big black beard. He put both his huge arms around me, hugged me to him and said in his deep, booming Cornish voice, 'Now Frank. You don't know that. You can't think that way.'

Day 58

After completing my stats from the last 24 hours, I ate breakfast and rested before starting a new day's rowing. I was exhausted and demoralised but felt a robotic detachment to getting out of the cabin and rowing. It almost felt like a habit or that it was happening to someone else. I'd come to terms with the fact that the rest of my time in the boat was going to be very unpleasant and had to just get on with it.

Each rowing shift was backbreakingly hard and I was still pulling *Hope* through thick treacle. I knew my daily rowing target of 50 nautical miles was unrealistic, so I set myself a new target of rowing further than yesterday's pitiful 44½ miles.

I opened one of the port side hatches to get a snack pack for lunch. I knew I only had a few more days left on the boat so could afford to look for one that contained something nice. When packing the rations, I'd mixed them up to provide a small piece of variety in the monotony of ocean rowing. Some contained nuts, while others contained flapjacks or jerky. Throughout the row I'd always just grabbed the first one that came to hand as I didn't want to deplete all the best snack packs at the start of the row. But now I saw little point in that discipline and rummaged around to get one that looked half decent. I piled the contents of the hatch up to one side and rummaged around the bottom. My hands closed around the unmistakably round shape of an orange. I'd forgotten I'd brought a dozen oranges and presumed this one would be rotten, but it felt firm. I pulled it out of the hatch and to my amazement, it looked as fresh as the day I stowed it. I sat on the deck, peeled the orange and ate it segment by segment. It was sweet, juicy and the first fresh thing I'd eaten in forty days.

I called Claire and told her excitedly about the orange, 'It tasted amazing.'

Claire laughed. 'We went to see the French Navy chaps this morning and on the way Billy noticed an ocean rowing boat outside a sailing shop. The chap who owns it is an ocean rower and we told him about you and he's going to talk to Leven about how you finish. We showed him where you are on the tracker and he says you are too far south.'

After speaking to Claire I gave Izzy my Social Media points. She told me that someone on Facebook had identified my hitchhiker as a Noddy.

Starting the process of planning the final approach made me more aware that as I got closer, navigationally I had little room for error. I wouldn't have the advantage of taking the path of least resistance and would have to stick to my heading whatever the ocean threw at me. I knew the final approach was critical and a lot could still go wrong.

After my evening meal, I clambered onto the deck for my first nighttime rowing shift and the Black Noddy from the night before hitchhiked again on the rear cabin. This time it had a friend who perched on my right oar. I said hello to both and grabbed my oars to start rowing. The Noddy on the oar took off and tried to land on the rear cabin with its mate, who was having none of it. It squawked and flapped its wings aggressively, stopping it from landing. After a couple of unsuccessful attempts it circled the boat and settled on the front cabin, where it stayed throughout the night.

With no moon and only the brightest stars shining through the haze of an otherwise pitch-black sky, I rowed through the night rows with no discernible sense of location. The boat rocked from side to side in nothingness and often I had the sensation of falling through space. The hard rowing continued, and I forced myself to pull on the oars hoping to beat yesterday's distance with the two Black Noddys keeping me company through the night.

Just after midnight, a huge flying fish hit me in the face like an Exocet missile, almost knocking me from my rowing seat. It flapped on the deck before I threw it back into the sea. On my last rowing session before the sun rose both Noddys had gone. I finished rowing then cleaned their pooh off both solar panels before entering the cabin and completing my stats. I was relieved that I'd beaten yesterday's distance by just a nautical mile and a half.

Day 58 Logbook Entry

Position at 0800hrs (L) (1100hrs UTC) on 8th Mar 2019
O4°44'. 282n 049°10: 083w

Distance travelled 46nm rowed at 263°t
Total distance 2920nm

182nm to Cayenne

Frustratingly slow progress again today. Now heading 223°t but will increase this to 225°t. Should hit the main Cayenne current at some point today and will then see what I can expect for the final few days rowing. Hopefully it'll be an increase in pace.

Had another hitchhiker on the end of the boat. Quite content to let me go right up to it. Its mate was sat on the end of my right oar. When I started rowing it tried to land on the rear of the boat but the bird that was there kept warning it off. Was also hit in the face by a massive flying fish.

After another well-earned post-deployment leave, I returned to Chicksands and was sent down to the course as directing staff. I remembered Vinny's words from when I was teaching on the basic course, that you only start to understand 'mechanics' once you start teaching them and now I was teaching Advanced Mechanics on the Advanced course.

Whereas before I felt like a massive fraud when teaching the basic course, having only just scraped a pass on the same course a year before, my time and experiences in Sangin gave me the self-belief that I knew what I was doing. I'd always enjoyed teaching, whether that was skiing and living in the Arctic or picking up and meeting with agents, the fundamental principles are the same. Either teaching a practical skill or a technical competency, the understanding the 'why' behind it is key. And now I had a good understanding of the 'why' I felt confident in my understanding of what I was teaching. I was part of a great team who all took immense pride in everything we taught and great care in grading the students on the course. I felt that I'd earned my place amongst my contemporaries. For the first time in my life, I was happy with who I was and the voice that had constantly told me that I was a coward, had told me that I 'wasn't really good enough', had gone completely.

Away from work, I had a loving wife who'd supported me throughout my life in the marines, two children I was immensely proud of and a home in a village on Dartmoor. I was as far as it was possible to be from that terrified little boy in Dagenham frozen with fear in the doorway whilst his Dad beat his Mum.

All DS took advantage of a couple of days where we were not needed on the course and went out in London ending up in the recently gentrified East End.

I woke up the next morning in my Dad's flat in Dagenham. I opened my eyes and at first I had no idea where I was or how I'd got there. Then almost instantly a vague familiarity gave way to being transported back 33 years to a child. Julie and I had stayed overnight and slept together with our Dad and his bedroom hadn't change in the intervening 33 years. My Dad would have drunken arguments and fights in his sleep. He would snarl, shout, threaten and swear at invisible demons and spectres that obviously stalked his subconscious mind. My Dad's nightmares were a regular occurrence whenever he slept after drinking and it had been frightening as a kid. His aggression was real, even if his enemies were not. It's why we didn't stay at our Dad's flat overnight and this one lone occasion must have been because our Mum was on a rare night out. Julie and I laid awake most of the night listening to him shout and swear. But when he woke up in the morning, he changed completely. He was happy and totally oblivious to a night filled with fights, arguments and terrors. He smiled and started telling us a funny story about being attacked by chickens in an attempt at cheering us both up. He grabbed his bedside lamp, the kind with a long, adjustable neck and it instantly transformed into an angry chicken in his hands. It attacked him and he screamed as it made a lunge at his neck. Between shouting, screaming and gurgling, he made funny chicken noises. Me and Julie were crying with laughter. He thrashed about the bed fighting with the lamp and then thumped the top of the shade to finally kill it. The bulb went out and we laughed louder at his now broken lamp. The memories of that night and the morning fight with the chicken, came flooding back. The lamp was still there with dent in the shade from where he'd hit it.

I got up and dressed in the clothes I had on the night before and went into the front room. My Dad was sat on his sofa watching the telly.

'How on earth did I get here?' I asked.

'I think you got a taxi last night.'

'What time did I get here?'

'About half past one this morning,' he smiled.

'Sorry if I woke you up.'

'I wasn't asleep.'

My Dad had no set routine and often watched TV all night and stay awake drinking and slept in fits through the day.

He made me a cup of tea and I wondered how I was going to get back to Chicksands. As I sat drinking it, I blurted out exactly what I did for a living. I'd not told any of my family what my job involved, they knew I'd done a different kind of job because I grew a beard before I left for Afghanistan and maybe they knew that I was on a secondment away from the Royal Marines, but that was all they knew. I hadn't planned on telling him and I was probably still drunk from the night before. But as I told him, about the course I'd passed and the job in Afghanistan, I felt that I was trying to convince him that I wasn't the wally I believed he thought I was. I felt like a small boy wanting his Dad to be proud of him. I can't imagine the thought process that led me to get a taxi to Dagenham and I don't know why I decided to tell my Dad about my job. I genuinely thought that wanting him to be proud of me was in the past and that I was over it. But it must have been there lurking in the depths of my subconscious waiting and it burst out of me like a levee breaking. I could see that he was shocked and I hoped a little impressed by what I was telling him and I felt stupid at needing to tell him.

My Dad died of a massive heart attack on 4 October 2011, a couple of months after I'd woken up in his flat. When my kids were young, he'd make them laugh telling them that Elvis died on the toilet. Maybe there is some karma that he died on the toilet as well.

That morning in his flat was the last time I saw him. Julie and I tied his ashes to a bottle of port and laid him to rest in the English Channel off Plymouth Sound in January 2012. After being expelled from Bishop Ward school for spraying the nuns with a hosepipe, my Grandad had sent my Dad to sea school and his first job was a merchant seaman. He always talked wistfully about his time at sea, so a sea burial seemed apt.

I returned to the DHU from being an instructor and started pre deployment training to return to Afghanistan. I deployed to Kandahar in March 2012 as the senior handler in the Det. The Det boss was a former RSM from the rifles called Sean. He'd gone through the ranks and was very experienced HUMINT operator. The Det sergeant major was a Bootneck and very good friend called George who'd been on my first tour. Both George and Sean were level-headed, experienced and were excellent to work for.

One case that dominated my daily work was a farmer on the fringes of the Taliban called Mahmood. He claimed to have fought the Russians along with every other Afghan in Helmand Province. In reality, most Afghans in Helmand fought each other depending on changing tribal alliances between Russian-backed government militias and Iranian or Pakistani Intelligence-supported Mujahideen. They fought for whoever gave them the most weapons to protect their tribal interests, which was mainly opium farming.

Mahmood had a good understanding of military tactics so probably did fight at a sub commander level and had a deep hatred for the Taliban. His deep-set eyes twinkled with mischief and his quick smile and constant laughter belied a bravery that bordered on stupidity. He'd often go out at night and disrupt Taliban IEDs and place himself in extreme danger to call in ambushes before they could be sprung. He'd become the most prolific agent in terms of reporting real-time threats to life and undoubtedly saved tens, if not hundreds of British soldiers' lives. I loved him. I'd hear his dedicated phone ring on the edge of a dream as I drifted awake ready to take his call and through the summer fighting season, he'd call in three or four times a day. Each with time critical and accurate lifesaving intelligence. My six-month tour in KAF was the most fulfilling time of my entire soldering career.

I returned home in the late autumn of 2012 and in January 2013 I started a secondment to the Foreign and Commonwealth Office in a mostly training role. It was a high-profile appointment and I often found myself in situations where I had to pinch myself in disbelief at what I was doing. A Royal Marines career is typically 22 years and as 2014 rapidly approached, so did my 22-year point. I now had the relevant skills and experience to look at going into the high-end security sector, something that was very well paid. But my time on secondment with the FCO opened up other opportunities that I hadn't even dreamed existed, certainly not for someone like me. I received a three-year extension to my military contract in November 2013. I had dreamed of being a Royal Marine and was told at 13 that I wasn't what they were looking for. I was told the same thing again at the careers office at 18 and when I finally got past the interview stage at 21, my uncle told me I would never pass. I had not only proven them all wrong, I had gone way beyond what I only dreamed was possible. After Christmas I was about to start a specialist job that only a few people knew existed and I felt that I was at the very pinnacle of what it means to be a soldier.

Between Christmas and the new year, Claire and I were awake in bed, both unable to sleep. I had an overwhelming need to tell Claire something. I had no idea where it was coming from, but as we were laying there in the dark, I said, 'Claire, if anything ever happens to me and I'm in a coma or something.'

'What?' asked Claire as she turned over to face me. 'What are you going on about?'

'I don't know,' I said. 'It's just, if I'm ever in a coma or something like that. I want you to know that I will be in there somewhere fighting to get out.'

'Why would you even say something like that?'

'I don't know.' I said. 'I just wanted you to know.'

'Silly arse,' she replied. We both turned over and went back to sleep.

Day 59

My first rowing shift of the day had perfect waves rolling from behind. I pulled on the oars and *Hope* nudged forward like the dead weight she had become. I rowed with a robotic monotony, resigned to two hours misery whist on the oars.

Halfway through the shift I finally hit the Southern Equatorial Current. *Hope* suddenly stopped. I pulled harder on the oars, but there was no relenting. It felt like I was rowing through setting concrete. There was no discernible difference in the ocean around me. Unlike previous patches of strong current where the sea appeared like it was boiling, this time the waves continued as they were. *Hope* changed direction and she swung dramatically round to face due west. The autohelm steered *Hope* into the current to keep the same heading. I wondered if now was the time to turn more north with the current but I wasn't due to speak to Leven until after lunch, so decided to keep the same heading until then. I continued to pull on the oars with all the strength that remained in me for a pitiful 1.2 knots. After two hours of exhausting effort pulling on the oars, I stowed them ready to collapse shattered into the cabin. I looked over the stern at the large rolling waves behind *Hope* and then a huge dark shadow appeared in the water. It was absolutely massive. As *Hope* crested a wave, I could look down over it into the water below. It must have been almost 15 metres long. I could just make out its large and obvious whale's tail as it followed just below the surface of the water. As *Hope* fell into a watery valley between the large waves, it turned its head to the side and used the wave to look down on me. It was too far behind the boat to have any hope of videoing it on the GoPro and my phone's camera only captured the glistening sun reflecting in the waves. It followed behind me for about a minute then suddenly shot away to the south with a speed that surprised me. After the whale disappeared, I reached into the hold to get a snack-pack for lunch and my hands closed around a tin of peaches. I don't think in the circumstances I could've been happier.

I called Leven and told him about the current, current situation.

'I've spoken to a local ocean rower in Cayenne,' said Leven. 'He's advised that we are too far south for the currents, and it would be remiss of me to not go with local knowledge. Come round to 260 true and any additional north you can get may pay dividends later.'

I changed direction and immediately *Hope* picked up speed. She still felt sluggish, but she surged forward compared to how she was rowing against the current. I tried to keep as close to 260 degrees as possible, but the waves were too big and I held a line as oblique to the waves as possible without going into irons. When I wasn't rowing, the battle between the waves pushing west and the current pushing north meant that the waves won out. I couldn't hold a course close to 260 degrees and *Hope* drifted west instead of my intended heading of north-west. Leven's words of 'any additional north you can get may pay dividends later' rang in my ears and after only a short rest in the cabin, I decided to get out and row. Every time I stopped rowing, *Hope* started to be pushed west and a slow realisation began to form, I may have to row constantly all the way into the Cayenne. As much as I was looking forward to finishing the row, I was dreading the next couple of days rowing.

As the sun set, the air around me seemed to be tinged with an orangey pink hue. The sea changed from a deep clear blue of the open ocean to a very slight orange tinge. I realised I was crossing into coastal waters. I remembered it was Morale Saturday. I allowed myself a quick ten-minute break to eat the tin of peaches. The syrup dribbled through my beard as I savoured every spoonful. I changed my pants before exiting the cabin to row through the night.

The first stars shimmered through a hazy evening sky and I understood that this Morale Saturday, despite the whale and tin of peaches, was going to be hard. With the exception of the ten minutes it took to eat the peaches, I'd been rowing for nearly six hours before reaching the point where I couldn't row anymore. As I shipped the oars, *Hope* immediately started to drift west. I entered the cabin and set my alarm to give myself one hours rest then fell immediately into a deep sleep. My two hitchhikers joined me at some point whilst I was sleeping and again kept me company through a night of near constant rowing. At four in the morning, I again stopped after falling asleep several times whilst sat rowing. I'd bounce back into consciousness with my arms pulling on the oars. I must have been asleep sat upright with my arms mechanically moving backwards and forwards. I set my alarm for two hours rest and woke to row the last two hours as the night drifted into dawn. I'd rowed 57 nautical miles. Ten more than I dared hope, and it seemed a large chunk out of the distance to Cayenne.

Day 59 Logbook Entry

Position at 0800hrs (L) (1100hrs UTC) on 9th Mar 2019
O4°35'. 805n 050°06: 237w

Distance travelled 57nm rowed at 256°t
Total distance 2977nm

128nm to Cayenne

Hit the Cayenne current @ approx 1100hrsL then after a conversation with Leven Brown and Pascal, a French Guianan, local ocean rower in Cayenne altered course from 250°t COG giving a COG of 260°t. Speed increased dramatically.

@ midday saw a huge whale, maybe 12m-15m in length in the water. Could only see its shadow as it was about 10 metres away, it swam off impressively fast.

Now I bloody hope it was a whale, if not it was a huge shark.

INVICTUS

On Sunday, 5 January 2014, I said goodbye to Claire and the kids and drove back to work after nearly three weeks Christmas leave. Most Sundays revolved around the impending evening drive back to work with a familiar television programme heralding the end of the weekend. When I first passed out from training it was *Last of the Summer Wine* before the train to Plymouth, but more lately it was *Countryfile* before the drive back to Bedfordshire. Sunday evenings after leave always felt worse with the added wrench back to work after time off.

'See you Friday,' I said to Claire.

'Bye, Dad,' said Billy and Harriet.

This was our family's routine. I preferred driving late at night avoiding the worst of the traffic. I'd bought a Volkswagen Transporter and converted it into a campervan four years before and it served as my day-to-day vehicle. I waved goodbye to Claire as she stood by the back door as I reversed out of the drive. The Met Office had issued another weather warning as the worst run of winter storms for two decades continued and the rain lashed against the windows as I drove out of the village and through the Devon lanes. The roads were unusually quiet and I hoped to be in my bed on camp by 1am. I presumed the weather had kept most people at home. I soon turned onto the first main road at Okehampton as I left the lanes behind. The rain stopped briefly but water glistened in my van's lights on the black tarmac.

As the dual carriageway skirts the northern slopes of Dartmoor, it traverses over several big hills and as I crested one, I noticed lots of small pieces of debris in the road. It looked like someone had scattered a load of pebbles across the tarmac. They were too small to see before it was too late and the road too wet to brake hard. 'Bugger' I thought as the van rumbled over them. I turned the radio off and listened to familiar sound of the van's wheels on the road surface. After a couple of seconds my heart sank as I felt the tell-tail judder of a flat tyre. I knew I'd just driven past one of the many parking laybys and reasoned that the next one would be too far to drive to without damaging the wheel, so I pulled over onto the soft verge. I came to a stop as far over onto the verge as I could possibly get with the outside two wheels only just on the tarmac of the road. I turned on my hazard lights and carefully checked in the side mirror before jumping out of the van to inspect the tyres. A gust of cold wind blew a fine drizzle into my face as soon as I got out. Even in the near pitch black of the moonless night, I could see that the nearside rear tyre was completely flat. The sodden ground squelched underfoot as I got my spare wheel out from under the rear of the chassis. As I fitted the jack to the van, I worried that it would sink into the sodden ground instead of lift the van up. I started to wind it up until it bit, and it started to sink into the ground. But after it sank a couple of inches the van started to slowly rise into the air. The ground was firmer than it looked and I quickly lowered the van again. I then got the spare wheel ready so that when I jacked it up again, I could work as quickly as possible and maybe, if I was lucky, I could change the wheel before the van sank back down into the muddy ground.

I twisted the arm of the jack as quickly as I could, the van creaked as it lifted with the wheel staying on the ground as the suspension sagged. Then as the van slowly lifted higher, the wheel started to clear the ground. I loosened the nuts then took them off and just managed to get the wheel clear of the floor as I pulled it away from the wheel hub. I could see that the jack was slowly sinking, so I wound furiously until the jack was at it maximum height, then grabbed the spare wheel. As I fitted it over the wheel hub, I could feel the van getting lower as the jack sank further into the soft, muddy ground. Then the wheel slipped onto the hub, clearing the ground by millimetres. Just as I managed to align the holes where the nuts would go, the wheel touched the ground. I only managed to get the wheel on by the merest of fractions. Before I tightened the nuts, I took a quick photo on my phone of the jack fitted to the bottom of the van and the wheel behind it then tightened the wheel nuts. I threw the spare wheel, jack and wrench in the back of the van and climbed into the front seat. I looked at my watch and thought, 'I could probably be in bed by two'. And feeling rather pleased with myself, I posted the picture of the jack and wheel on Facebook with the caption, 'well this journey can't get any worse', then pulled away.

A couple of uneventful hours later, I was driving along the M3 motorway, when I saw yellow hazard lights flashing in the distance. It was just before midnight and it had stopped raining, but the road was still very wet. Large patches of water reflected the lights from the signs for the upcoming junction with the M25. The yellow flashing lights were quite a way in the distance, but I could sense that they were not in the right place. It just didn't feel right. I immediately pulled my foot away from the accelerator and started to slow down. The road ahead was bending slightly to the right and as I approached, I began to decipher what was two sets of hazard lights, one to the left on the hard shoulder and one to the right that was now obviously in the middle of the road. I immediately put my hazard lights on and prepared to pull over. As I approached the vehicle in the middle of the road, I could see debris from a collision scattered across the fast lane. It looked as if the car had crashed into the metal barrier of the central reservation.

I pulled onto the hard shoulder and prepared to stop and slowly drove past the crashed car to my right. It was straddling the middle and fast lanes and pointing slightly towards the central reservation. Its front bonnet badly smashed up. I wondered if there was anyone stuck in it and if they were, they were in mortal danger. My priority would be getting them out.

I came to a stop behind the car on the hard shoulder, its orange flashing hazard lights illuminating the ceiling of my van. I turned off the engine, grabbed my phone and then pulled on the door handle to open the door. As I did, I felt something pull me back. Not physically. It was inside me. Kind of. It wasn't some kind of sixth sense hinting away in my subconscious. It grabbed me and stopped me dead in my tracks. I then heard in my mind, *'Careful. This is dangerous.'* I didn't actually hear a voice, it was more that I became aware of the words without actually hearing them. But they were so impactful, if it was a voice, it would've been screaming in my ear. I have never, before or afterwards, felt anything remotely like it. Not in Iraq. Not in Afghanistan. And it shocked me. All the battles, firefights, patrols through heavily mined areas, the helicopter ride through the Iraqi night with tracer streaking through the air behind. I've never had a warning reach up from the depths of my subconscious and scream at me to stop. I took note, steadied myself, opened the van door and stepped into the night.

I walked back along the wet tarmac and a couple of metres behind my van was a tall guy with long ruffled hair talking into his phone.

'Are you phoning the police?' I asked. He nodded. *'That's one job sorted,'* I thought

'Is there anyone in the car?' I asked him.

'I don't know, my mate is talking to the people out of the car there,' he waved back along the road with his free hand.

I couldn't see anyone in the gloom and hadn't noticed anyone when I'd slowed to a stop on the hard shoulder. I walked back towards where he'd gestured, the night eerily quiet. I took a few steps and a small group of people slowly emerged out of the shadows ten metres away. As I approached, I could make out that there was three men and a heavily pregnant woman stood on the hard shoulder next to the metal barrier.

'Is there anyone left in the car'? I asked.

'No, we are all here', said one of the men in a pronounced Polish accent.

'Are you sure no one is left in the car?' I again asked.

'No. No. We are all here. We all got out,' said one of the men.

'Is anyone hurt'? I asked.

They all began talking at once with the pregnant woman in obvious distress. One of the men was a lot younger and seemed to not be part of the group and I assumed he was the friend of the bloke on the phone I'd just spoken to.

'Is that your mate back there?' I asked.

He nodded back. I visually checked each one of them in turn, three tours of Afghanistan had given me a sound understanding of first aid. They all appeared OK if a little shaken up, but I was concerned about the pregnant woman and any hidden internal injuries.

I said, 'Has anybody got any injuries?'

The two men both started talking and pointing at the pregnant women's large bump. They were obviously shaken up by the crash and were clearly worried about her unborn baby.

I turned to her and asked, 'Are you OK?' She had long straight fair hair and I could tell that she was clearly beautiful, even in the dark night.

'I think, but my baby. My baby is come soon,' she said in broken English, holding her bump with both hands. All three looked OK but even with the worry of the pregnant woman, there was little that I could do.

'I'm going to walk along the road and use the torch on my phone to warn oncoming traffic.' I said to the young man whose friend was on the phone. 'Shout out if there's any change in anyone. If they feel sick or nauseous or faint, just shout and I'll run back.'

He nodded and I turned to walk down the road. As I turned, I heard a huge bang.

Day 60

After a quick breakfast I continued rowing on my heading of 260° True. The waves rolled in from the east, just behind and to the starboard side of *Hope*. *Hope* was flying along at an impressive three knots but again, every time I stopped rowing, she almost came to a standstill and was pushed too far west. I ate my lunch sat on the oars and as the sun traversed across the sky, I kept rowing. From the Cape Verdes where I turned west, sunsets happened behind me and I would have to stand facing over the front cabin to see them as *Hope* slowly headed west into the setting sun. As I headed north-west towards Cayenne, this sunset painted the whole western horizon a brilliant orange. A few wispy clouds glowed bright yellow as the sun dipped towards the ocean over my right shoulder. The first stars shimmered in the darkening sky to the east and as the sun finally dipped below the western horizon, I stopped rowing. I had rowed constantly for over ten hours. I cooked my dinner of two boil in the bag main meals and ate them in the cabin. Exhaustion filled every part of my being and I wondered how long I could rest for. I called Leven at our pre-arranged time of 7pm local time. 'Almost there now captain.' He said, 'But we urgently need to get some more north in. Come round to as close to 280° as you safety can,' He continued. 'The more north we get in the now, could prove crucial for the run in.'

Leven's tone more than his words, forced me straight back out on the oars. All through the row, Leven's calming voice had been a constant reassurance but the words 'urgently' and 'crucial' resonated. I set a new course on the chart plotter and could see that 280° True pointed me straight at Cayenne and the finish line. I also noticed how close I was to Brazil. It was just 30 nautical miles to my west and I would now be traversing its coast and at some point during the night I would cross into French Guianan waters. I rowed through the early evening almost beam on to the waves that thankfully weren't too big or breaking. *Hope*'s speed picked up to an impressive four knots. The speed was encouraging after my conversation with Leven. At about ten o'clock, I couldn't row any more. I stowed the oars, clambered into the cabin and fell immediately into a deep sleep. My alarm woke me at midnight and I crawled out of the cabin. My hitchhiker's had joined me again, one sat on the rear cabin and one perched behind me on the front cabin. I again rowed for as long as I could, which was until half past five in the morning, just as the sky to the east began to lighten. After an hour's rest, I started rowing again as the sun rose out of the sea for what I hoped would be the last time. At eight o'clock I completed my stats and realised that I had rowed further in the last 24 hours than was the distance left to Cayenne. Baring a disaster, this was likely to be my last day at sea.

Day 60 Logbook Entry

Position at 0800hrs (L) (1100hrs UTC) on 10th Mar 2019
O4°42'. 742n 051°15: 422w

Distance travelled 69.5nm rowed at 276°t
Total distance 3047.5nm

58.7nm to Cayenne ☺

Current heading of COG 270°t COG of 281°t is almost beam onto wind and swell. I'm following the coast of Brazil and soon French Guiana which is approximately 30nm to the south-west. I need to maintain at least 280°t to hit Cayenne which is proving difficult. Final run in is getting a little tricky.

The bang was followed by a crashing noise and screaming then, almost simultaneously I felt myself hit by what felt like the flat front of a huge juggernaut lorry. Then time slowed down. The screaming continued and I could feel myself moving through the air, but it was like I went into myself. I knew where I was and I could hear everything that was going on around me, but it all seemed removed. Also, I couldn't see anything. Not like when you close your eyes or when you are in absolute darkness. There is always the sense that you are looking at the back of your eyelids or even the absence of light. I wasn't looking at anything, as if absolutely nothing was there. Even 'there' was absent, like I was in between worlds, without substance or time. I tried to piece together what was happening. I knew that I was on the hard shoulder. I heard the bang, screaming and felt like I'd been hit by a lorry. I assumed that is what had happened. I knew that this was all very, very bad. I kept telling myself that when all this movement stops, I must check myself over for any injuries. I kept saying this to myself again and again. In the moment, there was no sense of time, but in my memory I have about three or four minutes of thinking that in reality could only have been a couple of seconds. Finally, in retrospect what seems like an age, I was wrenched back into the present. I was kneeling on a grassy bank. Immediately I moved my hands up to my face and rubbed and patted my jaw. I was worried that my lower jaw had been smashed away for some unknown reason, but it felt normal. I continued to feel around my face and head, but it all seemed OK. I looked down and patted chest hips and groin. As I was doing this, I became increasingly aware that something wasn't quite right with what I could see. I concentrated and looked again, then it became clear. I was kneeling on grass where typically both legs from the knee down should be behind you. But the bottom part of my left leg was angled sideways away from me. I thought 'Well that's not good' and I realized that I had been seriously injured.

I shouted 'MEDIC,' at the top of my voice, then shouted it again. In Afghanistan, if someone becomes injured by either explosion or gunfire, then whoever sees this immediately shouts 'MEDIC', followed by everyone else so that the whole patrol is aware that there is a casualty. I can't remember making the conscious decision to shout that out. It came from somewhere deep inside of me. At that point I hadn't been in Afghanistan for over two years. Training just kicked in. As I shouted it a second time, it occurred to me that no one would understand what that meant. No training had prepared me for this so I shouted the only thing I could think of and that was, 'I need medical attention.' As I shouted that, I thought to myself, 'That just sounds ridiculous.' All of this happed really quickly and as it was happening, I started to fall backwards. I had landed on the grassy slope, the other side of the metal barrier that separated the hard shoulder of the motorway from the grass verge on the other side.

Another car driving in the fast lane had hit the front of the crashed car with such force, it span it round three times flinging its engine out. The engine flew across the motorway and hit me. The force of the engine hitting me had tossed my body about 15 metres through the air over the metal barrier and onto the grassy slope on the other side. I tumbled backwards down the slope and then turned onto my front and crawled under the metal barrier and onto the wet tarmac of the hard shoulder. I could feel that there was also something wrong with my right leg. I rolled onto my back and propping myself onto my elbows, I looked down at legs. My jeans were covered in mud and my left leg felt alien to me, as if it didn't belong to my body, but my full attention was instantly drawn to the bottom of my right leg. The blue jeans were shredded from just below my knee, my right boot flopped sideways against to tarmac and my foot inside it was hanging on to the rest of my leg by odd bits of tendon and skin. I knew instantly that I had lost my leg. I wasn't shocked or even surprised, it felt that it was bound to happen sooner or later. Every time I walked out of the front gate in Afghanistan, on a subconscious level I had made peace with the real prospect that this would happen and now it had. 'Fuck, I've lost my leg,' was my first thought. I could see a pitch-black puddle of blood ooze across the ground that focused my attention. I was losing a lot more blood than I expected. My second thought was 'That's not important, I've got to stop that bleed.'

I couldn't sit up or bend my body sideways to reach the upper part of my right leg, I knew that I wouldn't be able to do anything to stop the bleed. I was aware of people on the grass verge the other side of the metal barrier and I assumed it was the three polish people from the crashed car. 'Help,' I shouted. 'I need someone to help me.' But nobody came. I felt angry that I had stopped to help them and now they weren't helping me. Then the young lad who was with the people from the crashed car appeared above me. 'Quick. I need a tourniquet now.' I said.

'OK. A tourniquet,' he repeated and looked confused. He then walked away back into the gloom. Realizing that he probably doesn't know what a tourniquet is, I thought 'I need to communicate what I need better.' Moments passed and the young lad didn't return. I could feel the situation slipping away from me. I knew that the police and hopefully an ambulance were on their way, but a sense of dread began to build within me as I tried estimate how long they would be. The math's weren't adding up in my favour no matter how I tried to work it and I slowly realized that I was now in a fight for survival. I felt incredibly vulnerable laying on the wet, dark tarmac of the hard shoulder and looked around for some kind of safety. To my left, through the gloom I could see the hulk of a badly smashed-up car about 30 metres away, its violently mangled hulk another sharp reminder of my precarious position. To my right, I could see my red van, its hazard lights still flashing and the blue lights of the motorway signs beyond. But in between my van and me was the unmistakable shape of a car's engine. It was about twenty metres from me. Then from the gloom, a breakdown truck appeared. It came to a quick stop right next to me and then the orange lights on top of its cab flashed into life. The passenger door of its cab opened and a man jumped out with a reassuring sense of purpose. He knelt right next to me and I said, 'I need a tourniquet now on my right leg.'

The man frowned as he looked from me down towards my shattered leg. His beard and glasses gave him an air of practicality that was encouraging.

'I can't go down there,' he said. 'I'll be sick.'

'But I need to stop the bleeding now or I'll bleed to death.'

He shook his head and said, 'It's alright. The ambulance will be here in a minute.'

'I don't have the time, I know what I'm talking about. I'm a soldier. I need a tourniquet now.'

'Honestly, I just can't go down there. I can't look at it. The ambulance is coming. It won't be long.'

His words were strangely hypnotic. I knew that I didn't have the time for the ambulance to arrive before I bled to death. I could already feel the onset of shock where your body takes the blood it needs from your extremities to keep your vital organs going. I could feal my fingers tingling as the blood that would normally be there was redirected to my abdomen. But to just lay back and believe that I was going to be OK, that the ambulance would be here in a moment, was so comforting. I wanted to relax back into a soft, warm cloud of cotton wool that would wrap around me. Everything would be OK if I would just let it. It was intoxicating. It overrode all of my survival instinct and I had to wrench myself away with some considerable effort of logic and fact over feeling.

'I am bleeding to death. I don't have the time for the ambulance to get here,' I half said to myself.

'I can't,' he said again and I knew I couldn't reach him. He was wrapped in the same soft cotton wool cloud of acceptance that I so nearly was. But he was also the only person here, now with me and I knew that I didn't want him to leave. I was stupidly scared of antagonizing him and him leaving me on my own. My fingers felt numb and the tingling extended into my arms. I could feal the cold wet tarmac right through to the core of my body. I had no idea how many minutes had passed since I had been hit by what I now presumed was an engine. I could feel what it is to be me with a sharpened clarity and I was filled with a cold determination to stay alive. The man with the beard and glasses from the breakdown truck was still there, but right next to me I could sense a huge abys. A portal to nothingness. I couldn't see it or feel it in any tangible way. But it was there. If I wanted, I could have reached out to touch it and I knew I was now on a knife edge between this life and whatever is next. I assessed the harsh reality of where I was and knew I had only moments left alive. I was aware for the first time that I still had my mobile phone in my left hand and I was slightly shocked that I hadn't let go of it. I thought that the right thing to do would be to call Claire and say goodbye. But the fear of giving in overrode the sensible logic of the situation I was in. And the brief thought of calling Claire was pushed completely out of my mind by cold hard survival

Day 61

After completing my morning stats and updating the logbook, I studied my finish point on the electronic chart plotter. The entrance to the Mahury river is guarded by two large islands, Iles Remire to the north and Le Mare to the south. I'd have to skirt around the southern island, Le Mare to access a dredged shipping channel that was marked by buoys with lights on them. This meant that I'd have to stay as far east of the French Guinian coast as possible. I measured the heading to the start of the shipping channel and knew that I couldn't drop below 280 degrees true. Any extra north I managed would be critical in the run into the finish line.

Pascal the local ocean rower would be meeting me in his powerboat and would shadow me across the finish line where the French Navy would then tow me to the marina a couple of miles upriver. I also knew that I'd now have to row constantly to the finish with no rest. I was exhausted. I'd only managed a few hours rest in the last couple of days. I forced myself out of the cabin for what I thought would be the last time and sat on the rowing seat. Down between my legs in the bottom of *Hope*, was hundreds of flying fish. I had no idea how or when they had jumped into the boat, but I spent a precious couple of minutes, fishing them out and turfing them overboard. I started rowing and set *Hope* on a course of 290 degrees true. This brought her around to face almost due north with the waves now beam on. It felt like *Hope* had gone into irons, the waves pushed her sideways and as I rowed it appeared that I wasn't moving in the water. The small splashes from the oars hitting the sea on every stroke, stayed next to me instead of flying behind as normal. I seemed to be stuck in the same patch of water, but according to the satellite navigation, the boat was moving north at 3.7 knots. I continued rowing through the morning trying to keep *Hope* heading as north as possible and started wondering when I might finish. The waves started to build in height as morning drifted into afternoon. I called Leven at 2pm and told him about my forward momentum but appearing to be stuck in the same patch of water.

'That's good. Keep as north as you dare. The current is working in your favour.'

I called Claire. 'Billy is going to come out and meet you on Pascal's boat,' she said.

'But he gets seasick?'

'He still wants to come out.'

After the call I settled back onto the rowing seat and continued the slow trudge to the finish line. Through the afternoon my speed slowly declined and with it my morale. I'd been flying along but doubted it would last.

The waves increased and made my heading of 290 degrees true unattainable. I was worried that a breaking wave that was side on to *Hope* would capsize her. I adjusted my heading to 285 degrees and with the slight change in direction my speed dropped to 2.5 knots. Any slight hope I had of the current carrying me all the way to the finish line dissolved. I continued the hard drudgery of rowing with the feeling that I wasn't moving anywhere. Only my speed readout at the end cabin gave any indication of any forward motion.

As the afternoon drifted into early evening, my speed slowly dropped until I was pulling on the oars with all the strength left in me for a pitiful 2 knots. The sun began to dip behind a few hazy clouds and lit the horizon bright yellow and as I strained to look at what I hoped would be my last sunset at sea, I noticed a small grey block rising out of the water approximately two miles to my west. It was unmistakenly land. It took a couple of seconds to sink in that this was the first land I'd seen for over a month since Mount Teide, the snow topped volcano on Tenerife slowly disappeared over the horizon. I punched the air and cheered at the incontrovertible evidence that I was closing in to the end of the row. I jumped into the cabin to check my position and confirm what I was looking at. It was Grand Connétable the larger of two Îles du Connétable islands. I also realised how precarious my position was and how close to disaster I'd come. I was now skimming dangerously close to the French Guinan coast and had zero room for manoeuvre. Any extra north in my heading I'd managed for the last three days had proven critical.

The sun set into the French Guinan jungle just over the horizon and the first stars appeared in the sky. The waves from the east became choppy, more coastal and I worried that a rogue breaking wave could end the row by capsizing me tantalisingly close to the finish. Further out at sea I could take the time to sort any problems that a capsize could cause. But here it would only push me closer towards the coastline.

A waxing crescent moon hung low in the sky in the north-west and seemed to point me towards the finish and then set into an increasingly choppy sea at around 10pm. I had my iPad with my position on the chart and handheld VHF radio, tied to the deck so I wouldn't have to get into the cabin to answer the radio or check my position. At midnight I strained to look around over my right shoulder. According to the chart on the iPad, I thought I should be able to see the outline of Le Mare Island but I couldn't. Worried that I wasn't where I thought I was I stood on the deck and looked over the bow. Right in front of *Hope* was the unmistakable black lump of an island with the twinkling lights of civilisation and just to the right, low in the sea, a line of flashing lights. I knew they were the buoys indicating the dredged shipping channel and my route into the Mahury River. I was bang on course. I settled back rowing and the Le Mare island loomed over my right shoulder. The waves were beginning to break and I worried that I wouldn't be able to hold my heading much longer, then my radio burst into life.

'*Hope Hope Hope*, this is . . .' then something unintelligible.

I picked up the radio and called back. 'Hello unknown callsign this is *Hope Hope Hope*. What is your position?' I stood again to try and see the boat that was calling me.

The radio called back again and it was clear that they hadn't heard my transmission from the handheld VHF. I jumped inside to use the cabin radio and gave my position. After they acknowledged I exited the cabin to continue rowing. A few minutes later a large coastal cruiser pulled up alongside and shone a huge light on me. It was Pascal with Billy, Ant the photographer and Stevie an old friend from the Marines who was now a cameraman.

'Alright Dad,' shouted Billy, and then was sick over the side of the boat.

I've never been so happy to see someone throw up in all my life. Pascal came out of his cabin and shouted for me to change course. I was heading towards the start of the dredged channel but now swung *Hope* around to face the entrance of the river. I looked over my shoulder and counted the buoys and saw the one that signified the finish line. Only then, with it in sight, did I allow myself to think, *'I might have just done this.'* The now breaking waves were behind me and they pushed *Hope* forward. I surfed the down them towards the finish line with the flash of Ant's camera capturing me as I rowed. Then pascal sounded the horn of his boat. It blasted across the waves.

Billy, Ant and Stevie shouted, 'Hip Hip. Hooray. Hip Hip. Hooray. Hip Hip. Hooray.'

Billy shouted over to me, 'Dad. How does it feel to row an ocean?'

It was 1.16am 11 March 2019.

I had done it.

Day 61 Logbook Entry

Position at 0800hrs (L) (1100hrs UTC) on 11th Mar 2019

Hotel bed ! Yay ☺

Last days rowing v hard, had to keep above 280°t which was a massive struggle. In the morning the boat was virtually in irons with the wind and swell beam on with the sea next to the boat not moving but the boat touching 3.7kts in current. Speed dropped slowly through the day with swell growing. The slightest North (above 280°t) I managed paid dividends later in the day when I had zero room for manoeuvre.

Official finish of the row 0106hrs L 11th March (L) (0406hrs UTC)

Official time for the row 60 DAYS 16 HOURS 6 MINS 40 SECS

A large figure loomed over me, 'Is there anything I can do?'

He was dressed in dark clothing, had very dark face and was wearing a huge rastacap. Next to him was a slightly-built young girl in glasses and shoulder length black hair who I assumed was his daughter.

'Yes. I need a tourniquet now!' I blurted out.

He looked at my leg, frowned then to my relief, immediately whipped of his belt. He knelt down next to my foot and I lifted my right knee so he could feed his belt under my leg. He pulled as tight as he could and fastened the belt. I knew it wasn't anywhere near tight enough to stem the flow of blood.

'It needs to be tighter,' I said.

'It's as tight as I can get it.'

I suddenly remembered my tyre wrench from when I changed my wheel earlier in the journey so looked over to where my van was parked. I thought that it could work as a windlass, placing it under the belt, and then forcing it around in circles, pulling the belt tighter. I calculated how long it would take to explain where it was and then what to do and realised that I didn't have the time. I remembered the young lad who'd disappeared earlier looking for a tourniquet and if I sent this man away, by the time he came back I'd most likely be unconscious and if that happened, I knew I was dead. I'd been totally focussed on getting a tourniquet on but now I knew that a tourniquet wasn't going to save me I had a sudden brainwave. I needed to get direct pressure on the femoral artery in my groin. The femoral arteries supply each leg with all the blood they need and there is a pulse in your groin where it comes close to the surface. *'Why haven't I thought of this before,'* I chided myself.

'What's your name?' I asked the young girl who I assumed was his daughter.

'Zanele.' She replied.

'OK Zanele. I need you to stand on my leg here.'

I moved slightly onto my right side, exposing the inner thigh of my right leg and pointed to groin. I thought it would be a waste of time to try and find the femoral artery by feeling for a pulse and I guessed where it was. Zanele placed her foot where I indicated and pressed down.

'Like this?' she asked.

'Yeah there but put all your weight on that leg,' I said.

She stood on one leg for a second, I didn't know I could feel my blood bleeding out of me until I felt it stop.

'That's it,' I said. 'Try and dig you heel in there.'

Zanele did her best to balance with all her weight on my groin and her father pulled as tight as he could on his belt wrapped around what was left of my leg.

'What's your name?' I asked him.

'I'm Frank,' he replied in a distinctive West Indian accent.

'Thank you, Frank.' I said.

I laid back slightly relieved. I knew I was in deep shock and still close to death, but at least the blood had stopped and someone was now helping me. I needed to concentrate on just staying alive. I thought about Claire and imagined her getting a knock on the door from some random police officer telling her that I'd been badly injured, so I decided to call her to warn her off. I pulled my hand up with the phone and dialled her number.

'Claire, I've been in a bad accident, I need you to get some help.'

'What do you mean, where are you?' she asked.

'I'm on the M3.'

Just then the guy I'd first seen calling the police as I got out of my van came up to me with the young lad I'd sent off looking for a tourniquet.

'I've gotta go." I said to Claire and hung up.

He was much bigger and heavier than Zanele and I figured he would be more effective at shutting of the artery, so I asked him to jump up and replace Zanele. He stood on my groin and dug his heel right in using all his weight. Again, I felt the artery close down. Time seemed to drag and I started to wonder if anyone had actually called the ambulance.

I asked the guy standing on my groin. 'The ambulance is definitely coming, isn't it?'

'Yes. One hundred per cent,' he answered.

I was shivering and felt a cold right down to my core. I could also feel myself right on the edge of consciousness and that if I relaxed, I'd fall straight into a deep sleep. I fought to stay awake and even though I could feel adrenalin coursing through me, it was still an effort. I absolutely knew that if I went to sleep, I'd never wake up.

The motorway was completely blocked and more people began to arrive and offer help, but there wasn't anything that anyone could do. I again thought about Claire and that she'd have to get someone to drive her to whichever hospital I'd be taken to. I also thought about my van. Someone would have to collect it. I rang her back and she answered straight away.

'I've been in an accident and I've been badly injured, you need to get some help.'

'What do you mean I need to get some help,' she said confused.

'Well, someone needs to get my van.'

Someone shouted, 'The ambulance is here.'

Someone else said 'No, it's the police.'

'I'll call you back.' I said to Claire and hung up again.

I gave the phone to Zanele and turned my attention away from practicalities back to survival. On the other side of the motorway a car with blue flashing lights sped past.

'It's the first responder,' said the guy stood on my groin.

I tried to remember how far back the last junction was, I thought it was about three minutes away, so six or so minutes until they got to me. For the first time I thought I had a fighting chance. I rehearsed in my head what I need to say to the first responder when they got here. I needed to give him the critical information quickly and succinctly if I was going to live. Whilst this was happening my phone rang and Zanele answered it. She was talking to Harriet and I was vaguely aware of her reassuring Harriet that I was going to be OK.

Six minutes later the first responder stopped next to me and got out of his car. I immediately said, 'Right I've got a catastrophic bleed on my lower . . .'

'Hold on,' he interrupted, 'I haven't got my high visibility vest on.'

I bit my lip and patiently waited as he delved into his car. He pulled it out and put it on in what seemed to me a painfully slow way.

'OK then,' he said.

'Right,' I tried again. 'A catastrophic . . .'

Again he interrupted me. 'I have to do a triage.'

A triage is where casualties are prioritised according to who needs medical assistance first. It was the first time I'd thought about anyone else. I hadn't considered that there might be someone else who was badly injured like me, I'd been concentrating solely on myself and staying alive. In my medical training I'd been taught that a catastrophic bleed is the highest priority. For a second the elation of thinking that I was going to make it was replaced by a panic. If there was someone more injured than me who would require the attention of the first responder, then I thought I'd die. I was filled by a selfishness of self-preservation that when I look back at, I'm ashamed of. It was survival instinct at its rawest.

'I've got a catastrophic bleed,' I said. 'I'm the priority here.'

'There are no other casualties,' said the guy stood on me. Thankfully there wasn't.

With what felt like a grudging reluctance, the first responder grabbed his first aid kit and settled down next to me. He opened his bag and got out a tourniquet, the same type as the ones I'd carried in Afghanistan. He applied it to where Frank had tied his belt as Frank stood to one side. The first responder applied the tourniquet over my jeans and then got up, picked up his medical kit and wandered off in search of someone else to help. The big guy then got off my groin thinking that his job was done. I was taught that a tourniquet is always applied next to the skin to ensure that it works and it was usual in Afghanistan to apply two or more to make absolutely sure.

'Can you stay where you are,' I said. 'I'm not sure the tourniquet is on properly.'

'OK,' he said and dug his heel back into my groin.

Moments later a police car pulled up and an ambulance finally arrived. As soon as the paramedics got out of the ambulance, I felt myself relax, I knew I was going to live. As relief set in, I felt a surge of pain washed over me. The paramedics firstly cut away the leg of my jeans and applied a couple of tourniquets to my leg just below the knee. As they were working, they were talking to me. I guessed they were keeping my attention so I didn't drift into unconsciousness. As they were working the pain was slowly building as the adrenalin subsided.

'Are you in the Army Lee?' asked one of the paramedics.

'No, I'm a Bootneck,' I replied.

'Well you've got an ex-Para looking after you now,' he said playing on the years old rivalry between the Royal Marines and the Paras.

He took my blood pressure then looked concerned. He went back into the ambulance and returned with a stretcher. Between the two of them they lifted me onto it and started to pack my foot together with the rest of my leg. All the time this was happening the pain was getting worse.

'They will try to save your leg,' he said.

'No chance,' I replied. 'My leg's gone.'

They lifted me up and carried me over to the ambulance and strapped me in. By now the pain was getting severe. 'Lads, give me morphine.'

'We can't,' replied the paramedic. 'You've lost too much blood. You must know what morphine does from your first aid training.'

'Yeh, it's a respiratory depressant,' I replied.

'There you go. We can't give you morphine until we can get some blood into you.' He then busied himself with applying a cannula, swabbing the inside of my arm and then looking for a vein. As they worked around me, I focused on dealing with the pain. It was almost overwhelming. My phone rang. At some point Zanele must have given it back to me and I looked at the screen. It was Billy.

'Don't answer that.' The paramedic said.

I thought for a second about Billy worrying but I decided to just do what the paramedics said. 'OK.' I replied and turned the phone off.

A doctor joined us from an air ambulance and they must have given me a transfusion because the paramedic said, 'We're going to give you something better than morphine Lee. We're going to give you ketamine.'

I felt the pain wash right out of my body as the drug took hold.

'This ketamine is brilliant,' I said to the doctor, 'Because I want to say that I was with you in Romford market yesterday, but I know that I've never seen you before in my life.'

I heard a laugh from the doctor and two paramedics as I drifted into unconsciousness.

I was flown to St George's Hospital in Tooting, South London and taken straight into surgery. My Mum and sister arrived whilst I was in theatre and were told that I'd lost my right leg.

Claire arrived at 6am and waited for me to be moved from recovery to the ICU. The surgeon spoke to Claire and told her that they'd have to keep me sedated for further operations before she was led into see me in intensive care. She was shocked to see me wired up to machines and saw that not only had I lost my right leg, but my left leg had metal rods and an external-fixator sticking out from my upper thigh and shin. Just as Claire was heading to my Mum's to get some rest she received a call from the hospital.

'Mrs Spencer, are you still on the hospital grounds?'

'No. I'm in the car on my way to my mother-in-law's,' she replied, heart in mouth fearing the worst.

'Your husband is awake.'

I'd fought my way out of the induced coma three times and after pulling drips out of my arm on the third time, the doctors decided it would be less traumatic if they were to leave me conscious. As I came round, I could just about see that my left leg had what looked like a Meccano set hanging out of it with two metal rods attached to my shin and upper thigh. My right leg had a mass of bandages at the end that seemed to form a ball with a thick clear tube extruding from it.

A doctor in green scrubs stood by my bed 'How are you feeling?' she asked.

'I'm OK,' I think I replied.

'I'm afraid I have some bad news, we couldn't save your right leg, I'm sorry but you've lost your leg below the knee.'

'I know,' I said. 'I'd have been surprised if it had been there.'

I remembered the night before and the fight to stay alive. As I was laying there in the intensive care bed, broken, bruised and shattered, I was almost overwhelmed with a feeling of relief. All I could think was how grateful I was to be alive. They called Claire to tell her that I was awake and put me on the phone to her. My voice was croaky from all the tubes that had been down my throat. The next morning, Claire remembered the conversation we had a week before about me being in a coma.

The accident had been in the news with the headline, 'Good Samaritan Royal Marine loses leg after being hit by flying debris when he stopped to help crashed motorist.' Social media went a bit mad with people calling me a hero. I remembered the overwhelmingly selfish compulsion for self-preservation and felt anything but a hero.

After a couple of days in intensive care, I was moved to a bed in a standard ward that would to be my home for the next five weeks. As I came down from all the drugs, I started to feel strange. I felt hyper-aware, as if my brain was running on rocket fuel. I was still running on adrenaline from the incident and I couldn't switch it off. My mind was spinning at a thousand miles an hour and I could feel it draining me. I kept waiting for it to stop naturally and finally, on the Friday, I asked a doctor if there was anything I could do to help me come down. She explained that the hospital psychologist was the person to help but had gone home for the weekend and wouldn't be back until Monday morning.

My whole life I'd striven to prove to myself that I was a person of worth and I felt that had just recently achieved it. I was finally confident in the person I was. I had been a Royal Marine for very nearly twenty-two years, I had been an Advanced HUMINT Operator in a Special Duties Unit and had worked undercover in Afghanistan. I felt that there wasn't anything that life could throw at me that I wouldn't be the equal of. Now every professional competence I had was useless. I had defined myself in terms of physicality, but I was now disabled. I felt like I was in the middle of a spinning hurricane with a thousand different emotions fighting for dominance. I feared a future as a disabled person. I felt like a fraud, I knew I wasn't the hero I was being called. I wrote a semi-coherent and slightly rambling post on Facebook about how I wasn't a hero. Almost immediately a comment pinged up from Corey, the American Marine I had worked closely with in Sangin, Afghanistan four years before.

> *I knew you were going to have a belly ache about the 'hero' word. I don't think they mean by this one particular instance which is the culminating event, but more so you're a hero in life. You served your country fearlessly, numerous combat deployments (hell we were in Sangin together) you come back and set the example for everyone, always smiling, always having fun, always helping people out, and you're one hell of a family man. To me that's a hero. You just continue to do the right thing and be a damn good person . . . So put your humble pie aside for a few minutes and accept that you are the knight in shining armour in people's eyes. . . . With that said, love you bud:)*

I read what Corey wrote and burst into tears. As I sobbed the levee broke, I felt every emotion that had built up during that first week after losing my leg, flood out of me like a tidal wave. With the outpouring of emotion, I finally relaxed as the tension from running on adrenalin drained out of me like a deep long sigh.

I awoke the next morning, a week after losing my leg, feeling eternally grateful that I was alive. I was woken from a mid-morning snooze by the hospital psychologist.

'I've been told that you are experiencing some difficulties,' she said.

'Not any more.' I replied. 'I'm fine now, honestly. I was feeling like I hadn't switched off from the accident and I was getting exhausted. But I'm fine now.'

The psychologist looked down at me with a slight quizzical frown and said, 'Is it OK if I check back in on you?'

'Yeh, if you want to, but honestly I'm fine.'

And I was.

CAYENNE

I drifted from the depths of unconsciousness to repeated beeping. I could hear the emergency alarm signifying that *Hope* was again drifting aimlessly in a big ocean. As the real world slowly came into focus and I mentally readied myself to put on my life jacket and dive out of the cabin, the beeping subsided and I felt the cold, crisp cotton of the hotel bed. Realising it was a dream, I opened my eyes and revelled in the unbelievable luxury of a proper bed as the blessed relief at not being at sea washed over me.

After crossing the finish line, I was met by the French Navy in a river patrol boat. They shouted their congratulations and I threw them the bow line. They towed me a couple of kilometres up the Mahury River to Îlet La Mère, a tiny collection of pontoons forming a small marina on the edge of the jungle. Pascal followed in his boat and I concentrated on steering *Hope*. The French Navy left me just outside the small marina and after shouting my thanks, I lit a red flare in celebration as Ant took lots of photos and Stevie captured it all on video. I rowed around the end of a pontoon into the marina where I saw Claire stood on the jetty. I turned *Hope* round to point at the jetty and pulled on the oars for the last time. Izzy and Claire were joined by Ant, Stevie and Billy as I pulled the oars in and drifted up next to them.

I felt empty. I had no emotions, nothing. I wasn't happy. I wasn't even relieved at finishing. I felt like a husk. I threw the boat lines to Stevie and Billy who tied *Hope* alongside. I went into the cabin and grabbed the bottle of whisky I'd carried across the whole ocean but been too scared to drink. There followed interview after interview and I tried to look interested, but I couldn't care less. Not because I was tired or even because I found it tedious. I knew how important this was. I just felt hollow. I had nothing inside. It wasn't an anticlimax, I was empty of every emotion, I had absolutely nothing left to give. In between interviews I pulled on the whisky as the sky grew lighter and the jungle began to wake.

After the interviews finished, I clambered off *Hope* and onto the jetty. Billy and Stevie held me up, one each side with me clutching the by now half-drunk bottle of whisky. After 60 days at sea, I'd still be rocking from side to side and wouldn't be able to stand unaided for a few days. They led me up to the waiting vehicles and we drove to the hotel in Cayenne just in time for breakfast. The hotel dining room was half full and I was carried in by Billy and Stevie, looking and probably smelling like I'd been at sea for 60 days. The hotel residents looked at me in shock, probably wondering which storm drain I'd just been scraped out of. After breakfast I fell asleep sat in the shower and after Claire woke me up and helped me into the bed, I fell into a deep sleep.

For months, I couldn't think about the row in a positive way. I'd smashed the able-bodied record by 36 days and was featured in numerous online and print media articles. But the last two weeks' rowing were so mentally traumatic, it was almost impossible for me to even think about the row. Whenever anyone mentioned it, I'd deflect the conversation away with a self-deprecating joke. But as the trauma of the final two weeks slowly subsided, I slowly became aware of what I'd achieved. Almost six months after finishing the row, I opened the new *Guinness Book of Records* and saw myself on the last page. I was instantly transported back to a Christmas long ago and the frightened little boy I was. My Dad had acquired a box of *Guinness Book of Records* off the back of a lorry a few weeks before Christmas and I knew that was going to be my present. I was so excited to get it. As I looked at the picture of myself clutching my prosthetic leg, I thought about that little boy in Dagenham. I wished I could go back and tell him not to worry. 'I promise you it will all be OK.' I'd tell him. 'You *will* be a Royal Marine, in fact you'll lead Royal Marines in war. And one day you'll be in there, the *Guinness Book of Records*.'

The End